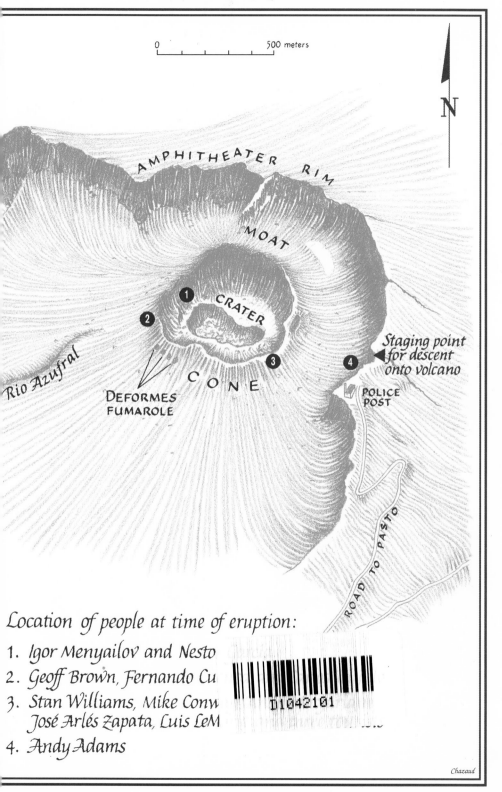

0 500 meters

N

AMPHITHEATER RIM

MOAT

CRATER

CONE

Rio Azufral

DEFORMES
FUMAROLE

Staging point
for descent
onto volcano

POLICE
POST

ROAD TO PASTO

Location of people at time of eruption:

1. Igor Menyailov and Nesto

2. Geoff Brown, Fernando Cu

3. Stan Williams, Mike Conw
   José Arlés Zapata, Luis LeM

4. Andy Adams

Chazaud

SURVIVING GALERAS

SURVIVING GALERAS

STANLEY WILLIAMS AND FEN MONTAIGNE

HOUGHTON MIFFLIN COMPANY
BOSTON · NEW YORK
2001

For information about permission to reproduce selections from
this book, write to Permissions, Houghton Mifflin Company,
215 Park Avenue South, New York, New York 10003.

Visit our Web site: www.houghtonmifflinbooks.com.

Library of Congress Cataloging-in-Publication Data
Williams, Stanley, date.
Surviving Galeras / Stanley Williams and Fen Montaigne.
p.   cm.
Includes bibliographical references and index.
ISBN 0-618-03168-5
1. Williams, Stanley. 2. Galeras Volcano (Colombia)—
Eruption, 1993. 3. Volcanologists—United States—Biography.
I. Montaigne, Fen. II. Title.
QE22. W45 A3 2001
551.21'092—dc21   [B]   00-068246

Printed in the United States of America

Book design by Robert Overholtzer

VB 10 9 8 7 6 5 4 3 2 1

Endpaper map by Jacques Chazaud

THIS BOOK IS
DEDICATED TO MY FRIENDS,
COLLEAGUES, AND
FELLOW VOLCANO LOVERS
WHO LOST THEIR LIVES
ON GALERAS.

These superb creatures, these geological beasts, every man should see one up close at least once in his lifetime.

— Maurice Krafft

When I chose volcanoes for my field, Shaler said, "You have certainly selected the hardest." It was a missionary field, for in it people were being killed.

—Thomas A. Jaggar,
My Experiments with Volcanoes

CONTENTS

SURVIVING GALERAS

PROLOGUE

M Y COLLEAGUES came and went in the clouds. Banks of cumulus drifted across the peaks of the Andes, enveloping us in a cool fog that made it impossible to see anything but the gray rubble on which we stood. Perched at 14,000 feet on a cone of volcanic debris in southwestern Colombia, we were checking the vital signs of Galeras — gases, gravity, anything that would tell us whether the volcano might erupt.

As morning gave way to afternoon, the clouds occasionally dispersed, offering a heartening glimpse of blue sky and revealing Galeras's barren, imposing landscape. At the center of the tableau was the cone, 450 feet high, and its steaming crater. Surrounding the cone on three sides were high walls of volcanic rock, known as andesite. Forming an amphitheater 1.3 miles wide and open to the west, these ramparts were a subtle palette of dun, battleship gray, and beige. The top of the escarpment was composed of crumbling columns of hardened lava, the bottom a steep incline of rock and scree. All of it was the remnant of an earlier volcano that had collapsed thousands of years ago, spilling its contents down the mountain in a vast debris field. Occasionally I glimpsed in the west a forested, razorback ridge sloping toward the equatorial lowlands 9,000 feet below. That was the flank of an ancient volcano, which imploded 580,000 years ago after a massive eruption.

For miles around, the landscape was defined by these vestiges of earlier Galerases in various stages of decay and erosion.

Around one in the afternoon, I stood with four other geologists on the crater's lip and gazed into the steaming pit. Like the craters of most explosive volcanoes, this was not a cauldron of lava. It was a moonscape. Some 900 feet wide and 200 feet deep, the mouth of Galeras was a misshapen hole strewn with jagged boulders. Much of that rubble came from a hardened magma cap, or dome, that had been blown to pieces six months earlier in an eruption. At first glance, the crater seemed a sterile place, its colors running a dreary spectrum from dark gray to brown to beige. But on closer inspection the mouth revealed pockets of color — rust-hued swaths of rock breaking down in the heat and gases of the crater and canary-yellow patches of sulfur that had accumulated next to a gas vent, known as a fumarole. These vents were small fissures where high-pressure gases were released from the magma body beneath the volcano. The gases, which assaulted the nostrils with a melange of sharp, acrid odors right out of the chemistry lab, shot from the fumaroles with a hiss, obscuring the landscape in a swirl of vapors.

Galeras's fumaroles were relatively quiet that day, emitting a *whooshing* sound much like that of a steam machine used to clean buildings. When you step down into such a crater, the howl of the wind at 14,000 or 16,000 feet is instantly replaced by the eerie quiet of the earth's interior. The exception is when volcanoes are riven by high-pressure, high-temperature fumaroles. Then you feel as if you are planted behind a jet engine as it prepares for takeoff. Such fumaroles are not encircled by yellow sulfur crystals, which form at lower temperatures, but rather by a bathtub ring of expelled minerals in black, orange, blue, and white.

I divide volcanoes — and their craters — into two types, hot and cold. Galeras falls into the cold category, which has its own mix of discomforts. Chief among them are the thin air and the frequent shifting between overheating and freezing as you sweat during the ascent, then shiver when the sun disappears behind clouds and you work at high elevations. With hot, lower-altitude volcanoes, such as those in Costa Rica and Nicaragua, you sweat all the time, your clothes stiffening from the salt when they dry. Nearly all craters are awash with acidic gases so strong they can corrode the metal eyelets on your boots and leave your skin feeling as if it has been rubbed raw with Brillo pads.

That afternoon on Galeras, steam clouds often obscured my friend Igor Menyailov, a highly regarded Russian volcanologist who was sitting amid a jumble of rocks thrusting a glass tube into a fumarole. From deep inside the earth, gases streamed out of the vent at 440 degrees Fahrenheit and bubbled into solution in Igor's double-chambered collection bottle. Taken over time, these samples of sulfur and chlorine might reveal the volcano's secrets. Was the magma body rising? Was an eruption imminent? It was Igor's first time on Galeras, his first time in South America, so he could tell little about this particular mountain yet. But the fifty-six-year-old Russian — a short, handsome man who learned English by listening to black market recordings of Elvis Presley — looked content, smiling, smoking a cigarette, swiveling his head away from the shifting gas clouds as he talked with the Colombian scientist Nestor García.

Circling the rim of the crater, appearing and reappearing in the fog like a phantom, was the English volcanologist Geoff Brown, accompanied by the Colombian scientists Fernando Cuenca and Carlos Trujillo. Brown, a rangy, affable man who also had never set foot on Galeras till now, was taking the volcano's pulse with a sophisticated contraption called a gravimeter. One hundred million times more sensitive than a grocer's scale, the gravimeter gauges the forces of gravity on a mountain as it heaves under the power of rising, molten rock. Geoff was trying to map the innards of Galeras, hoping, like Igor, to determine if magma was on the move or if an eruption was likely. We all used different methods, but our goal was the same — to understand what makes a volcano tick, to forecast eruptions, to save lives. We all wanted to save lives.

I know now what a tricky and elusive thing memory can be, particularly after a calamity such as Galeras. I sustained a grave head wound, but was nevertheless able to piece together a picture of the last minutes before the eruption. Over the years, as I underwent sixteen operations, as Galeras greeted me every morning when I awoke, as I slogged through a recovery that continues to this day, I came to believe unshakably in my version of what had transpired on the crater rim before Galeras blew. But I am less certain now. Three of my colleagues, standing just feet from me, remember things differently. Are they right? Can their stories really be true? Some of my memories are vivid, others less so. But no matter. This is what I remember of the moments before Galeras exploded. About the eruption itself — well, we're all more or less in agreement on that.

On January 14, 1993, around 1:40 P.M., I was on the lip of the crater next to José Arlés Zapata, a young Colombian volcanologist. Three tourists, who had hiked up to see what the scientists were doing on the volcano, stood a few feet away. Near them, moving diagonally down the volcano's flank, were two geologists from the United States and one from Ecuador. I was in charge of this foray onto Galeras and just minutes before had asked these scientists to begin walking off the volcano. As a rule, I like to wrap up work on Andean volcanoes by early afternoon, since the heaviest clouds tend to obscure the peaks later in the day.

Igor Menyailov and Nestor García were in the crater, resting after taking their final samples. Geoff Brown, Fernando Cuenca, and Carlos Trujillo were on the crater's western rim, carrying out their last gravity readings. Geoff was too far away to hear me, so I just waved at him, indicating it was time to go.

A rock tumbled off the inside wall of the crater — a common occurrence that at first aroused no concern in me. But a second rock clattered down the crater mouth, then a third, and soon a cascade of stones and boulders rained onto the floor of the volcano. It was an earthquake or an eruption. Either way, we needed to flee.

"Hurry up! Get out!" I shouted in English and Spanish.

The volcano began to shake, and I turned to run down the scree-covered flank. I had made it only a few yards when the air was rent by a sound like a thunderclap or a sonic boom. Immediately afterward I heard a deafening *craaack*, the sound of the earth's crust snapping. Instinctively, I hunched my shoulders and hiked my backpack over my neck and head. I did not get far.

My fascination with volcanoes, now a quarter century old, taps into something universal and timeless. As they watched fountains of lava spew from Mount Etna in Italy or Popocatépetl in Mexico, the ancients believed they were witnessing a phenomenon linked to the origins of the universe. The flames and magma gushing from a volcano came from a place as mysterious as the heavens above. Small wonder that the Mayas, Aztecs, and Incas tossed virgins into the mouth of this beast; it was capable of destroying villages, towns, entire civilizations in an instant. Human sacrifice, they believed, would placate the monster.

To the Greeks, volcanoes were a direct conduit to Hades. The Romans believed the entrance to hell was in the Phlegraean Fields, next to Vesuvius, where gases poured out of hundreds of fumaroles. Vulcan — the Roman god of fire — lived deep inside a mountain on Vulcano, in the Aeolian Islands. There, at his underground forge, he rocked the earth and unleashed eruptions as he made weapons for Apollo, Hercules, and the other gods. The Icelanders, living on an island that was but a mound of volcanoes, believed hell's gateway was the crater of the massive fire mountain Hekla.

Like any grand and destructive spectacle, volcanoes have alternately attracted and terrified humanity through the ages. The difference between ordinary people and volcanologists is that, with us, the appeal far outweighs the terror. Ours is a counterintuitive endeavor. Most people flee from erupting volcanoes. We head straight for them.

From the moment I first set foot on a volcano — at Pacaya, Guatemala, in 1978, where I stared into a crater with dozens of hissing fumaroles — I have found it an exhilarating experience. The spectacle, especially at lava-spewing volcanoes, is impressive. On later visits to Pacaya, I watched as the volcano — with a big *KAVOOM!* — repeatedly launched blobs of magma as big as trucks 200 yards into the air, whereupon the projectiles disintegrated and fell back to earth in hundreds of glowing, baseball-size pieces. At that same volcano, a group of students and I witnessed a lava flow, 9 feet thick and a half mile long, slowly ooze out of Pacaya's flank. We tossed banana peels into the flow and watched them turn to ash with a hiss. Rocks tumbled out of the black stream, revealing the incandescent, orange-yellow core of the lava tongue. We clocked the flow's speed, about 15 feet per hour, and took its temperature, 1,970 degrees F. You could only insert the temperature probe when the wind was blowing away from your body; otherwise you started to cook.

Lava is pretty to look at but rarely dangerous. Eruptions are driven by the explosive power of pent-up gases. (Think of the cork blasting off a bottle of champagne.) But the lava that pours out of Kilauea and other picturesque Hawaiian volcanoes tends to be relatively fluid and depleted of its gases, hence not explosive. The volcanoes with thick, pasty magma — from which gases cannot readily escape — pose the greatest danger of eruption. On these mountains there often isn't a river of lava in sight.

The subtler, extraterrestrial beauty of these explosive volcanoes is, to me, no less stirring. Gases roar out of fumaroles. Hunks of basalt the size of small cars litter the landscape, vestiges of earlier eruptions. I always sense that, despite the barren surroundings, I am perched on a conduit to the most basic energy of the universe, a pipeline to the beginnings of the planet. No other place leaves me as keenly aware of man's powerlessness in the face of nature and the inconsequence of a single life.

I also take pleasure being in a place where, with good reason, few people ever set foot. The splendid loneliness of our work was brought home to me recently when I looked at a series of photographs of a colleague, David Johnston of the U.S. Geological Survey, sampling gases on the summit of Mount St. Helens on May 17, 1980, the day before it erupted. The volcano's northern flank was bulging out as much as 12 feet a day from the increasing pressure of rising magma. The governor had ordered the evacuation of nearly everyone within 8 miles of the volcano. Yet Johnston and another young volcanologist, Harry Glicken, rode a helicopter to the top of the volcano, landed on its swelling hide, and took gas samples.

The first picture, an aerial, shows the gray northern face of Mount St. Helens, with an arrow pointing to the area where Johnston was working. The second and third photographs, taken by Glicken with a telephoto lens, show a speck of a man, dressed in blue jeans, bending over a fumarole. That was Johnston. I can imagine the fear and excitement that stirred inside him as he hurried to collect his samples and get off the volcano, whose ever-distending flank promised that it would soon blow. He was alone on top of the mountain, riding the back of a monster.

By the next morning Johnston was dead. Studying the volcano from an observation post 5.7 miles from the summit, he was incinerated and buried in a blast as powerful as five hundred of the atomic bombs dropped on Hiroshima. Glicken was not killed at Mount St. Helens. He died eleven years later in an eruption in Japan.

My colleagues and I don't harbor a death wish. But despite the progress we've made in taking a mountain's measure using seismometers and other remote sensing devices, the best way to understand a volcano is still, in my opinion, to climb it. I study volcanic gases, which indicate how much magma is rising inside a volcano and how explosive it is likely to be. The most accurate way to sample gases is to descend into a volcano's crater and insert pipes into the fumaroles expelling steam, carbon dioxide, sulfur dioxide, and other compounds. This is dangerous work, as I know from personal experience and the loss of a dozen friends and colleagues. But the goal, which has driven me throughout my career and has taken me to more than a hundred volcanoes in two dozen countries, is a worthy one: to improve our ability to forecast eruptions.

All the volcanologists I admire, whether they've died in eruptions or lived to old age, share a passion for working *on* volcanoes. Most geologists are like pathologists, scrutinizing dead systems for clues of cataclysm and violent demise. Volcanologists are emergency room doctors. We work in the here-and-now, plunging into crises as the earth's fifteen hundred active volcanoes take turns popping off. We clamber on volcanoes because it is the best way to understand their behavior. But we're also hooked on the thrill of climbing into the crater, of confronting so monumental a force. No place on earth leaves me feeling as alive as a volcano does.

In the quarter century since I began studying geology, our knowledge of volcanoes has grown dramatically, testimony to how young the discipline is. Only in the last few decades has the cornerstone theory of plate tectonics become fully understood and accepted. I have witnessed and played a small role in these recent advances in our knowledge, yet a quarter century of work has not diminished my awe of the power of volcanoes and their role in creating our planet. Our atmosphere and our oceans appeared roughly 4.4 billion years ago, when the new planet — an accretion of star dust — began to vent gases and water through primitive volcanoes in the form of steam. Over the past 2.5 billion years, the earth's plates have collided, separated, collided again, and thrust under one another to create our landscape. Drive down the spine of the Appalachians and you are cruising over the remains of ancient volcanoes that ceased spitting magma more than 200 million years ago. Visit Yellowstone Park and you are in the midst of three gigantic calderas, circular depressions formed when a volcano ejects its contents and then collapses in on itself. The three eruptions in the Yellowstone Basin, which occurred from 2 million to 600,000 years ago, blasted out several thousand times more pumice, rock, and ash than the 1980 eruption at Mount St. Helens. One Yellowstone eruption alone created a caldera about 30 miles long and 50 miles wide.

West of Yellowstone, in eastern Oregon and Washington, sit the vast basalt canyonlands of the Columbia River. In this basin, about 16 million years ago, fissures in the crust opened up and, over the course of 1 million to 2 million years, oceans of magma poured out onto the surface from a source hundreds of miles inside the earth. Piling up in pancake-like layers, the basalt reached a depth of nearly 10,000 feet in some places. The accompanying ash and gas would have blocked some of the sun's rays, drastically lowering temperatures worldwide. But the Columbia River "flood basalts" were dwarfed by two earlier basalt outpourings in India and Siberia.

Those events, one occurring 248 million years ago and the other 65 million years ago, radically altered the earth's climate and may have played a role — possibly along with meteorite impacts — in the mass extinctions of dinosaurs and other animals.

Such calamities are almost beyond comprehension. Easier to grasp are the great eruptions of recent times, minuscule by comparison but still awesome in their destructive power. In the past 225 years alone, volcanic eruptions have killed at least 220,000 people. Only a handful died in lava flows; the rest perished in ways that do not readily come to mind. In 1783, in Iceland, the earth was split by a 17-mile volcanic fissure, which gushed ash, lava, and gases for several months. Nobody died in the actual eruption, but the poisonous fluorine gas that rushed out of the vents blanketed the countryside and killed half of the nation's cattle and three quarters of its sheep. In the ensuing famine 9,300 people died, one fifth of Iceland's population.

In 1815, in what was probably the largest eruption of the last 10,000 years, Tambora exploded on the island of Sumbawa in Indonesia. About 12,000 people died immediately, either incinerated by speeding clouds of gas and ash, known as pyroclastic flows, or drowning in huge volcano-induced waves, known as tsunamis. Later, at least 44,000 people — some say as many as 100,000 — perished of famine and disease on neighboring islands when thick layers of ash ruined crops and killed livestock. Volcanic aerosols and dust in the stratosphere made temperatures drop around the world, causing "the Year Without a Summer" in New England and creating the vivid red sunsets painted by the English artist J.M.W. Turner.

In 1883, also in Indonesia, Krakatau erupted, its blast heard as far as Rodrigues Island in the Indian Ocean, 2,900 miles away. An estimated 36,000 people died, most of them in towering tsunamis that swept the island of Sumatra.

Nineteen years later, in 1902, Mont Pelée erupted on the island of Martinique, unleashing a pyroclastic flow that sped down the mountain at 100 miles an hour and, in minutes, killed 27,000 people in the city of St. Pierre.

In 1985 a small eruption at Nevado del Ruiz in Colombia melted glaciers at the volcano's summit and created a mudflow that swept through the town of Armero, killing 23,000 people in several hours. Two days later I was on the scene, measuring the gases streaming out of Ruiz and flying over the entombed town. Scientists from both Colombia and the United States had warned of such a disaster but were ignored by local civil defense officials.

I left Armero keenly aware that if we don't improve our ability to forecast eruptions and educate local officials, another eruption will kill tens of thousands, perhaps hundreds of thousands, of people someday. Burgeoning populations, particularly in Third World countries, have pushed many people even closer to active volcanoes. Today, roughly 500 million people live within reach of an eruption. The famed eruption of Vesuvius in A.D. 79 killed several thousand people at Pompeii and Herculaneum. Dr. Peter Baxter, a good friend and the world's leading expert on how volcanoes kill, says that if a similar eruption occurred without warning today, and if the evacuation of Naples and its suburbs moved slowly, more than 100,000 people might perish in a few minutes.

Six years after the eruption at Galeras I stood again at the crater's rim, scarcely recognizing the blasted, gray pit spread out before me. The ledge on which Igor Menyailov and Nestor García knelt and sampled gases had disappeared. The western rim, where Geoff Brown, Fernando Cuenca, and Carlos Trujillo stood, had been partially blown away by the eruption. Portions of the crater's southwestern lip had collapsed. Even the outer flank of the crater, where I had run for my life, had changed, its lower reaches littered with boulders — some as big as washing machines — thrown from the volcano. The truth is that few places on earth are as mutable as a volcano's peak, where high-pressure gases force open new fumaroles and eruptions scour the crater's bottom and sides.

Gazing into the crater, I was struck by how tiny, in a geological sense, the eruption had been. As the steam from fumaroles drifted past me and wafted down Galeras's western flank, I reminded myself that the deadly eruption was a mere hiccup, a blast so small that geologists decades hence will find no sign of it. Yet the power of the eruption, to those of us who lived through it, was staggering. It wiped five of my colleagues from the face of the earth. It killed nine men, injured six others, and continues to ripple through the lives of dozens of people. It nearly killed me.

The volcano runs like a fault line through my days, dividing my existence into life before Galeras and life after.

1

. . . .

GALERAS

PASTO, population 300,000, sits at 9,000 feet in a wide green bowl in the northern Andes. The city's central square is 5 miles from the crater of Galeras, and on a clear day residents can sometimes see steam rising from the volcano, whose squat, barren silhouette looms over the city. Local Indians long referred to the volcano as Urcunina, the Fire Mountain. But to the Spanish colonists, the gas clouds that formed over the volcano resembled sails, and its long, gentle slope looked like a ship's hull. In the nineteenth century, they rechristened the mountain Galeras, from the Spanish *galera* — a boat with large, open sails.

As Pasto and its surroundings have grown, the population has gradually crept onto the flanks of Galeras. Today, on all sides, the volcano's apron is colored green, brown, and gold by a patchwork of crops — corn, wheat, potatoes, and vegetables. The soil is enriched by volcanic ash, and Galeras seems to be a generally benign presence. Occasionally it explodes, shooting a black column several miles high and dusting Pasto and the towns of Consacá, La Florida, Nariño, and Jenoy with fine gray ash. The Fire Mountain also rumbles, its earthquakes shaking the region's adobe and stucco homes with such force that nervous residents take to sleeping in the streets. Despite these reminders that they live under a volcano, Pastusos are quick to point out that Galeras has never killed anyone in recorded history — never, that is, until the scientists angered the mountain by prodding it with their equipment.

The landscape around Galeras — verdant and breathtaking — does not inspire foreboding. The lower realms of the mountain, at around 5,000 to 6,000 feet, are thick with white-flowering coffee bushes, yellow-flowering guava trees, red and purple bougainvillea, 6-foot poinsettias, orange and avocado trees, and banana plants. Tall, ramrod-straight eucalyptus trees line many roads, which campesinos follow by mule or on foot. Driving down these winding, vertiginous thoroughfares, where 2,000-foot drop-offs are common, the traveler is treated to expansive vistas where the heavily cultivated Andes ranges unroll to the horizon. Patches of thick jungle dot the slopes, but increasingly they are being cleared by farmers, who think nothing of planting a stand of coffee bushes on a 45-degree incline.

As a geologist, I see a different — and more threatening — landscape. Driving into town from the airport, I see in a succession of forested ridges the eroded walls of ancient volcanoes, vestiges of four previous incarnations of Galeras, the oldest of which formed 1.1 million years ago. Arriving in Pasto, the capital of the Department of Nariño, I see beneath parks and streets the deposits of massive pyroclastic flows that swept over this terrain as recently as 40,000 years ago — the blink of an eye in geological time. Scattered around Galeras are numerous quarries, where workers scrape away at high, gray, striated walls for stone and gravel. In these quarries and wherever a highway slices through a hillside, I see the geological record of countless volcanic eruptions, a yellow and gray layer cake of ash, pumice, and lava. On the western side of Galeras, near the valley of the Río Azufral, villagers pay no mind to a high, rounded hillock, covered in cornfields, that rises abruptly from the landscape. I see it for what it is — a 150,000-year-old satellite cone of a long-extinct embodiment of Galeras.

Geologists have two ways of divining the threat a volcano poses: by studying its current activity or reading a record of past eruptions in the landscape. A close look at Galeras's geological pedigree leads to an inescapable conclusion: this volcano is anything but benign.

Another fact should give pause: Galeras has been the most historically active volcano in Colombia. Over the past 500 years, it has erupted nearly thirty times. One eruption, in 1866, sent a lava stream 3.5 miles long and 90 feet deep down the western slope of the volcano toward Consacá. Galeras has disgorged pyroclastic flows — deadly clouds of hot ash, gas, and volcanic ejecta — on many recent occasions, including 1580, 1616, 1641, and 1936. The August 27, 1936, pyroclastic flow, captured by a photographer, sped several kilometers down the northeastern slope toward Pasto. Today, thousands of people live around the volcano on the deposits of pyroclastic flows 1,000 to 2,000 years old. Indeed, the town of Jenoy now sits on the remnants of a pyroclastic flow that swept over the area roughly 180 years ago. A similar event today would probably kill thousands of people.

I ascribe Galeras's low death rate to serendipity and historically lower populations. But convincing people that they live in the shadow of a potentially lethal volcano is not easy. The politicians often don't want to hear about it; such talk can be bad for business. Residents can stick their heads just as deeply in the sand, confident that recent behavior is a guarantee of future tranquility.

But there is no such guarantee. The most famous eruption of all time — that of Vesuvius — caught its victims completely by surprise. Most residents of Pompeii, Herculaneum, and other towns had no idea that Vesuvius was, in fact, a volcano. It had been dormant for so long that thick underbrush grew near its summit and wild boar lived at its mouth. The top of the wide crater was so overgrown that Spartacus and his band of seventy-eight gladiators retreated there in 73 B.C., during their slave rebellion, by descending the throat of the volcano on ladders made of vines.

A century and a half later, on the morning of August 24, A.D. 79, Vesuvius was convulsed by an eruption that threw a column of ash and pumice 16 miles into the stratosphere and shot out pyroclastic flows and suffocating ash falls that killed people 10 miles away. As many as 5,000 people died; some of their remains were disinterred 1,700 years later at Pompeii and Herculaneum. As the enormous ashfall turned the day pitch-dark, few people even realized that the beautiful mountain covered by vineyards had caused the cataclysm.

"Some people prayed for death because they were so frightened of dying," wrote Pliny the Younger, an eyewitness to the events at Vesuvius and the author of the first detailed description of an eruption. "Many begged for the help of the gods, but even more imagined that there were no gods left, and that the universe was being plunged into eternal darkness forever more."

Scientists love to convene, and the tribe of men and women who work on active volcanoes — about three hundred to four hundred people worldwide — is no exception. Roughly fifty hard-core volcanologists, and an equal number of geologists in related fields, were flying into Pasto for a conference scheduled for Monday, January 11. They came from fourteen countries — including Canada, Iceland, Japan, Ecuador, the United States, Guatemala, and Colombia — because Galeras had been selected as one of fifteen volcanoes worthy of study under a United Nations program, the International Decade for the Reduction of Natural Hazards. The decade in question was the 1990s, and the U.N., working with the U.S. National Academy of Sciences, had been prompted to act after two natural disasters in late 1985 — the Mexico City earthquake, which killed more than 20,000 people, and the eruption of Nevado del Ruiz, which cost 23,000 people their lives.

Galeras was a prime candidate for a "decade" volcano: it was active, it was near a large population center, and it hadn't been heavily studied. We planned to hold two days of meetings in Pasto, to conduct six field trips on Wednesday — including a research foray into the crater — and to hold two days of roundtable discussions on Thursday and Friday. Many scientists, including Igor Menyailov and Geoff Brown, would continue working on the volcano after the conference. The goal was to launch several long-term research projects that would focus on Galeras, deepening our understanding of the volcano and assessing the threat it posed to the region.

Foreign tourists — and scientists — are wary of visiting Colombia, and with good reason. A half century of leftist guerrilla insurgencies, right-wing paramilitary atrocities, drug-related violence, and political assassinations and kidnappings have left several hundred thousand Colombians dead and made the country one of the most dangerous places on earth. But Pasto is a relatively safe back-water, more like Ecuador, just 40 miles to the south, than the infamous cities of Cali, Medellín, and Bogotá. The Pastusos are often of Indian heritage and are likely to have the short stature, copper-colored skin, and sharp features of their Andean cousins to the south. Indeed, many Colombians dismiss the residents of Nariño as bumpkins, an image not helped by the fact that Pastusos are fond of eating grilled guinea pig, considered lowly peasant fare. With narrow streets lined with colonial buildings, tree-lined squares, and tall, handsome, stucco churches, Pasto — founded five hundred years ago — is a fine spot to keep a pack of volcanologists entertained. Only scientists from the U.S. Geological Survey (USGS) backed out at the last minute when the American government prohibited their traveling to Colombia.

On Saturday and Sunday, January 9 and 10, old friends and colleagues began arriving in Pasto. Helping me welcome them — and run the conference — was Marta Lucía Calvache Velasco, my good friend and prized graduate student. A petite, striking woman with short black hair and dark blue eyes, Marta was a native of Pasto who also headed the local geological observatory that was run by INGEOMINAS, Colombia's geological survey. She was doing her Ph.D. work on the history of Galeras's eruptions, knew every bit of its terrain, and hiked the Andes with an ease I could admire but never match. By the end of the week she would lead the effort that saved my life.

Two good friends in the volcanological community, Minard "Pete" Hall and his wife, Patty Mothes, drove in from Quito. Pete had been in Ecuador since 1972 and had helped found the Geophysics Institute at the National Polytechnical University. Patty arrived in Ecuador in 1985, married Pete a few years later, and continued to work with Pete, studying Ecuador's many active volcanoes and improving the country's forecasting and evacuation plans.

A child of the sixties, Pete was now a reticent man of about fifty with a graying walrus mustache and thinning, light brown hair that fell over his collar. His specialty was seismology — interpreting the subterranean signals emitted by a volcano. Patty was a sincere and instantly likable woman in her early forties with green eyes, a ruddy complexion, and straw-colored hair. She was interested in electronic distance measurement, which involved shooting a laser beam at a mirror on a volcano to see if its flank was swelling from growing gas pressure.

I knew Pete and Patty well and had great respect for both of them. They had gone thoroughly native, speaking excellent Spanish, living mainly off their meager Ecuadorian salary, building their house themselves, and generously sharing their knowledge with their Ecuadorian colleagues. Pete and Patty felt none of the condescension some expatriates display toward the indigenous culture and treated Ecuadorians with decency and respect. Whenever we traveled into the countryside to work on volcanoes, Patty gave newspapers, rolls, and other gifts to the people we met and always took a few minutes to chat.

On Thursday, January 14, she was at Marta's side during the rescue operation.

The weekend before the conference, as I walked into Pasto's geological observatory, I was greeted warmly by two of my favorite Colombian colleagues, Nestor García and José Arlés Zapata. I had known Nestor, a former judo champion, since 1985. A geochemist by training, he was a true volcano lover who, unable to support his family doing pure research, had taken jobs at the state hydroelectric company and a distillery while working in the crater in his spare time. He had studied Nevado del Ruiz with Werner Giggenbach, one of the world's foremost experts on volcanic gases, and was familiar with Igor Menyailov's work. As we talked at the observatory, Nestor told me how excited he was at the prospect of working with someone of Menyailov's renown.

José Arlés, a good-looking man in his late twenties who always seemed impeccably attired, was a rising star at INGEOMINAS. One of a dozen children from a poor campesino background, he had risen by dint of his intelligence and hard work to become the first high school and university graduate in his family. I had known him for five years and had worked with him on Galeras several times. He was planning to give his first major talk at our conference — a summary of Galeras's recent activity — and was plainly nervous about it. But he, too, was looking forward to working with the likes of Menyailov and Brown.

That Sunday, a team of scientists led by a friend and fellow Dartmouth alumnus, Chuck Connor, flew into Pasto's tiny airport with heaps of scientific equipment. Chuck, a geophysicist at the Southwest Research Institute in San Antonio, had studied the circulation of gases inside volcanoes in Mexico and Colombia. After the conference, he and his group were planning to spend several weeks performing gas studies on Galeras. Accompanying him were two men. Mike Conway, a postdoctoral fellow at Florida International University in Miami, was a geologist who had worked on volcanoes in Guatemala. An affable man of thirty-seven, he spoke Spanish well and seemed comfortable in South America. I had met Mike once before and liked him. With him was Andy Macfarlane, who had just received his Ph.D. from Harvard in isotope geochemistry and was now teaching at Florida International. Andy spoke Spanish and had never been on an active volcano.

On Galeras, Chuck's team would be joined by an Ecuadorian geochemist, Luis LeMarie, who had arrived at the workshop with Pete Hall and Patty Mothes. Luis, who had been educated in Ecuador and Europe, was a slight, unassuming, forty-three-year-old professor with a dark, neatly trimmed beard. I first met him in Ecuador in 1988 when we descended into the massive crater of Guagua Pichincha, the 15,695-foot volcano that rises over Quito, to perform gas studies. He had worked once before at Galeras with José Arlés Zapata and, like José Arlés and Nestor, was pleased to have the chance to ascend Galeras with Menyailov.

As the conference opened on Monday, my colleagues were still straggling into Pasto. At 10:30 that morning, during a coffee break at the Hotel Cuellar, where we were meeting, I looked up and saw an old friend from England, Dr. Peter Baxter. A droll, adventuresome Englishman, Peter was the world expert on how volcanoes kill and injure people. He had wandered into this offbeat niche in medical science when, as a physician at the Centers for Disease Control in

Atlanta in 1980, he went to Mount St. Helens to study how people had died in that eruption. We met in 1980 at Masaya, in Nicaragua, where Peter was studying the effects of toxic gases that were wafting out of the volcano, defoliating the landscape and threatening the health of the residents. Since then we'd worked together a few times and kept in close touch.

Peter was accompanied by Geoff Brown, his lanky compatriot who knew more about how to read a volcano's innards with a gravimeter than anyone else on earth. Gregarious and charismatic, Geoff — whom I had met a decade before — greeted me with a big handshake and said how glad he was that we finally had the chance to work together in the field. We had talked for years about collaborating on Galeras, and I was pleased he was about to apply his gravimetry techniques to the volcano at the center of my current research. Geoff and Peter seemed excited to be in Pasto, although I learned later that both men initially had had second thoughts about the trip, which included a week's work in Costa Rica and Nicaragua before the conference.

"We met at Heathrow, not sure why we were going when we were both busy at work and so soon after Christmas," Baxter told me later. "It was a cold, cloudy day in the U.K., but we soon forgot all that on what was the first trip for both of us to the Andes. I think the sense of exhilaration was very strong. Our first view of Galeras along the airport road was awe-inspiring."

The last of my close friends to arrive was Igor Menyailov. Tuesday morning, as I was leading a workshop about Galeras, Igor — short, slight, and spry — came striding into the room, a backpack slung over his shoulder, a beat-up suitcase in his hand, and a cigarette in his mouth. Seeing each other, we both smiled, and I introduced Igor to the group. As soon as I finished talking, we stepped into the hallway, and Igor gave me a Russian bear hug. He looked exhausted, having spent nearly two days traveling from Moscow to Kamchatka, then on to Havana, Bogotá, and Pasto. I helped him get settled, and we ate lunch at my favorite hangout in Pasto — the Punto Rojo, or Red Spot, a twenty-four-hour cafeteria on the central square. As always, Igor asked me what to eat, and I steered him to the *ajiaco,* or chicken stew. We spent an hour catching up on our work and talked for the first time about our families. I told him about our plans to visit the crater, and he seemed keen. It was Igor's first visit to the Andes as well.

Returning to the hotel, Igor slept for eighteen hours. The next day we met again for lunch, this time with two Soviet-trained Colombian geophysicists who worked for INGEOMINAS — Carlos Corral and Fernando Cuenca. Corral, a supervisor at the geological agency, seemed hostile to Americans — a trait he may have acquired in Russia — and we rarely spoke to each other during lunch. Cuenca was an inexperienced, unassuming man in his twenties who sat and listened to his older colleagues. In the beginning, Cuenca — who was married to a Russian — and Corral began speaking Russian with Igor. But Igor, seeing I was left out, would have none of it and insisted we speak Spanish.

The first two days of the conference were going well; in a babble of Spanish and English, my colleagues discussed Galeras and the volcanoes they were studying around the world. The language barrier was not the impediment I had feared, with people like Patty Mothes, Mike Conway, and John Stix — who helped organize the workshop — translating during both the presentations and informal conversations. My colleagues asked me about Galeras, which was, as usual, shrouded in clouds. I told them, as I told a Colombian TV reporter, that the volcano appeared quiet, as it had for six months. But two random events — one the work of man, the other of nature — would intersect and place us on Galeras just as it stirred to life.

The first happenstance involved electricity. Due to a shortage of generating capacity, the authorities regularly cut electrical power to different sections of Pasto for a few hours each day. As the conference got under way, the management at the Cuellar informed us that the next blackout was scheduled for Thursday, when we had planned to be at the hotel. I discussed the problem with Marta Calvache, and we decided it would be best to hold meetings at the hotel on Wednesday, when we would have power, and move the field trips to Thursday, January 14.

The second turn of fate involved Galeras itself. After slumbering for forty years, it awoke in 1988 with a series of minor earthquakes. Police officers at a post perched on the amphitheater above the active cone noticed small explosions and a stronger smell of sulfur and other gases. In March 1989, with its earthquake activity continuing, the volcano coughed up a cloud of ash that fell on Pasto. In May an eruption ejected ash and rocks, sending a plume 2 miles high and sprinkling volcanic dust on the surrounding towns.

The volcano continued chuffing and generating minor earthquakes until August 1991, when this activity rose sharply and scientists noticed an increase in the number of *tornillos*, screw-shaped signals on the observatory's seismographs. About 1,000 tons of sulfur dioxide began streaming out of the volcano each day, the sharp increase indicating that more magma was rising from inside the earth. By November, Colombian scientists saw that a hardened lava dome was being squeezed up out of the volcano. The dome, charcoal gray with hues of rust, eventually grew to a height of 150 feet with a diameter twice as long. For a few months Galeras quieted down. Then, on July 16, 1992, the volcano could contain the growing pressure no longer. The dome was blown to pieces, catapulting 12-foot boulders throughout the amphitheater and sending a column of ash 3.5 miles above Galeras.

Afterward, the volcano grew quieter than it had been for four years. By the time our conference opened in Pasto six months later, seismic activity had dropped to an extremely low level and the volcano was releasing a minuscule 100 tons of sulfur dioxide per day. A faint twitch of seismicity occasionally etched a *tornillo* onto the black, smoke-covered seismograph drums in the geological observatory.

At the time, my colleagues and I couldn't appreciate the significance of this screw-like signal. As we studied the seismographs on January 12 and 13, Galeras looked quiet, or at least as quiet as an active volcano can be. But it fooled us. Galeras was not sleeping. It was plugged, the low gas emissions and minor earthquake activity reflecting a volcano that had sealed itself and was poised to blow.

The most memorable talk at the conference was Peter Baxter's presentation about the many ways volcanoes kill, accompanied by gruesome slides. Volcanoes, Peter explained, can kill at close range by shooting out clouds of bombs or from afar by triggering giant waves, or tsunamis. They can kill immediately by discharging pyroclastic flows or many months later by destroying crops with ashfalls, causing famine. Even volcanologists are often surprised to learn the mortality statistics from past eruptions: 30 percent died in famines and epidemics after the blasts, 27 percent in pyroclastic flows, 17 percent in mudflows caused by volcanic activity, and another 17 percent in volcanic tsunamis.

Peter's slides were horrific, especially those of pyroclastic flow victims. In addition to some of the plaster casts taken of the victims at Pompeii, he flashed photos of the cooked corpses of *nuées ardentes* casualties from Mont Pelée and Mount Lamington in Papua New Guinea, where 2,942 people died in a 1951 eruption. In medical argot, the corpses had been "carbonized," but to laymen they simply looked as if they had been barbecued. The glowing clouds of ash and gas, which can reach temperatures well over 1,000 degrees F, had burned off hair, reduced digits to stubs, charred lips and noses into indistinguishable globs of flesh, and melted body fat. Some of the victims, subjected to slightly lower temperatures, looked as if they had been mummified, their skin desiccated and cooked to an eerie yellow-orange hue.

Peter showed other pictures of flash-burned corpses frozen in rigid poses, some standing, some prone. These slides represented the so-called pugilistic effect, which occurs, Baxter explained, when extremely high temperatures cause powerful muscle spasms and contractions, locking the deceased in a fighter's stance. The sudden charring can also cause muscles to experience instant thermal coagulation, known as heat rigor mortis. At Mont Pelée, some victims were found in sitting or walking positions. At a 1911 eruption of the

Taal volcano in the Philippines, a doctor discovered a pyroclastic flow victim still holding an umbrella over her head.

Although it seemed to us that the victims had died from burns, Baxter said that autopsies at Mount St. Helens actually showed that a majority of victims expired after inhaling the fine ash and suffocating on plugs of mucus and volcanic dust. The burns might have eventually caused death had the victims not suffocated first. But what was clear to everyone was that perishing in a pyroclastic flow was an agonizing way to meet your maker. Baxter mentioned, however, that there are ways to survive some pyroclastic flows, by either barricading yourself in an airtight building or — if caught in the open — diving into a depression, covering your body, and trying to hold your breath until the worst of the *nuée ardente* has passed.

To those of us in the audience, the most unsettling slides were of the victims of the 1991 eruption of Unzen in Japan, in which 43 people died in a pyroclastic flow. Among the dead were the American volcanologist Harry Glicken and two of the world's most passionate volcano lovers, Maurice and Katia Krafft from France, renowned for their photography of erupting volcanoes around the globe. Their deaths had shocked the volcanological community. Later that week, as we climbed Galeras, these images remained all too vivid.

The day before we were to work on Galeras, José Arlés Zapata stood before the assembled volcanologists and, with a slight show of nerves, gave his first talk at an international symposium. His subject was the reactivation of Galeras as shown by its gas emissions, and he did a fine job. That night he called his wife to tell her about his talk. He said how excited he was to be meeting so many foreign volcanologists and how much he was looking forward to working with Igor Menyailov the next day on Galeras. His voice, she later recalled, was full of optimism.

As usual at conferences, the most meaningful communication often took place in hallways and restaurants. Years later, Baxter still remembered his breakfast discussion with Gudmundur E. Sigvaldason, a tall, slender, white-haired Icelander who was director of the Nordic Volcanological Institute. The subject was volcanology's ability to forecast eruptions.

"I said to Sigvaldason, 'You're no more able to predict that volcano than I'm able to predict whether anyone's going to drop dead tomorrow,'" recalled Baxter. "I tend to take the piss out of volcanologists, you know, because their understanding of volcanoes is much worse than our understanding of the human body. There's a very good analogy between the human body and volcanoes. Both volcanologists and medical people are trying to find out what's going on *inside*. But the techniques of volcanologists are much worse than ours. So when they say, 'Well, we think this volcano is safe,' I tend to say things like, 'No. You really don't know that. That volcano could pop off tomorrow, and you wouldn't be able to predict it.'"

The evening before our field trip, I had dinner with Baxter, Geoff Brown, Pete Hall, and Patty Mothes. We ate at Sausalito, Pasto's best restaurant, renowned for its smoked and fried trout raised in ponds on the slopes of Galeras. Patty had never met Geoff before and was impressed with his soft-spoken manner and exhaustive knowledge of gravimetry and volcanoes. "I thought he was quite a gentleman," she said later.

The topic of the next day's trip arose and we briefly discussed the risks. Then Brown related a conversation with his family just three weeks earlier in which he had acknowledged the dangers of working on volcanoes. He told us, as he had told them, that he would rather die on a volcano than in a car accident on an English road.

The next morning I was up at 5 A.M., preparing for the trip to the crater. I attached a rock hammer, knife, and compass to a wide, brown belt I would strap around my waist. I put on cotton field pants, a turtleneck shirt, a chamois shirt, and a fleece jacket lent to me by my student Tobias Fischer after mine had been stolen earlier in the week in Pasto. I wore tough, leather hiking boots, essential on the scree and sharp rocks of Galeras. In my blue backpack I placed a Gore-Tex rain jacket, rain pants, fleece gloves, leather gloves for scrambling on rocks, a lightweight "space blanket," some candy bars and water, sunscreen, a field notebook, a camera, and — perhaps most important — a flashlight. One should always prepare for the worst on a volcano, and that might mean getting lost and spending a night at 14,000 feet.

Before leaving the hotel, I tried to find the manager so I could put $10,000 in cash — expense money for running the conference — in a safe deposit box. But I couldn't track him down and wound up stuffing the wad of hundred-dollar bills in a pants pocket.

When the sun rose around 6 A.M., I saw clouds piled over the summit of Galeras and mused that we might have to cancel the trip if the weather deteriorated further. If we did proceed, I was determined to get out of town and on the mountain as quickly as possible. The weather is generally clearer in the morning, for by afternoon the earth warms up — Galeras is only one degree north of the equator — and thick clouds often blanket the mountains, sometimes making it hard to see more than a few feet away. A volcano's landscape is already a monotonous, gray world, and being enveloped there in clouds vastly increases the chances of becoming disoriented and getting lost or falling.

About 40 people wanted to visit the crater, but I had whittled the number down to 15, almost all of whom were either performing tests on the volcano that day or studying the topography to prepare for work after the conference. More than 75 people had signed up for six field trips around Galeras. In addition to the group heading to the crater, another contingent was touring neighboring towns to consider evacuation and crisis plans, still another was studying seismic monitoring of the volcano, and several were studying pyroclastic flow and avalanche deposits from precursors of Galeras. We were to meet at 7 A.M. in front of the Hotel Cuellar, then pile into an assortment of old Toyota Land Cruisers and minibuses and hit the road. In addition to the group going to the crater, about two dozen others wanted to drive up to the amphitheater wall to get a glimpse of Galeras, then head back down and begin their excursions.

Not surprisingly, we were late. Leaving Pasto around 8 A.M., we drove west, toward the impressive mass of Galeras. The temperature was in the forties, and thick clouds drifted slowly across the mountaintops. Soon we were passing the corn and potato fields at the volcano's base. We sped by white stucco farmhouses, through stands of eucalyptus, and then, on an increasingly bad dirt and gravel road, began to zigzag up the caldera's eastern flank. This landscape was typical of the *paramo,* the more barren ecosystem found in high altitudes of the Andes. A few pines and cedars grew on the lower slopes, but as we rose the vegetation became scrubbier. About 2,000 feet from the summit we entered a national park, where the mountainside was thick with *frailejon* (*Espeletia wedellii*), a succulent plant with silvery-green, velvety leaves and vivid yellow flowers. Found throughout the Andes, the plant was believed to be named for the traveling friars — *frailes* — who once ranged across the region and whose cassocks resembled the plant's hooded leaves. Left alone, as they were in the park, the *frailejon* grew 10 feet tall.

Interspersed between the stands of *frailejon* were short grasses and violet, orange, and yellow wildflowers. Occasionally, a large dove would take flight as our convoy struggled up the mountain on the rocky road, cautiously negotiating its switchback turns.

Marta and I, in separate jeeps, pointed out Galeras's eruptive history, as written in the landscape: dark gray, 100-foot-thick lava flows from several hundred thousand years ago and more recent detritus, including layers — from several inches to several feet thick — of unusual yellow deposits sandwiched between the more typical light gray deposits from pyroclastic flows. Embedded in the layers were charred twigs, which often made it possible to tell the precise date of the eruptions using carbon-14 dating techniques. Near the summit, many of the pyroclastic flows were only 1,000 to 2,000 years old.

Before entering the clouds, I caught a final glimpse of Pasto a few thousand feet below. Hemmed in by the mountains, the city was a low, beige and white agglomeration of houses and apartment buildings. Above the red tile roofs, wisps of smoke drifted from the chimneys.

Near the summit, our caravan passed a cluster of towering TV and radio antennas, and then, after bouncing through deep, muddy holes, we reached the top of the mountain. We were actually on the rim of the old volcano, which had collapsed more than 5,000 years ago. Perched on a craggy, dark gray, andesite promontory was a small white stucco building, a police post to guard the government communications towers from leftist guerrillas who, though they had never attacked the antennas, operated no more than 30 miles from Pasto. Barbed wire lined the road near the post, and signs warned of a minefield seeded across the steep flanks of the amphitheater.

The caravan of a dozen jeeps reached the summit around 9:30 A.M. Enveloped in cool clouds that limited visibility to 50 feet at times, several dozen scientists, with about fifteen drivers and workers from the geological observatory in Pasto, milled around the police post and walked along the ridge, hoping to glimpse the crater. The temperature was in the low forties. Patty Mothes looked at the ground and saw a small patch of ice. The mood was relaxed but subdued, in part because of the gloomy weather, in part because the prospect of hiking onto an active volcano tends to bring on a certain quiet.

A Colombian TV reporter approached Patty, who was standing near the police post. Wearing a blue parka, a wide-brimmed, royal-blue rain hat, and a pink scarf over her ears, she looked more like the head of an English gardening club than a volcanologist.

"Is there a possibility of an eruption in the next five years?" the reporter asked.

"This is really the purpose of what we're doing here now — to understand the volcano's activity and the pattern that characterizes that activity," she replied in excellent Spanish. "There is no volcanologist who is going to be able to say if the volcano is going to erupt next week or in the next five years ... At this time the signs we are receiving from the volcano indicate that it is calm ... INGEOMINAS has all the seismic instruments, and from these there's no indication it's going to reactivate in the next few days. But you always have to be watchful when you're near a volcano."

The reporter wasn't satisfied. He wanted a prediction. "Is there any danger it's going to erupt?" he asked.

"Well, yes, but I can't say whether it is going to erupt," Patty replied. "At the moment the volcano is not emitting many gases and there is not a lot of seismic activity. But a scientist has to be very aware and very watchful of the changes that occur day to day."

Poised on the lip of the old volcano, Marta Calvache did her best to explain Galeras's layout to a small gathering. But the weather did not cooperate, offering only an occasional view of the crater's gray flank. Wearing a yellow parka, Marta was reduced to pointing into the foggy void behind her at invisible landmarks.

Having been to the volcano many times, I knew its topography well. The horseshoe-shaped amphitheater is more than a mile wide and open to the west. Rising in the middle of it is the present cone of Galeras, 1,500 feet in diameter. In the center of the cone is the crater, which is about 900 feet wide and 200 feet deep, and rises 450 feet above the floor of the amphitheater.

Standing at the police post, you gaze down at the active volcano; its crater lip is about 300 feet lower than the top of the amphitheater wall. The distance from the post to the crater is about a half mile, and to get there you descend the declivitous wall of the old volcano, with layers of hardened gray lava at the top and scree at the bottom. Then you cross the amphitheater floor, about 150 feet wide, before reaching the cone, a scree slope that rises at a 45-degree angle. An old wooden soccer goal sits in pieces on the amphitheater floor, placed there by police and soldiers who once played on what was undoubtedly the world's most dangerous soccer field.

Sixteen people, including Igor Menyailov and Geoff Brown, checked their gear and moved to the lip of the scarp above Galeras. Three other scientists were supposed to join us but failed to make it. Chuck Connor, the head of the group studying the physics of degassing at Galeras, was sick in bed at the hotel with the flu. His absence almost certainly saved his life and those of three of his colleagues, for he and his team would no doubt have been in the crater.

Werner Giggenbach, a German living in New Zealand and one of the world's premier experts on volcanic gases, dropped out when Colombian officials botched his airline ticket. He, too, would probably have been in the crater. As I stood with José Arlés Zapata and

Nestor García, waiting for our group to assemble for the descent to the cone, both men said how disappointed they were that Giggenbach couldn't attend.

Yuji Sano, a friend as well as a highly respected young geochemist from Japan, had more mundane problems. He had left his hiking boots in Tokyo and showed up on the amphitheater rim that morning in tennis shoes, hoping to join us on the crater. But I took one look at his feet and told him to forget it; the descent down the scarp was tricky even in good boots. Embarrassed, Yuji muttered his apologies and reluctantly went on another field trip. By the end of the afternoon, Yuji would be safely back in Pasto.

Not far from him were two men intent on studying the composition of Galeras's magmatic fluids for the U.S. government's Los Alamos National Laboratory. One was an American, Andy Adams, and the other was Alfredo Roldan, a Guatemalan. Following U.S. government guidelines, both were wearing hard hats and Adams had a tan, fire-resistant jumpsuit. None of the rest of us was wearing protective clothing, which Adams found odd. But each of us had weighed the risks and decided that good boots and warm clothing were sufficient.

"I remember people looking at me in my coveralls and hard hat and I felt like they were thinking, 'Who is this guy all dressed up?'" Adams recalled later. "We were the only ones who thought about safety before going in. We discussed what we would do in case of an eruption. It's a shame no one else put any thought into that."

As we prepared ourselves on the top of the amphitheater wall, a university administrator, his teenage son, and his son's best friend were hiking to the volcano from Pasto for a day's excursion on Galeras.

Shortly before descending onto the volcano, Geoff Brown and the Colombian scientist Fernando Cuenca gave interviews to the TV reporter. The footage shows Brown — in an open blue parka and blue crewneck sweater — hunched over his gravimeter, a white box the size of a car battery. Resting on a round metal disk, the sensitive instrument had three black knobs on top and a black wire leading from the side. Brown, his wispy, gray hair blowing across his forehead, stood on the foggy mountaintop and, in rudimentary Spanish, did his best to explain his work.

"Could there be an eruption at Galeras and at what time?" asked the reporter.

"I don't know," replied Brown. "It's necessary to know the volcano much better in order to make a prediction. It's not possible to predict an eruption at this time — perhaps [we'll be able to predict eruptions] in ten more years or in a hundred."

Cuenca, a slight, handsome young man with jet-black hair and wearing a rose-colored sweater, helped Brown place the gravimeter in a blue knapsack. Then they headed for the scarp.

Watching us, Patty said good-bye to the group, then added, "Be really careful." Accustomed to working on far larger volcanoes in Ecuador, she thought Galeras looked benign. Her only concern was that most of us were not wearing hard hats and that someone might be struck on the head by a rock as we clambered down the escarpment.

Before hiking onto Galeras, José Arlés Zapata followed his customary ritual of making the sign of the cross and saying, "God will help us." Then he added a few words: "I hope we finish our work quickly."

Around 10 A.M., we began to descend the amphitheater wall. Most of us held on to a thick, yellow nylon rope for the first 50 yards; only the agile and experienced local geologists could make it down without the rope. I was in good spirits, happy, after three days of sitting in meetings, to be on the volcano with my colleagues at last.

The clouds were still dense, and after a few dozen yards the yellow rope disappeared into a gray void. I had negotiated this drop many times and felt at ease. But being poised on the precipice in the fog, looking straight down, could be unsettling to a newcomer.

It was, a friend said, like stepping off the edge of the earth.

2

....

PUZZLES

M Y INTRODUCTION to volcanology was a black rock the size of a softball. At the age of twenty-two — having dropped out of one college and one university, gotten married, and built homes and warehouses for a couple of years — I was sitting in Professor Hank Woodard's mineralogy class at Beloit College in Wisconsin when the professor held up the black rock.

"Can anyone tell me what this is?" asked Dr. Woodard.

Blank looks. Then someone ventured, "Lava?"

No, he replied, but it does have something to do with volcanoes. In fact, he said, that angular fragment had forever changed science's understanding of volcanic eruptions.

The rock came from the slopes of Mont Pelée, on the Caribbean island of Martinique. On May 8, 1902, in the deadliest eruption of the twentieth century, Mont Pelée spewed out a pyroclastic flow — *nuée ardente,* or "glowing cloud," in French — that roared down the mountainside at 100 miles per hour at temperatures as high as 1,500 degrees F. Witnesses described the flow as a billowing, incandescent avalanche, hundreds of yards high, that threw off bolts of lightning and moved with a *whoosh* and a grinding of rocks. The dark cloud engulfed the city of St. Pierre, and within minutes 27,000 people, nearly the entire population of the city, were either dead or dying. They had been instantly "carbonized" by the *nuée ardente,* suffocated by the thick clouds of hot ash, or burned to death when the city burst into flames.

Only two people in the direct path of the pyroclastic flow survived, including a prisoner in a stone bunker–like solitary confinement cell. That man, twenty-five-year-old Louis-Auguste Sylbaris, later toured America with the Barnum and Bailey Circus, billed as THE ONLY LIVING OBJECT THAT SURVIVED IN THE "SILENT CITY OF DEATH" WHERE 40,000 [SIC] HUMAN BEINGS WERE SUFFOCATED, BURNED OR BURIED BY ONE BELCHING BLAST OF MONT PELÉE'S TERRIBLE VOLCANIC ERUPTION.

In fact, about 70 other people on the fringe of the *nuée ardente* lived through the disaster, but "a lone survivor" made better copy for reporters and press agents. The suddenness and thoroughness with which the eruption wiped out a city, the photographs printed worldwide showing the charred and flattened ruins of St. Pierre, and the gruesome tales of surviving eyewitnesses in the city's harbor all captured the world's imagination for decades to come. The deaths from the pyroclastic flow were excruciating. Relatively fortunate victims were burned to death in seconds or minutes or quickly suffocated. The unlucky lingered for hours with burns over much of their bodies or with scorched throats, windpipes, and lungs. Unable to drink, they endured agonizing thirst. To an observer today, Hiroshima comes to mind.

Two months later, a pair of volcanologists from the Royal Society of London, John S. Flett and Tempest Anderson, were anchored in the same harbor when another pyroclastic flow, two miles wide and nearly a mile high, came streaming down Mont Pelée. The two men were the first scientists to observe a *nuée ardente* directly.

> Suddenly a great yellow or reddish glare lit up the whole cloud mass which veiled the summit. It was like the lights of a great city on the horizon, or the glare over large iron furnaces . . . Then from the mountain burst a prolonged angry growl, not a sharp detonation . . . but a long, low, rumbling sound, like the sullen growl of an angry wild beast.
>
> Then in an instant a red-hot avalanche rose from the cleft in the hillside, and poured over the mountain slopes right to the sea. It was dull red, and in it were brighter streaks, which we thought were large stones, as they seemed to give off tails of yellow sparks . . . Its velocity

was tremendous . . . Its similarity to an Alpine snow avalanche was complete in all respects, except the temperature of the respective masses. The red glow faded in a minute or two, and in its place we now saw, rushing forward over the sea, a great, rounded boiling cloud, black, and filled with lightnings . . . The pale moonlight shining on it showed that it was globular, with a bulging surface, covered with round, protuberant masses, which swelled and multiplied with a terrible energy. It rushed forward over the waters, directly toward us, boiling, and changing its form every instant . . . The cloud itself was black as night, dense and solid, and the flickering lightnings gave it an indescribably venomous appearance.

After rolling over the abandoned city, the *nuée ardente* stopped short of Anderson and Flett's boat, sparing them.

From earlier descriptions, the men realized they had witnessed the same phenomenon that had destroyed St. Pierre. After seeing the *nuée ardente* with their own eyes, Anderson and Flett correctly deduced its genesis: Under immense pressure from gases pent up under its dome, the volcano had erupted, releasing so much heat and energy that frothy magma was torn into pumice and minute particles of ash. "It is," the men wrote, "lava blown to pieces by the expansion of the gases it contains."

Sweeping down the mountain, the lighter and more gaseous elements of the *nuée ardente* continued on while the heavier particles settled, dropped out, and — still superheated — fused together to form the lava-like icing on Mont Pelée's flanks. Anderson and Flett, as well as a renowned French geologist, Alfred Lacroix, studied these dark deposits covering the volcano and the city. Scientists had seen these rocks — angular, densely fused specimens — on Vesuvius, Krakatau, and scores of other volcanoes and assumed they were from lava flows. Incredibly, before Mont Pelée's eruptions, no one had figured out that the ubiquitous rocks were the remnants of pyroclastic flows. (The word comes from the Latin *pyro*, "fire," and *clastic*, "broken.") After the disaster at St. Pierre it became clear: All these deposits on volcanoes around the world, and all that destruction, were the result of the *nuées ardentes* — boiling, swiftly moving "avalanches" of gas, ash, pumice, and hot lava blocks.

That, Professor Woodard said, was the secret Mont Pelée revealed to science. And, like so many advances in volcanology, it came on the heels of a disaster. As we students hefted a piece of that discovery, what struck me was that only by directly observing the pyroclastic flow were scientists like Anderson and Flett able to fathom its mysteries. I was determined to see such things with my own eyes.

"This is what I want to do!" I scribbled in my notebook. "I want to be a volcanologist."

My guide through this nascent science was an aging, potbellied, profane, eternally curious, and tireless professor at Dartmouth College named Dick Stoiber. Legendary for his brilliant lectures on geology and his love of clambering on volcanoes with students, Stoiber was sixty-five when I wrote to ask if I could study with him at Dartmouth. On a tattered piece of paper, he replied in his jerky scrawl, "I haven't died yet and don't plan to anytime soon, so why don't you come and work with me?"

For two decades Stoiber and I were close collaborators, making twenty-five field trips around the world. We spent one night on the rim of the crater at Momotombo in Nicaragua, turning constantly from side to side as the heat rising through the scree baked our flanks. In the 1980s, during the civil wars in Nicaragua, Guatemala, and El Salvador, we survived more unnatural dangers as well — car crashes and attacks by teenaged rebels. We studied Mount St. Helens and Krakatau and Sakurajima in Japan, where the white-haired, white-mustachioed Stoiber was venerated and known as "Chicken San" for his resemblance to Colonel Sanders.

Stoiber had a restless and unconventional intellect, as shown by one of his most inspired ideas. After learning that heavy industry was using an instrument known as the COSPEC (short for correlation spectrometer) to measure the sulfur dioxide pollution pouring from smelters and power plants, Stoiber asked a question no other scientist had considered. Since sulfur dioxide is one of the main gases escaping from volcanoes, why not point the COSPEC at the vapors steaming from a crater? He did and it worked, giving science a rough tool to gauge how many tons per day of SO_2 were escaping from volcanoes. As a rule, the more gas, the more active the magma. Stoiber and I used the COSPEC at dozens of volcanoes and trained scientists in the Third World to use this simple, relatively cheap device.

Stoiber had similar hunches throughout his career, and, recognizing how little science still knew about the inner workings of the earth, he would refer to them as "fairy tales." Some turned out to be just that. Others, such as his work with the COSPEC, were brilliant.

As I began my graduate studies, I knew I wanted to devote my life to working on active volcanoes. But Dick understood the value of classic geological sleuthing and urged me, for my master's thesis, to reconstruct the massive 1902 eruption of the Santa María volcano in Guatemala by studying deposits from the blast. Flying with me into Guatemala in January 1978 — my first visit to a volcanically active region — he pointed out a glaring fact: the country is a vast volcanic landscape. Most of the houses and fields rest on pyroclastic flow deposits or the flanks of both active and dormant volcanoes. As we landed in Guatemala City, we saw in the distance Pacaya, which regularly spouts off with benign, Strombolian eruptions — named for the volcano near Sicily that routinely shoots out small columns of lava. (Since Roman times, Stromboli has been known as the "Lighthouse of the Mediterranean.") Farther on was Fuego, then Lake Atítlan, a stunning, 10-mile-wide, 1,000-foot-deep body of water that fills the caldera from a massive eruption 75,000 years ago. Around the edge of the lake are the much younger volcanoes Atítlan, Tolima, and San Pedro, each with fields and forests covering the fertile lower slopes and a dark gray scree of ash and lava above. Stoiber, trained in looking beneath the surface of the lush countryside, remarked that if an eruption like Atítlan were to occur today, 90 percent of Guatemala's 12.4 million people might perish.

In 1979, I spent two and a half months in Guatemala and southern Mexico, much of it on my hands and knees sifting through the clues left by Santa María. Believed to be extinct, Santa María roared to life on October 25, 1902. In one of the most powerful eruptions of the century, it spewed out a volume of pumice and ash that I demonstrated was ten times greater than that from the 1980 Mount St. Helens eruption. Though the exact number of casualties was never determined, the Santa María eruption killed at least several thousand people, many when the roofs of their homes collapsed from the weight of the ash. The blast sent an ash column 22 miles into the air, darkened the sky over Guatemala for days, and covered 106,000 square miles — an area the size of Virginia — with pumice, ash, and other debris.

Evidence of the eruption was there for anyone to see, concealed just beneath the fields and forests of western Guatemala. A layer of pumice — the light, porous rock that forms when frothy, gas-rich magma explodes — was readily identifiable by its snow-white color and texture. Piled as high as 6 feet on Santa María's flanks, the layer of pumice, ash, and rock fragments fanned out to ever shallower depths hundreds of miles away. Measuring the thickness and extent of the deposits as well as the diameter of the pumice lumps and old rock fragments, I was able to compile a detailed map showing the distribution of the deposits. I then calculated the energy and duration of the eruption and the total volume of material Santa Maria ejected. The eruption had created a classic Plinian column, named after Pliny the Younger, who first described the towering, pine tree–shaped eruption column over Vesuvius in A.D. 79. In a Plinian eruption, constant explosions blast out a stream of ejecta at up to 675 miles per hour, the superheated column rising as high as 26 miles until it usually collapses. It's a bit like pointing a fire hose of pumice, ash, and gas into the sky.

Digging in the dirt, piecing together the record of a little-studied eruption, was a valuable academic exercise, but I craved work on active volcanoes. Within a few months, I got my opportunity, at Mount St. Helens. And by the time I left there, with one of our colleagues dead and the scientific community caught flat-footed by the scale of the eruption, I had learned much about the ways of volcanoes and the woeful limits of our knowledge.

Before the blast, Mount St. Helens was a sublime volcanic form. Situated in the Cascade Range of western Washington State, St. Helens

— a symmetrical, 9,677-foot, snow-covered cone rising above ever-green forests — prompted comparisons to Japan's Fuji. Part of the Pacific "Ring of Fire," Mount St. Helens had been dormant for 123 years. But in 1979 the U.S. Geological Survey (USGS), well aware of St. Helens's past activity, had warned that it was the Cascades volcano most likely to erupt by century's end.

On March 27, 1980, Mount St. Helens discharged the first of the preliminary eruptions that culminated in the catastrophic blast of May 18. At Dartmouth, Stoiber and I learned of the initial eruption around 1 P.M. That afternoon, the USGS called to ask Dick to come help monitor the volcano. That same evening, he and I were on a flight from Boston to Portland, Oregon, with fourteen cases of equipment, intent on using the COSPEC to measure the sulfur dioxide pouring out of the volcano.

On March 29, in a plane rented by NBC News, Dick and I got our first look at the volcano. It was erupting as often as once an hour, propelling gray ash columns a mile into the air. Mount St. Helens was massive, and the first thing I noticed was that the pristine snow covering its flanks had been sullied by repeated coatings of ash. As we circled, the sight of this volcano coming to life set my stomach churning.

We stuck the 2½-foot COSPEC out the window and pointed its telescope skyward at clouds of gas and ash. Our research goal was simple. Was all this activity just another example of what Stoiber called "nature's noise," with the volcano rumbling and popping off but not threatening a major eruption? Or was it gearing up for a big blast? Given all the new activity, Stoiber suspected that a magma body was swelling under the volcano, which would release large quantities of sulfur dioxide. But again and again the COSPEC told us there was almost none. Was our instrument broken? Were we doing something wrong? We were the first scientists to have observed such an eruption accompanied by almost no release of gases.

In subsequent days, we returned to the volcano a dozen times. On March 30, the volcano let loose with ninety-three small eruptions. More than seventy planes — carrying reporters, geologists, and sightseers — flew around St. Helens that day. Armed with the

COSPEC, we were among that group. The result was always the same: virtually no SO_2 was being released. Finally, Stoiber and I reached an inescapable conclusion: Although a magma body was no doubt beneath the volcano — the USGS was picking up deep, subtle "harmonic tremors" below St. Helens, indicating the movement of magma — the current eruptions were not caused by exploding magma. They were strictly phreatic, or steam driven, a process in which groundwater seeps into a volcano, comes in contact with the hot interior, and causes small explosions. It's like throwing handfuls of water onto hot coals.

After sixteen days at Mount St. Helens, Stoiber and I returned to Dartmouth and wrote a paper for *Science* concluding that the eruptions were phreatic. But we ended on a note of caution. The last significant eruption of a Cascades volcano — Lassen Peak, in California, in 1914 — had started as a series of phreatic eruptions but had eventually devolved into a much more dangerous magmatic eruption. The same thing could happen at St. Helens.

David Johnston was a lean, kinetic, thirty-year-old volcanologist with the USGS. A gas specialist, he wanted to monitor the volcano with our COSPEC, and we agreed to leave it with him when we returned to Dartmouth. When we first ran into him, he had just been reprimanded by his superiors for flying to Mount St. Helens with a television news crew and telling the truth about the threat. The mountain, he said, was capable of a massive explosive eruption that could cause devastation for miles around. They were all in peril and should clear out.

"This is an extremely dangerous place to be," Johnston told the *Portland Oregonian.* "If it were to erupt right now, we would die. We're standing next to a dynamite keg and the fuse is lit. We just don't know how long the fuse is."

The young geologist knew what he was talking about. He had written his doctoral thesis on the evolution of magmas beneath the St. Augustine volcano in Alaska, which unleashed a large eruption in 1976. In describing the dangers of such a blast, Johnston wrote words that, in some ways, served as a warning of the forces that would kill him at Mount St. Helens.

"High-temperature and high-velocity shock waves extend far beyond the limits of discernable deposits," he said. "Hazard zones defined on the basis of deposits [alone do not] reflect this more extensive shock wave hazard, which at Augustine extends many kilometers offshore."

Johnston also knew about Bezymianny, a Russian volcano on the Kamchatka peninsula. On March 30, 1956, an unstable flank of 10,121-foot Bezymianny collapsed, causing a horizontal "directed blast" that cut off the top of the mountain, formed a crater 1.2 miles wide, sent an eruption column 21 miles into the air, devastated an area extending 15 miles from the volcano, and disgorged nearly a cubic mile of smoking ash and debris over an area of 200 square miles, in places to a thickness of 160 feet. No one was killed in the eruption only because Bezymianny was far from civilization. Such a blast, he realized, could take place at Mount St. Helens.

Johnston was one of the most enthusiastic volcanologists I'd ever met. Like the best in our field, he strove to work *on* volcanoes. He didn't ignore the risks. He just didn't fret endlessly about them. Either you were comfortable being on volcanoes or you weren't, and those who constantly worried about what might happen quickly found another line of work.

Born and raised in my home state, Illinois, Johnston got his Ph.D. at the University of Washington and spent much of the late 1970s working on volcanoes in Alaska and the Pacific Northwest. In the summer of 1979, he and Wes Hildreth, a USGS colleague, spent nearly two months in Alaska's remote Valley of the Ten Thousand Smokes, the site, in 1912, of the most powerful eruption of the twentieth century. "Ten Thousand Smokes" refers to the countless fumaroles dotting the vast debris field that remained after the Novarupta volcano exploded, spewing out 25 times more pumice and ash than Mount St. Helens would in 1980. Hildreth and Johnston were studying ashfall and pyroclastic flow deposits that extended 12 miles down the upper Ukak River valley as well as taking gas samples at Mount Mageik, part of the same volcanic complex.

There the USGS team tried to sample gases rushing out of fumaroles in the crater. Roped together, the geologists climbed up the glacier on the 7,100-foot volcano. At the crater's lip, they stared down into a steaming lake gone yellow from the sulfur emitted by Mageik. Vigorous fumaroles under and around the lake stirred up waves on the water's surface, and the gaseous hiss was deafening. They wanted to descend to the bottom of the crater and sample gases on the edge of the highly acidic lake, but feared they might be asphyxiated by lethal concentrations of sulfur dioxide and carbon dioxide. Johnston volunteered to go into the crater first.

"Dave was our canary in the coal mine," recalled Hildreth. "He went down on a rope and he didn't pass out, so we all went down. It turned out to be all right; it was so windy that there wasn't enough accumulated gas to kill us."

Dave Johnston was also the first volcanologist on St. Helens after it awakened, measuring gases at fumaroles near the summit. In April, another of Stoiber's students flew out to train Johnston how to use the COSPEC, and for the next month he monitored the volcano with the instrument. It was still emitting only a trace of sulfur dioxide.

Back at Dartmouth, Stoiber and I closely watched the events at St. Helens. The bulge on the volcano's upper, northern flank, first noticed at the end of March, continued to grow. Washington's governor, Dixy Lee Ray, declared a state of emergency on April 3, restricting access to an area of up to 8 miles from the crater. When the eruptive activity slowed in late April and early May, loggers, vacationers, and others complained bitterly about being kept out of the "Red Zone." But the geologists knew that something bad was afoot; only a fool would ignore the swelling hump, which by late April measured 1.5 miles across and protruded nearly 300 feet.

All the while, Johnston kept monitoring gases and studying the volcano from a USGS observation post known as Coldwater II, 5.7 miles north of Mount St. Helens. Located on Coldwater Ridge, 1,500 feet above the valley floor, the post initially seemed to provide a safe vantage point; pyroclastic flows, the USGS reasoned, would not reach such an elevation. But as the northern flank continued to bulge, the scientists worried that 5.7 miles might be too close to the mountain if it blew. The USGS was even planning to move an armored vehicle to Coldwater II to protect Johnston and other geologists should the volcano erupt.

Johnston took part in discussing the safety of Coldwater II. On some people's minds was Bezymianny, the Russian volcano. Johnston argued that a Bezymianny-type eruption was possible at St. Helens, an opinion shared by Jack Hyde, a geology professor at Tacoma Community College.

"I have a gut feeling that as the bulge continues to grow, something dramatic is going to happen soon," Hyde told the *Tacoma News Tribune* twelve days before the eruption. "It could come suddenly without any leakage of magma gases . . . The blast from the explosion of a Soviet volcano in 1956 blew down trees 15 miles away."

Then he warned that the scientists observing Mount St. Helens from places like Coldwater II could be pressing their luck. "I hope they're not in a direct line," he said. "That's like looking down the barrel of a loaded gun."

A week later Johnston left Coldwater II — where he lived in a house trailer — and turned the post over to his field assistant, Harry Glicken, a young, temporary worker for the USGS. The day before the eruption, Johnston and Glicken flew a helicopter to the top of Mount St. Helens, where a series of photographs taken with a telephoto lens capture Johnston's work at a fumarole on the bulging flank.

That evening, May 17, Johnston replaced Glicken at Coldwater II. He was up early the next morning, a clear, cool Sunday. At 8:32 A.M., an earthquake measuring 5.2 on the Richter scale shook the volcano, triggering the collapse of the bulging, unstable northern flank. One side of the volcano disintegrated in a huge landslide. Freed from the confining pressure of the mountainside, the exhumed magma body exploded with unfathomable force. Photographs taken 10 miles away show the mountain sliding down, followed by an angry, dark gray cloud expanding so rapidly — 300 miles an hour — that soon the billowing form blackened the entire horizon. Alone at his post, Johnston may have felt the earthquake. He may have been watching the volcano as it opened up, then reached out to consume him. He managed to shout over his radio to the USGS command post in Vancouver, Washington: "Vancouver! Vancouver! This is it!"

A volunteer observer, 1.8 miles behind Johnston, saw the geologist swallowed up, then reported his own imminent demise. "The whole north side is giving way!" Gerald Martin said over the radio. "The camper and car over to the south of me are covered. It's consuming the USGS people, and it's going to get me too!"

No trace of Johnston was ever found. In fact, nearly everything on Coldwater Ridge vanished, obliterated by an explosion that swept away trees 6 feet in diameter and scoured the earth down to bedrock. Similar to the situation at Bezymianny, a zone of devastation extended roughly 15 miles north of the volcano, covering a total of 230 square miles. The eruption decapitated the top 1,300 feet of the mountain, turning the snow-covered summit into a bare gray stump. Roaring out of the volcano for nine hours, the eruption column reached a height of 16 miles and covered central and eastern Washington in inches of ash. A total of 58 people died.

The eruption blew down trees in a wedge-shaped area measuring 12 by 20 miles. Sixty-five people — loggers, campers, hikers — were in the blowdown zone; 48 of them died. Another 10 people just outside the zone also perished. Of the people who lost their lives in the eruption, 23 of the bodies were never found.

Autopsies were performed on 25 victims. From those studies and from interviews with survivors, it's evident that Mount St. Helens's surge suffocated many of its victims. Seventeen of the 25 died from asphyxiation, 5 from burns, and 3 from being struck in the head by falling trees or rocks. Most of the asphyxiated died immediately as thick clouds of ash filled their throats, windpipes, and lungs, forming plugs of ash and mucus that prevented breathing. As a team of doctors reported in the *New England Journal of Medicine,* "Once one became enveloped in the ash cloud, it would probably take only a few minutes to suffocate." Others lingered for up to 16 days, their lungs eventually overwhelmed by the assault of heat and ash.

Four loggers were working 12 miles from the summit when the volcano blew. They heard the roar of the pyroclastic surge heading their way through the forest. When it hit, the surge flung them to the ground and engulfed them in searing heat and darkness. They, too, felt as if they were suffocating and choking on ash. The men, all in their thirties, were badly burned over a third to a half of their bodies. When the surge passed and light returned, they struggled over to an ash-covered stream and dunked themselves to ease the pain of the burns. Seeking help, they began to walk out of the forest, but a landslide blocked their way. They soon found a spring and drank ceaselessly but were unable to quench their infernal thirst. Two of the men stayed by the spring; rescued by a helicopter, they reached the Oregon Burn Center in Portland 10 hours after they were injured.

The other two tried again to walk out. One eventually could go no farther and expired. His body was discovered several weeks later. Rescuers found the other man and took him to the burn center 13 hours after the blast.

The loggers had third-degree burns on their arms, legs, and backs. Their tongues and throats were also seared. One thirty-six-year-old man remarkably survived after receiving several skin grafts. He never needed a breathing tube. The other two had difficulty breathing, and within hours doctors intubated them, blowing oxygen into their burned lungs. One lingered for 10 days before expiring, the other 16. They might well have survived their external burns, but the damage to their lungs brought on infection and what doctors call "respiratory distress syndrome." Their lungs were never able to function properly and finally gave out.

The devastation at Mount St. Helens, which included $1 billion in property damage, was caused by an eruption that was puny in geological terms. About once a decade, a blast this size occurs somewhere in the world. The cataclysmic eruptions that shaped the face of the earth, altering the climate and perhaps leading to mass extinctions, were hundreds or thousands of times larger than the blast that held America's attention for months.

By 5 A.M. on the morning after the eruption, Stoiber and I were back in Portland, where we spent several days analyzing the ash that had fallen over central Washington. The volcanological community was in shock, not only at the loss of one of its own, but at the sheer force of the eruption. We had discussed the possibility of a "sector collapse," but few had believed that a horizontal blast of such magnitude would actually occur.

In the following weeks, our sadness was mixed with guilt and anger that we had not been able to forecast so large an event. As volcanologists started to study the enormous debris avalanche and related mudflows, which left chunks of the mountain the size of houses scattered for several miles, they shook their heads in recognition. The debris flow was similar to others around the world in which an unstable flank of a volcano had crumpled, setting off a titanic explosion. Bezymianny in Kamchatka, Bandai in Japan, Colima in Mexico, Galunggung in Indonesia — all had left the same geological signs that now surrounded us at St. Helens.

As a young volcanologist, I was fascinated by the complexity of trying to forecast the behavior of so elemental, hidden, and devastating a force of nature. Deciphering what was going on inside a volcano was like trying to put together a complex, three-dimensional puzzle for which you had only a quarter of the pieces, requiring you to fill in the blanks with your best assumptions.

Under Mount St. Helens, seismic activity had been telling us that magma was on the move. In the air, gas activity had been telling us that the eruptions were driven by steam, not magma. And on the surface we had watched the flank of the volcano distend, even measuring its menacing rate of growth. Yet no one had put it all together — that magma was stirring, that the volcano was plugged, and that St. Helens was about to experience a massive explosion that would kill people 15 miles away. If we had figured it out, Dave Johnston and fifty-seven others would be alive today. As is often the case in volcanology, understanding and progress follow disaster.

More than a decade later, in January 1993, as we began to descend the escarpment onto Galeras, not a thought about Mount St. Helens crossed my mind. Perhaps it should have. On a different continent, at a smaller volcano, several thousand miles farther south on the Pacific "Ring of Fire," explosive gases were sealed tightly under a dome of rock, giving scant hint of their mounting pressure.

Once again, my colleagues and I would be fooled.

3

·················

COLLEAGUES

A S THE MEMBERS of our group held on to the thick mountaineering rope and backed carefully down the face of the amphitheater wall, I stood on the rim with José Arlés Zapata, the young INGEOMINAS geologist, and waited my turn. Shortly before 10 A.M., José radioed the geological observatory in Pasto to check on any changes in seismic activity at Galeras. All was quiet.

The temperature was around 40 degrees F, the winds light, and the mountain still so socked in that we couldn't see the crater from where we stood. Negotiating the escarpment's steep upper reaches may be psychologically easier in the fog, for if the inexperienced or faint of heart could actually see the sharp drop, they might entertain second thoughts. If you hang on to the rope, however, there is little danger of falling. The only real threat is that someone above you might dislodge a rock and send it caroming off your head. After the eruption, some of my colleagues criticized me for not requiring everyone in our party to don hard hats and fire-resistant jumpsuits. It's a good idea — in theory and in hindsight. But at the time few geologists wore such gear when working on active volcanoes. Other than ensuring that our group wore sturdy boots and warm clothing, I was not about to enforce a dress code. We were all professionals. Even if I had forced everyone to put on protective clothing, I am confident that not a single life would have been saved.

The amphitheater wall is 450 feet high, and about a third of the way down the scarp changes from a 60-degree face of andesitic rock to a gentler 45-degree slope. The lower surface is covered with blocks and scoria — loose lava cinders — and after a series of easy zigzags you find yourself at the base of the scarp, standing in a moat between the amphitheater wall and the cone of the active volcano. About 50 yards wide, the moat is covered in volcanic ejecta ranging from the size of a pea to that of a small car. The moat's surface is pocked with impact craters, some 10 feet wide, left by boulders heaved out of Galeras in recent eruptions. Despite these unsettling reminders of the volcano's power, the moat is a good place to catch your breath and chat before heading on to the more dangerous terrain of the cone, where the aim is to quickly take your measurements and get out.

Our group was divided into four teams. The first, led by Igor Menyailov, was to sample gases at fumaroles in and around the crater. The second, led by Geoff Brown, was measuring gravity at various points on the cone and the crater rim. The third, led by Mike Conway of Florida International University, was planning to insert special thermometers, known as thermocouples, inside fumaroles to study the temperatures and physics of volcanic gases. And the fourth, led by Andy Adams from Los Alamos, was reconnoitering Galeras for later research on its magmatic fluids. All of these projects had the same goal: to take the volcano's pulse, enabling us better to forecast Galeras's future behavior based on the movement of magma and gases. I was overseeing the foray onto the crater.

At fifteen people, the group was larger than I had wanted, and we moved slowly. Later, my friend Mike Conway would say that we should have moved with more dispatch. "We were certainly not prepared," he said. "We were kind of dilettantes. We should have taken better precautions. We were all too cavalier."

I disagree. Our size did slow us down, but no one was so nonchalant that we tarried or squandered time in idle conversation. Whenever I walk onto a volcano, a clock is ticking in my head. I'm not counting down toward a feared eruption, merely aware that volcanoes are unpredictable and the sooner I clear out the better.

My sense of urgency stemmed, in part, from my own experience of being suddenly fogged in as I descended craters and scaled caldera walls, a predicament that greatly increases the likelihood of becoming disoriented or stumbling over a cliff. What made me especially wary, however, was the bitter experience of my mentor, Dick Stoiber.

In 1975 Dick and his brightest graduate student at Dartmouth, Gary Malone, climbed the relatively benign, 3,038-foot Sicilian volcano, Stromboli, to observe its constantly fountaining lava. The twenty-seven-year-old Malone grew up in a small town in southern Illinois, the son of a safety engineer at a coal mine. His rise from this modest background, coupled with his enthusiasm and first-rate mind, had endeared him to Dick.

Stoiber and Malone climbed to the crater in late afternoon and stayed after it grew dark, absorbed by the spectacle of lava jets spurting into the sky. Dick figured they could either descend Stromboli at dawn or use their flashlights to walk down at night on a well-worn trail. It began to rain, so rather than spend a miserable night on the volcano, they started down the mountain shortly after midnight. Stoiber had lost his flashlight and the rain had ruined Malone's, but they carried on, carefully picking their way. In the rain and darkness they wandered off the main trail, inadvertently stumbling onto a secondary one, and headed for the lights at Stromboli's base.

Walking slightly ahead of Stoiber on the narrow trail, Malone fell over a cliff, landing about 40 feet below. Stoiber first lost sight of Malone, then heard, "Dick! Dick! Don't move. I've fallen."

Stoiber crept toward the voice and, sensing an abyss, stopped. He couldn't see his student but could hear him well. Malone said he thought he had a badly broken leg but that he'd be all right. Then he warned Dick not to go any farther until first light.

They talked until 4:45 A.M., when the sky over the Mediterranean showed a hint of the sunrise. "I'll get you out as fast as I can," Stoiber promised as he left, thinking that Malone's injuries were serious but not fatal. Walking, then running, the professor threaded his way through the slowly brightening landscape, gradually recognizing where Malone had fallen. In less than an hour, Stoiber had reached the bottom of the volcano and contacted the police. They formed a search party and went to rescue Malone, leaving the exhausted, sixty-four-year-old Stoiber to rest. A few hours later they returned with a body on a stretcher. Malone had died of internal bleeding.

"It just about killed me," said Stoiber. He accompanied the body back to southern Illinois for Gary's funeral.

A series of small miscalculations had doomed Malone, but foremost was the decision to linger on the volcano too long. And so at Galeras, as we assembled in the moat around 10:15 A.M. to catch our breath, I was impatient to herd the group up the cone and begin to work, knowing, as always, that we were racing the clock and the weather. Igor — a slender, five-foot-seven man with bright blue eyes and gray hair — had arrived in Pasto only two days earlier and was tired but excited to be working on a South American volcano at last. Wearing a red rain jacket, khaki pants, and a black and white baseball cap, he was, as usual, smoking a cigarette, yet seemed the least winded of us all. As always, I was impressed by his relentless pace.

The lip of the crater, 300 feet above, was shrouded in fog.

As we made our way toward the first fumarole, following a path in the scree that cut diagonally upward across the cone, Igor and I talked about his daughter, Irina, whom he hoped might study with me at Arizona State University. I was scanning the surface of the volcano as we walked, looking for any evidence of new rocks tossed out by the July 1992 eruption. But Igor, who had a one-track volcanological mind — gases — seemed uninterested in the geology as we steadily climbed higher on the volcano.

Breaking off from Igor for a minute, I spoke with José Arlés Zapata and Nestor García. "He seems like such a nice man," Nestor told me, surprised that an acclaimed volcanologist could be so friendly and unpretentious. As we trudged up the cone, Nestor rattled off the dates that some of Igor's best-known papers had appeared in scientific journals. He and José Arlés spoke of them as if they were scripture.

We heard the first fumarole, Deformes, before we saw it. Located about three quarters of the way up the cone on Galeras's southwestern flank, Deformes is a cluster of several holes, up to a yard in diameter, which release gases emanating from inside the earth. The *whooshing* sound falls somewhere between the roar of the ocean and the howl of a jet engine.

We then smelled Deformes as its acidic vapors hit us in the face. At last we saw the fumarole, with thick columns of steam shooting out of its vents, forming clouds above the volcano that rapidly broke apart and drifted down the western slope. The rocks around the fumarole were encrusted with bright yellow sulfur deposits. Farther downwind, for at least 125 feet, Deformes's gases had painted the scoria-covered slope a paler shade of yellow, fading to a faint hue of yellow-gray.

Deformes's final sensory assault hit the taste buds, as our mouths filled with the bitter flavor of burned matches.

We probably reached Deformes around 11 A.M., although nearly everyone has a different recollection of that day, especially when it comes to times and the sequence of actions. Most of us remember heading straight for Deformes, but Andy Macfarlane recalls that he first climbed to the crater's lip to look inside, then walked down to Deformes. But I'm convinced that our first stop was Igor's main goal, Deformes, where the Russian took the lead in sampling gases. After pausing briefly to look at the fumarole, Geoff Brown — accompanied by the Colombians Fernando Cuenca and Carlos Trujillo — walked to the rim of the crater. He pulled out his gravimeter and began circling the volcano, taking measurements.

Dense streams of gas hissed from Deformes at about 440 degrees F, with shifting winds blowing the noxious clouds in different directions. A handful of us watched Igor pull out a new double-chamber collection bottle that he hoped would further improve the quality of his samples. Others, like Luis LeMarie of Ecuador, prepared to sample gases when Igor was finished at the main Deformes fumarole. Deformes did have satellite vents, but everyone wanted to tap into the large fumarole because it offered the hottest and purest gases.

The choking fumes forced most of us to put on respirators — "It was terrible when that gas cloud came your way," recalled LeMarie — but Igor was unfazed. Without a mask, a cigarette dangling from his lips, he inserted the silica glass tube — capable of withstanding temperatures up to 2,550 degrees F — into the mouth of the large fumarole. Then he knelt and did what he had done for countless hours on dozens of volcanoes: watched patiently as the gases bubbled through his collection bottles, slowly revealing the earth's secrets.

The first time I worked on a volcano with Igor, in Nicaragua in 1982, I knew immediately that he was my kind of scientist. He arrived in Managua with two boxes of supplies. The first contained his gas sampling equipment and other scientific paraphernalia. The second contained homemade pickles, black bread, sausages, and vodka. He generously shared everything, be it his latest professional insights or his *Russkaya kolbasa*.

I had met Igor the year before at a conference in Japan. Stoiber had known the Russian for a decade, and I recognized that he was a leading gas specialist with a superb geochemical pedigree: Both of his parents were renowned Soviet volcanologists, and his mother had reportedly climbed Kamchatka's highest volcano while pregnant with Igor.

Igor had risen to international prominence because of his meticulous work on what gases tell us about a volcano's behavior. His research excelled for a simple reason: He had the grit and courage to sit on a volcano for hours and sample gases. He loved being in the crater, as I saw immediately on Momotombo, a picturesque volcano whose conical shape soars 4,128 feet above the scrubby northwestern shore of Lake Managua. Momotombo is famous for its pure, hot gases; heat from its fiery magma body fuels a geothermal system that produces a third of Nicaragua's electricity.

Even the way Igor walked onto a volcano was impressive. Momotombo is not tall, but its flanks are covered in black scoria, and hiking into the crater is like walking uphill on marbles. Igor slowly and relentlessly trudged up the mountain — no pauses, no complaints. Once inside the 450- by 750-foot crater, Igor was in his element. The volcano's magma body is very close to the surface, so it releases gases at extraordinarily high temperatures. Generally we're satisfied to sample gases at 600 degrees F. We're very happy to find gases at 1,000 degrees F. But at Momotombo, the gases blew out of fumaroles at an astonishing 1,740 degrees F, not far from the melting temperature of rocks. For gas specialists, it's about as close as you can get to stepping inside the earth.

Hovering around the roaring fumaroles, Stoiber and I quickly donned full-face gas masks. But Igor and his assistant, Slava Shapar, eschewed such niceties. I can still picture Igor inside the infernal crater, his head turned away from the suffocating gases, his feet planted next to the fumarole, which glowed bright orange from the heat. Shoving his silica tube into the hole, he watched as the force from the gases sent shudders through his sampling bottle. Without a mask, he remained in the gas stream for minutes at a time, intently collecting bottle after bottle of samples. In hell on earth, the Russian had found heaven.

In the three weeks I worked with Igor in Nicaragua, we returned to Momotombo four times, as it was best to have a range of samples. Igor achieved no dramatic scientific breakthrough at Momotombo, but he did add important samples to his growing collection of data. His goal was to understand when magma was on the move, and he was an expert at deciphering the messages encoded in the gases released from a rising magma body. As magma nears the surface, increasing the chances of an eruption, water is the first — and by far the dominant — gas to escape, in the form of steam. Then comes carbon dioxide, sulfur dioxide, and finally hydrogen chloride, mixed with traces of others, such as fluorine. When a magma body is at a depth of, say, 6 miles, small amounts of sulfur and chlorine are generally released in certain stable proportions. But if Igor began to measure increasing concentrations of sulfur and low concentrations of chlorine, and if that discrepancy continued to grow, he could be fairly certain that magma was struggling up toward the earth's surface. In Kamchatka, Igor had shown that concentrations of sulfur increased before eruptions at six different volcanoes.

My friendship with Igor, forged in the crater, grew as we spent many evenings together in Managua, Nicaragua's capital, then ruled by the leftist Sandanista government. Igor learned English after listening to Elvis Presley records and reading illicit Western publications in the 1950s and 1960s. I helped him polish his English slang — and his profanity. He was an avid pupil. One hot evening, we were returning from Momotombo to Managua on a dirt road. Exhausted, thirsty, and caked in grime, we were about halfway there when a Russian truck pulled in front of us, kicking up a cloud of dust that engulfed our jeep. "Fucking truck!" yelled the normally low-key Igor, beaming at having mastered the American vernacular.

One night we ate at Managua's best restaurant, an open-air place with excellent steak. Our party of six polished off two bottles of Nicaragua's superb rum, Flor de Caña, then devoured the beef, which Igor liked to call "the big meat." At one point, Dick Stoiber's steak flew off his plate and skittered across the table, knocking over rum-and-Cokes like bowling pins. Dick, not known for his table manners, merely picked up the big meat and finished it with his hands.

Igor was not boisterous, but he did have the proverbial Russian hollow leg. By the end of dinner, which also included a bottle of vodka, our two Nicaraguan colleagues were nearly unconscious. Dick and I were pretty drunk, but Igor seemed in fine form. A few days later, a boozy celebration of Igor's forty-fifth birthday culminated with his loudly singing Elvis Presley songs. I remember how fascinated he was by his birthday cake's trick candles, which he would blow out, only to see burst into flame again.

Igor and I didn't see each other for another decade. We exchanged letters and Christmas cards and published an article together in a Russian volcanology journal. In the meantime, Mikhail Gorbachev had come to office, changed the world — and Russia — with perestroika, then fallen from power as the USSR disintegrated. Igor and I got together again in 1992 in San Francisco, where we boarded a plane to Hawaii and spent a week at a conference on volcanic gases. Sharing a room, we spent a lot of time together. The freedom and chaos of the new Russia alternately vexed and excited him. He was upset over the breakup of the Soviet Union and the ensuing collapse of funding for Russian science, but he was not blind to the advantages of the new Russia, including its opening up to the world. We discussed my finally traveling to Kamchatka. A strikingly beautiful peninsula in the Russian Far East, it is studded with some of the world's most active volcanoes but had been off-limits to foreigners for years because of its many military bases. I considered Igor a close friend and was anxious to learn more about his life in Russia and to work on the volcanoes to which he had dedicated his career.

The day before we left Hawaii, we went shopping for souvenirs. He had a paltry travel budget, so I asked him if I could buy some Hawaiian shirts and a dress for his granddaughter. He consented, and I spent $32 on a few gifts. Walking out of the store, Igor turned to me and said, "Well, Stan, you've just spent what the director of our institute of volcanology makes in a month."

Igor's was a classic Russian story, a tale of stoicism, courage, high achievement, and overcoming adversity.

As I learned much later when I visited Moscow, the legend of his traveling to the top of the 15,862-foot Klyuchevskoi volcano in his mother's womb was true. In 1999 in Moscow, I met Igor's ninety-year-old mother, Sofia I. Naboko, an elfin, redheaded woman with a vibrant mind and keen memory. She recounted the story of how Igor, three months in utero, ascended the giant volcano.

Sofia was married to Alexander A. Menyailov, a noted Soviet volcanologist, and in 1936 they were offered a position at a new volcanological station, Klyuchi, in east-central Kamchatka. Klyuchi was a remote village near three of the peninsula's most active volcanoes — Klyuchevskoi, Bezymianny, and Tolbachik. Surrounded by tundra inhabited by wolves, reindeer, and aboriginal Kamchadals, the station was little more than a few cabins. In late summer, the couple moved into one of them, which was still unfinished. Their first item of business was to climb Klyuchevskoi.

Traveling 15 miles on horseback and fording rivers, Naboko, Menyailov, four other scientists, and several workers took several days to reach a camp on the flank of the volcano, at around 9,500 feet. Naboko had told only her husband and one other scientist that she was pregnant.

It was early September, and after resting a day or two the group set out at 4 A.M. to climb to the crater, a twelve-hour trip that took them up the icy flanks of the volcano. Klyuchevskoi is a classic stratovolcano formed by millennia of lava flows piling on top of layers of lava and ash. Its massive, symmetrical flanks are several miles long. Reaching the summit in the afternoon, they found the volcano chuffing away, spewing thick, black gas and ash that prevented them from descending into the crater. Instead, they took temperature and gas samples from fumaroles on the flank and collected minerals and rocks. A flamboyant topographer named Dyakonov measured and roughly mapped the crater. They had planned to begin their descent around 6 P.M., making use of the late summer, northern light to help them negotiate the most treacherous parts of the trail. If all went well, they would be back at base camp before midnight.

Sofia Naboko, then twenty-seven, had just become the first woman to climb to the top of Klyuchevskoi. Dyakonov, standing near the crater rim, began to celebrate the occasion by shouting, "Long live the first woman on Klyuchevskoi! Long live the Communist Youth League!" In the midst of his antics he lost his balance, fell, and slid a mile down the glaciated flank of the volcano, eventually gliding out of sight. After a few minutes, his colleagues could hear his cries from far below. It was 4 degrees F below zero and perhaps four more hours of daylight remained. The group realized they now had to descend an unknown, treacherous flank of Klyuchevskoi to look for the fool who had just fallen.

"It was all ice, the most terrible place, a steep slope of about 45 degrees," recalled Naboko. "We had to rope ourselves together. I was sliding on my rear end. We were angry with him. We could have died ourselves. I was constantly thinking about my child. I remember it now, and my voice still trembles."

After a harrowing nine-hour descent — most of it in darkness — they found Dyakonov before dawn. His surveyor's tripod, strapped to his back, had finally stopped his fall when it became lodged between two boulders. Miraculously, he suffered only bruises and minor cuts.

Arriving back at camp at midmorning, Naboko found her lips swollen and raw, her hands cut, and the bottom of her special cotton climbing pants ripped out. But Igor was fine. Returning home ten days after they had set out from Klyuchi, Naboko was hailed as a hero, her picture published in the *Kamchatskaya Pravda* newspaper. "I think our heroism was not in the fact that we climbed up," said Naboko. "This is our work. Our heroism was in rescuing him."

Six months later, on March 14, 1937, she gave birth to Igor in a small hospital in the village near the observatory. It was a harsh place for a newborn. Temperatures fell to 60 degrees below zero. Igor was raised on breast milk, porridge, and dried fruit and vegetables. He slept in a sled. He often spent time with a babysitter when his mother was working on volcanoes.

In the USSR, Stalin's terror was at its peak in 1937, and the secret police arrested many people in the village, including the postmaster and the principal of the school. Igor's mother and father were convinced they were next, for anyone who had achieved prominence seemed bound for the gulag. They made plans to leave Klyuchi, hopeful they would be safer in the more anonymous world of Moscow. "We were sitting on our bags and waiting for them to come and arrest us," recalled Naboko. The secret police never showed up.

When Igor was eight months old, the family took two months to journey to Moscow by boat and train. In 1941, when Hitler invaded the Soviet Union, Naboko evacuated her son to the relative safety of the Ural Mountains, where they lived on war rations. After the war, the family returned to the volcanological station at Klyuchi for several years. Igor lived a tranquil, bucolic existence. A quiet, pensive child, he played with wooden blocks made by the station's workmen and was fascinated with the horses, cows, chickens, and pigs in the village. His parents were often away on volcanoes, traveling to the mountains in winter by dogsled.

Igor spent his youth living alternately in Kamchatka and Moscow. He loved Klyuchi, and during the summer he sometimes accompanied his parents on their trips to Kamchatka's majestic wilderness, an experience that instilled in him a love of fieldwork.

He entered a geological institute in Moscow and began his formal study of volcanoes. In 1958, still a student, Igor went to a public phone station on Leninsky Prospekt. In line there he met a pretty young woman, two years his senior, with wavy blond hair, named Lyudmila Pavlovna Nikitina. She was a student in chemistry and physics at the Institute of Nonferrous Metals and Gold. They quickly fell in love, discovering a mutual passion for Elvis and the jitterbug. Soviet society had loosened up considerably since the death of Stalin in 1953, and without fear of execution or exile to the gulag, people such as Igor and Lyudmila — or "Mila," as he called her — could obtain bootleg copies of Elvis's records and play them at private parties. Igor did an uncanny imitation of Elvis, singing "Hound Dog" and "Heartbreak Hotel" as he gyrated his hips and shook his shoulders. In the evenings he would sometimes adopt the Elvis look, slicking his hair back and wearing short, tight pants as he strolled along Moscow's wide, dreary avenues.

In or out of costume, he cut a handsome figure: blond hair, blue eyes, finely sculpted nose. "I just shut up and watched him for the first three years," his wife told me. The couple was married in 1959 and shared a cramped apartment with Igor's mother, who was divorced by then. After graduating from the geological institute, Igor felt the pull of Kamchatka and Klyuchi — a yearning heightened by the couple's weariness at their lack of privacy in Moscow. When an opening arose at the volcanological station in Klyuchi in 1962, Igor persuaded his bride to embark on a new life eight time zones and 5,000 miles to the east. After finally arriving in the village, Lyudmila realized she had gotten far more than she had imagined: rough country living, a one-room cabin, rats chewing off the cat's tail.

"I cried for four months nonstop," she recalled.

"Igor wanted so badly to go to the station — it was his motherland," said Sofia Naboko. "Lyudmila did not want to go. She was a born Muscovite."

Eventually the grandeur of Kamchatka and its volcanoes won

over Lyudmila, who began to collaborate on Igor's research projects. Four months after they arrived she became pregnant, and in 1963 she delivered a daughter, Irina Igorovna, in the same hospital with some of the same doctors and nurses who had delivered Igor twenty-six years before. The baby spent a year with her parents. But it was a strain to rear a child in such primitive conditions, where only salmon and caviar were plentiful, so Igor and Lyudmila sent Irina to live with Mila's mother in Moscow. Irina was essentially raised by her grandmother in the capital. Her parents — especially her mother — visited regularly, and she returned to Kamchatka for a year when she was six and for three years when she was eleven. The long absences were hard on everybody, but the family accepted the separations as a necessary condition of Igor and Lyudmila's research.

"He never said anything about the separations," Irina Menyailova told me. "He was not the kind to say anything sentimental . . . I remember lying on the couch with him as he told me fairy tales. We would watch TV together, play piano with four hands. At times I would play and he would sing Elvis Presley."

Igor and Lyudmila's stint in Kamchatka, originally supposed to last three years, stretched into three decades. Living both in Klyuchi and in the peninsula's capital of Petropavlovsk-Kamchatsky, Igor, often with Lyudmila, worked on many of Kamchatka's volcanoes. In the early days, four times a year Igor and a small team of scientists would set out on horseback for month-long expeditions to Klyuchevskoi, Tolbachik, Sheveluch, and other volcanoes. He quickly earned a reputation as a bold researcher and had many close calls. Once, sampling gases during a trip one winter to 10,770-foot Sheveluch, he fell backward and slid 100 yards down the volcano's icy slope before being stopped by a boulder. Shortly afterward, in 1964, a pyroclastic flow obliterated the cabin on Sheveluch's flank that Igor's group was using as a base camp.

Doing research for his doctorate on Bezymianny, the site of the massive, St. Helens–style eruption in 1956, Igor spent so much time measuring gases that he became violently ill from inhaling too much fluorine. Camped on the volcano, he and Mila were visited every few days by a worker bringing food, water, and mail. The man also carried telegrams from the chief of the volcanological station ordering Igor and Lyudmila off the mountain. They refused to budge until their work was completed.

While performing gas studies on Ebeko, just south of Kamchatka on the Kurile Islands, Igor calculated the intervals between the volcano's small eruptions — about every thirty minutes — and gauged the farthest point of the rockfall. Standing just outside the rain of ejecta, Igor, Lyudmila, and the other scientists would wait for an eruption to end, then run in, sample gases, and get out before the next blast. Igor refused to let an erupting volcano interfere with his customary afternoon nap. On Ebeko, he would merely lie down on the scree after lunch and nod off, oblivious of the periodic rumbling from the volcano a few hundred yards away.

Several times Igor, Lyudmila, and others were stranded on volcanoes for days or weeks when cloudy weather prevented helicopters from reaching them. Slowly running out of food, they would eat dried bread and pick wild mushrooms and berries, confident the weather would clear.

When Irina was eighteen, Igor took her — his only child — to the top of Sheveluch to collect gas samples. Leaving Lyudmila in a cabin on the volcano's flank, father and daughter spent a night near the crater, waking early the next day to begin sampling. Suddenly the volcano cleared its throat, throwing a cloud of stones into the air.

"Dad said, 'Look up at the stones! Watch them as they fall!'" said Irina, who would go on to became a volcanologist. "I could see the stones falling right onto me and I turned, ran away, fell down, and cried. I heard a big boulder land right near me. I lay there, being covered with hail-like stones, for some time. When I finally stood up and saw my father, he was so worried about me he was just gray. He told me that there was a special skill to being in a stonefall, to look up and dodge them as they land. We did not tell my mother about this."

Igor loved the solitude of his work. It was in the field, not the lab, where he renewed himself. "He was not exactly an unsociable person, but he liked to be alone with his thoughts," recalled Lyudmila. "He was a lone wolf."

His colleagues saw and respected this side of Menyailov. Anatoly Khrenov, a young graduate student when he went to work with Igor in 1969, spent seventeen days with him on the 7,073-foot Kambalny volcano. When Khrenov thinks of Menyailov now, two images spring to mind: Igor crouching next to a fumarole for hours, taking gas samples, and Igor sitting by himself in the evening, smoking and listening to the radio.

Another colleague, Viktor Sugrobov, remembers the contrast between the refined, sensitive Menyailov — a man who never pulled rank on his subordinates — and the difficult and dangerous work he had chosen to do.

But Igor wasn't always as cultured as Sugrobov believed. He told me of an unusual experiment that he and a Russian colleague conducted during an eruption at Kamchatka's 12,080-foot Tolbachik volcano. The two men rode to the volcano in a helicopter, and shortly after the chopper left, Tolbachik began spewing large quantities of ash. They moved away from the crater as ash darkened the sky and quickly blanketed the mountain like gray snow. Walking along, they generated "St. Elmo's Fire," a phenomenon in which freshly fallen volcanic ash crackles with lightning and brilliant colors as you walk through it. Soon, the ash-thickened air was so highly charged with static electricity — the tiny, expelled particles of rock, torn apart in the eruption process, bristle with energy — that they could literally throw lightning bolts off their hands at each other. The eruption slowed, and it wasn't long before Igor and his colleague dropped their pants to urinate and began flicking lightning bolts off their penises.

In his fifties, Igor achieved the scientific prominence he deserved, heading a volcanological laboratory in Kamchatka and traveling throughout the world to work on volcanoes and attend conferences. One of the world's two or three experts on volcanic gases, he knew more than anyone else about the sulfur-chlorine relationship and its use in forecasting eruptions.

In the early 1990s, he rued the chaos that followed the collapse of the USSR and the schism that split his institute in two. Though hardly a zealous Communist, he disapproved of his colleagues who hastily deserted the party. "He was too preoccupied with his work to meddle in politics," said Lyudmila. "But he could not tolerate betrayal. When everyone had turned their Communist Party membership cards in, he was still paying his party dues. He said he could not understand such hasty decisions."

Through all this upheaval, work and family remained the anchors in Igor's life. He and Lyudmila had an extraordinarily close relationship and spent much of their time together. Lyudmila was the tougher of the two and protected her husband from the politics of the institute.

When Irina got married, Igor and Lyudmila danced the jitterbug as the wedding guests formed a circle around them and cheered. In 1987 Irina gave birth to a daughter, Dasha, and Igor spent more time in Moscow, helping his daughter — who was already divorced — take care of her little girl. In later years, the family's favorite place was their small, wooden dacha, or country home, in the remote woods of Ryazan province, 250 miles south of Moscow. Igor picked mushrooms and berries by the bucketful, worked in the potato and vegetable garden, drew water from wells, and chopped wood for the stove.

"Before he left for Colombia, he said that when he came back, he wanted to go to the dacha in the winter," said Irina.

Hunched over the Deformes fumarole, with a half-dozen scientists watching, Igor continued sampling with his new, double-chambered collection bottle. In each chamber he had placed two different chemical solutions. The silica tube, inserted in the fumarole, transported the magmatic gases into the chambers, where they bubbled into solution. Whereas previous, single-chambered bottles had enabled scientists to tell how much sulfur was being released by the volcano, Igor's system made it possible to differentiate how much sulfur was present in the form of sulfur dioxide, or SO_2, and how much was from hydrogen sulfide, or H_2S. He hoped that by fine-tuning the measurement of sulfur emissions he could get a more accurate picture of what the magma was doing. SO_2 is released more readily from hotter magma, while the presence of H_2S indicates a cooler magma that is farther from the surface. Igor theorized that increasing amounts of SO_2, as compared to H_2S, indicate a hotter, more active, and potentially more dangerous magma body under the volcano.

Assisted by the Colombian Nestor García, Igor spent about an hour at Deformes, from roughly 11 A.M. until noon. Two other groups were waiting to work at the main Deformes fumarole. As he stood there, José Arlés Zapata sampled gases from an opening just a few yards away. Andy Macfarlane and Mike Conway took several temperature readings at other fumaroles near Deformes, with an average — according to Macfarlane's log — of 390 degrees F.

Igor finished his sampling and moved 15 yards away from Deformes, at last able to breathe fresh air. He seemed happy to be working with gases at a new volcano on a new continent and pleased that his new collection bottle was working well.

"It's good," he told me. "Very good."

Variable winds blew plumes of sulfurous gas in all directions, forcing our group to continually put on, then shed, our respirators. Luis LeMarie, from Quito — his full name was Luis Fernando LeMarie Chavarriga — stepped in front of the main fumarole and took two samples in separate bottles using a titanium tube. As the gas bubbled through the bottle, he periodically shook it to dissolve the compounds into a solution.

"It really was difficult because the temperature of the fumarole was very high, there was a lot of gas, and I did not have a gas mask," recalled LeMarie, who was forty-three at the time. "But the mood of everyone was very good."

After Luis had finished his work, which took around fifteen minutes, Nestor approached him, remarked on how well his collection apparatus had worked, and asked to borrow part of it to sample gases inside the crater with Igor. Nestor then said, "Why don't you come with me? We're going inside the crater to take the final samples." Luis demurred. He'd inhaled some gas and wanted to rest.

Igor and Nestor, their gear on their backs, hiked about 100 feet to the crater lip and prepared to descend. Meanwhile, Macfarlane and Conway set up their equipment at the main Deformes fumarole and began to take their own gas samples. In an account written a month later, Macfarlane described the scene:

> After we finished taking our sample, we got out of the gas and caught our breath for a little bit . . . The clouds were starting to clear slightly by this time and we could see down into the [old] caldera valley to the south and west from Deformes, the long, steep western slope of the cone, and some of the caldera wall. It was an impressive view, and the weather, while foggy, was quite comfortable — maybe lower sixties, not raining, and good weather to work in.

The temperature was probably cooler than Macfarlane estimated, more likely around 50 degrees F, given that we were at 14,000 feet. As the clouds occasionally parted, the view that greeted us was of the forested, razorback ridge — the caldera wall of an older incarnation of Galeras — sloping dramatically down to the lowlands on the western side of the mountain. Macfarlane had never worked on an active volcano, and he remembers that after taking gas samples I joked that he had "sucked gas" at a fumarole, a rite of passage for a volcanologist. He asked about Igor and Nestor García, and I told him that they were on their way to the crater. "They're a couple of mountain goats," I said. "They know their way around volcanoes."

Around 12:30 or 1 P.M., Macfarlane, Conway, José Arlés Zapata, and I walked to the southern rim of Galeras's crater. Clouds still swept over the volcano, but we generally had a clear view of Igor and Nestor García, about 250 feet below on the crater floor. After scrambling down the jagged wall of the crater, they worked at a fumarole near the lava dome that had plugged the volcano. The crater's interior was mostly shark gray, with scattered brown, yellow, and rust-colored patches of rocks and fumarolic minerals. Gases from a half-dozen fumaroles partially obscured the view. Crouching low to avoid being incinerated by the 1,200-degree F gases *whooshing* out of the fumaroles, Igor got to work. He smiled, pleased to be picking up excellent samples — pure, hot gases straight from the magma column.

Working in the alien territory of the crater — few places on earth feel as inhospitable — you may allow yourself a brief thought about what would happen if it were to blow, but you quickly move on to more mundane concerns: Where are the best fumaroles, and how much gas has accumulated at the bottom of the crater? You can see the steam when it condenses 5 feet above your head, but it's the gases you don't see that you have to worry about. I've walked into pockets of gas in craters that robbed my lungs of oxygen, leaving me gasping for breath as I either outran the invisible cloud or threw myself to the ground, where the concentrations are lower.

With a steady wind swirling around the crater, Igor and Nestor did not seem concerned about asphyxiation. I remember their being roughly opposite us, near the bottom of the crater wall, and don't recall their traversing the crater floor. My colleagues do. Macfarlane and LeMarie remember seeing Igor near the center of the crater. Conway vividly recalls the pair walking across the floor over fragments of the hardened lava dome, a small hillock that had formed near the far side of the crater.

"They went all the way down to the dome," said Conway. "They were walking across the crater floor . . . I remember them smoking, waiting for gases to accumulate [in the sampling bottles]."

Conway and Macfarlane stood with Luis and me on the edge of the crater, surveying the terrain for the study they were planning. Proposed by Chuck Connor, who was in bed with the flu at the hotel, and funded by the National Science Foundation, it was designed to determine where Galeras's gases originated and how long they stayed in the volcano. As part of the study, Connor's team wanted to measure temperatures and pressures at five different fumaroles. Conway and Macfarlane had planned to place thermocouples in the fumaroles that afternoon. But when they actually stood on the rim and saw the scale of the crater and how widely dispersed the fumaroles were, they had second thoughts about beginning that day. Their hesitation saved their lives.

What gave them pause was a lack of wire to connect their thermocouples. They had hoped to insert the devices in fumaroles on the crater floor and at several points on the cone, including Deformes. But they had only about 300 yards of wire to connect the thermocouples to the data logger, which would record the temperatures. Perched on the rim, Conway and Macfarlane thought it best to forgo monitoring the fumaroles on the northern and northwestern sides of the cone. Instead, they decided to monitor the fumaroles on the crater floor as well as at Deformes, placing the data logger in the crater. But it was Connor's show, and, given his absence, they resolved to discuss the matter with him when they got back to Pasto.

As Macfarlane later wrote, "We left that equipment in a shallow depression with large rocks on top of it to hold it down if high winds came up. Also, Stan remarked that we could either start on some new exploration and then maybe be late getting back to the caldera rim and the ride back to town, or leave now and have an easier time going back. This information also swayed me to leave at that time."

Conway said he, too, was persuaded not to enter the volcano because of the relatively late hour. "It would have taken us at least a couple of hours to do the work and we decided that this was not a good thing," he recalled. "You shouldn't go in on the first day on an active volcano and say, 'Let's get eight hours' work done in two or three hours.'"

Had Chuck Connor been with them, Macfarlane and Conway are certain that the three of them, and possibly LeMarie, would have begun their work — and would be dead today. "Connor is a gung-ho guy," Macfarlane said later. "If he had not been sick, there is absolutely no doubt in my mind we would have been on the floor of that crater."

Around 12:30 P.M., I felt it was time to begin wrapping up our work and get off the volcano. The Colombian TV crew had left earlier. Andy Adams was plainly ready to go. Overweight and wearing a hot jumpsuit, he was short of breath in the thin air and tired. I suggested he leave and, accompanied by the Guatemalan geologist Alfredo Roldan, he headed down the cone, across the moat, and up the amphitheater wall.

Igor and Nestor remained in the crater, finishing their work. Andy Macfarlane, Mike Conway, Luis LeMarie, José Arlés Zapata, and I stood above them on the lip. And Geoff Brown, assisted by Fernando Cuenca and Carlos Trujillo, was circling the rim, taking readings with his gravimeter. From time to time, they disappeared into one of the passing clouds.

Our group of five began walking counterclockwise around the crater rim as we got ready to leave. On the southern lip, we met the gravimetry team coming from the opposite direction. Brown was in the lead, moving briskly forward with his gravimeter in a backpack and his unruly gray hair blowing in the breeze.

Brown's gravimeter was quite a gadget. Some idea of how finely calibrated and accurate it is can be gleaned from a story told by John Simmons, a documentary filmmaker and close friend of Geoff's. Working on a film at the Poás volcano in Costa Rica, Geoff, John, and Geoff's former student and closest collaborator, Hazel Rymer, stopped at a church near the volcano. Hazel pulled out the gravimeter and placed it on the steps of the building. She took a reading of the gravity from that step to the center of the earth, 3,959 miles away. She then moved the gravimeter one step higher, adjusted a few knobs, and — to Simmons's astonishment — showed that the device had picked up the difference. Indeed, if she'd moved it only eight tenths of an inch, it would have given her a different reading of the gravitational pull toward the earth's core.

At first, many geologists and volcanologists were skeptical about Brown's use of "microgravity" to study a volcano. But over the years, the geological establishment was persuaded that it was an important tool, similar in some ways to using an ultrasound or CT scan on the human body. I thought Brown's research had great promise, and at many scientific meetings we had discussed working together on a volcano. That never came to pass until January 1993, when Brown showed up in Pasto with the white breadbox that he would use, at last, on Galeras.

Geoff was born in 1945 and grew up in Yorkshire, in northern England. His early years there instilled in him what the British call "Yorkshire grit" — a formidable determination. As a young boy, he needed such pluck. When he was four, his forty-year-old father, a chemistry teacher, died of a heart attack. For the rest of his life, Geoff worried about dying at an early age, a concern that drove him to frequently monitor his pulse and blood pressure in his later years. Left to raise her only child alone, Geoff's mother ran a guest house, then taught piano, and finally became a teacher and headmistress at a local primary school. According to Geoff's wife, Evelyn, she doted on her handsome, brown-eyed, dark-haired son.

Geoff began studying geology in high school, then continued at Manchester University, where he received his bachelor of science degree in 1966 and his Ph.D. in 1970. He and Evelyn met as undergraduates, and though he at first seemed to her like "a bit of a weedy wimp" — tall, gangly, and shy — they soon fell in love. Evelyn was drawn to his sincere, friendly nature, his passion for science, and his wit. Geoff also had a beautiful, soothing voice that would have served him well had he gone into another career he was considering, the ministry.

Married in 1966, Geoff and Evelyn quickly had three daughters — Miriam, Ruth, and Iona — in the space of four years and lived in near-poverty on his graduate student's stipend and Evelyn's wages as a geology teacher. For a year, Geoff took care of Miriam so his wife could commute the two hours to her job. From their early years, the girls remember an even-tempered, devoted father who would take them swimming on Sundays but who otherwise almost always seemed to be working.

As a geologist, Geoff initially studied the origin of granites and the possibility of using granitic rocks as a source for geothermal energy. In 1973 he joined the Open University, an unconventional yet respected institution where students learned through correspondence, computer, and video courses. Beginning as a part-time tutor, Geoff rose to full-time teacher in 1977, professor in 1982, and head of the Department of Earth Sciences in 1983. By then his research interest had shifted from granites to monitoring volcanoes using microgravity. He was convinced that the best way to learn more about volcanoes — and better forecast eruptions — was to understand their magmatic "plumbing systems."

He was a pioneer in the field. A basic law of physics is that all bodies — be they a rock and the center of the earth or the earth and the moon — pull on each other. The greater an object's mass or density, the greater the force with which it pulls on other objects. This pull is the force of gravity, and in recent decades scientists have devised extremely sensitive instruments — gravimeters — to measure it. Essentially, a gravimeter is a box in which a steel ball is suspended on an extraordinarily sensitive quartz spring. Geoff knew that the interior of a volcano was likely to have varying densities of material. Solid rock is denser than magma, and magma with a high gas content is lighter and less dense than magma that has lost most of its gases. Using the gravimeter, Geoff reasoned that he could map a volcano's inner workings. Taking readings at various points around a volcano would produce a three-dimensional snapshot showing magma bodies, rock, and ash deposits. Comparing measurements taken over time could indicate potentially dangerous developments — whether magma was rising, changing shape, or degassing, for example.

His first serious work with gravity began on Poás, an 8,884-foot volcano in a heavily populated region of Costa Rica. In Simmons's 1987 BBC documentary about Brown and his work, the scientist stood in front of Poás's large, steaming crater and explained his goals.

"Beneath my feet, a few hundred meters down there, is red-hot molten rock, called magma," Brown said in his mellifluous voice. "I'm standing on one of the most active volcanoes in Costa Rica. Now, this volcano has undergone violent explosions in the past. We know that. And I can't tell you when it's going to happen again in the future. But we need to know, and one of the things we're interested in is developing viable monitoring techniques that allow us to predict when there's going to be an eruption. Because if this volcano does go bang, it won't be a million trees that suffer, like at Mount St. Helens, it will be a million people who live in the central valley of Costa Rica."

Working with Hazel Rymer, who had gone on to become a distinguished Open University researcher, Brown took gravity readings in and around Poás. They had expected to find that the magma column beneath the crater was less dense than the surrounding rock, so they were surprised when their readings showed just the opposite. It turned out that wrapped around the column of magma was a mass of loosely consolidated ash from previous eruptions, which had a lower density and gravity than the magma column. Moving out from the active volcano, they picked up gravity readings that indicated the presence of two older calderas, through which the current magma body was forcefully rising. Using their data, Geoff and Hazel came up with a rough idea of where the magma body was and what it was doing over time. Much of the work was intuitive, with the pair making educated assumptions about the layout of Poás's plumbing.

It took an unconventional mind to work in the new terrain of microgravity research. Geoff applied his offbeat approach to teaching as well. Once, making a film on earthquakes, Simmons and Brown devised a gimmick to demonstrate the Richter scale. The prop department made a shed out of cardboard, which they took to a quarry in Derbyshire. Brown then squeezed into the shed behind a small table, on top of which rested a teacup. Simmons photographed the crew setting off charges (actually dummy blasts) at different distances from the shed as a way of illustrating the variable power of earthquakes. In fact the shed, with Geoff in it, was not being rocked by explosions but by a crew member shaking the hut — and hence the table and the teacup — with increasing force.

On the film, it looks as if the intrepid Brown is at risk as someone sets off dynamite nearby. Simmons remembers, most of all, what fun Brown had as the crew struggled to pull off this trick, their task complicated by a steady rain that began to soften the cardboard hut.

Many English academics would have shied away from such an undignified stunt, said Simmons. But not Brown, who saw it as an excellent way to teach viewers about the Richter scale.

Other friends, such as Peter Baxter, marveled at Geoff's determination. Baxter was on Mount Etna with Brown when he decided to take a shortcut across open ground. The group was in an ordinary car and should have stayed on the road, but Brown insisted on going cross-country. Finally, he hit a stretch that looked impassable.

"Anybody else would have just turned around and driven back to the road," said Baxter. "But Geoff said, 'No, we've got to go ahead.' We all got out of the car and looked at the problem. Geoff got back in and tried several times to get over this rough ground. The rest of us just stood outside the car, waiting. Eventually he got through this area with smoke coming out of the clutch, and we got in the car and drove off. I actually learned a little lesson then. You know, as you get older, you tend to sort of run down. And I said to myself, 'No, no, you mustn't run down. This guy's right. You don't let these things stop you — you find a way around.'"

In England, Geoff was a notoriously fast driver. Once he almost lost his license after being ticketed by the police three times for going more than 100 miles an hour. It wasn't just that he liked to speed but that he always crammed far too much into his day — teaching, research, running the department, and family obligations. Afraid of dying at an early age, like his father, Geoff went full tilt.

All of his daughters played in school orchestras, and he was perpetually late to their concerts. Iona, now a professional violinist, said, "He was trying to please everyone. He felt he could be everywhere at once. But at every concert he would always miss the overture."

Still, his daughters consider him an ideal father in many respects — affectionate, understanding, helpful. Miriam, the eldest, even accompanied him on occasional research expeditions. He was more even-tempered than Evelyn, and when the girls wanted something they went to him first. When they were grown, he gave them money for down payments on apartments or houses, then helped them paint and repair them. He also talked for hours with them about the one area of turmoil in his life — his marriage.

As Geoff rose steadily in his field and traveled widely — evolving from a shy academic to a dynamic, widely respected scientist — Evelyn was left home in the unglamorous role of housewife.

"He was tremendously insecure when I first married him," said Evelyn. "I would break the ice for him, introduce him to things, lead him forward . . . The difference between the later Geoff and the early Geoff was phenomenal. Of course, as he grew more confident, he became attractive to women and he was attracted to them, which led to all sorts of tension."

Increasingly, as Geoff and Evelyn drifted apart, his work overseas became a refuge from the tensions at home.

Standing on the crater's rim, Geoff and I talked for a few minutes. He, Carlos Trujillo, and Fernando Cuenca had taken a handful of readings on the southern and eastern side of the crater and were heading clockwise to get a reading or two on the northern rim. It was 1:15 P.M., perhaps a little later, and I told him that our group was finishing its work and that he should do likewise. He seemed in fine spirits. But he mentioned that he had been getting some strange readings on his machine — rapid fluctuations in gravity. He suspected that the gravimeter had been damaged in Costa Rica, where he had worked before coming to the conference, and said he'd check on it later. But he didn't seem concerned, and neither was I.

Later, I wondered: Had Geoff's gravimeter detected a throbbing in the volcano, a signal that Galeras was about to blow?

4

....

INNER FIRE

F AR FROM THE CONE, on the mountain's outer flank, Marta Calvache peeled back the layers of Galeras's history. Each eruption had left its signature on the landscape — sheets of pyroclastic flows, ashfalls, and lava piling on top of one another, century after century, millennium after millennium, slowly building a volcano. Surrounded by ten scientists from a half-dozen countries, Marta stood on the earthen path of the colonial Camino Real, or Royal Road, and led her colleagues on a tour through Galeras's past. They had started higher on the volcano in the morning and, by one-thirty that afternoon, had driven and walked to a point about a half mile below the top of the 14,028-foot mountain. Still in the clouds, their visibility restricted to a swath of mountain covered in scrubby bushes and *frailejones,* they couldn't see Pasto spread out below.

Stopping at embankments where the Camino Real and a newer road cut through the mountainside, Marta pulled out her slender rock hammer and scraped away at the yellow and gray deposits layered in the ancient soils. The deposits crumbled like old adobe, tiny pieces of stone and ash sifting to the ground. Embedded in these cross sections of the mountain were blackened twigs, carbonized thousands of years ago when pyroclastic flows streamed down the flank, incinerating everything in their path. Also suspended in the solidified ash strata, like raisins in pudding, were small bits of pumice that had been swept along in the pyroclastic flows.

Poking around Galeras and its previous embodiments as she

worked on her master's thesis and doctoral dissertation, Marta had made many fresh observations and a true discovery. Sandwiched between the classic, gray pyroclastic flow deposits were thick yellow strata, at first believed to be mudflows or debris flows. But after months of work, Marta was able to prove that the yellow layers were actually deposited when the volcano first blew open its vent during an eruption, spewing old, decayed rocks. Colored yellow by the highly acidic water percolating inside the mountain, these tiers of weathered stone were vestiges of the first coughs of old eruptions. Afterward, as the eruption proceeded, Galeras then disgorged more traditional pyroclastic flows, whose deposits rested on the yellow layers. Marta's most intriguing find was that the throat-clearing eruptions behaved like pyroclastic flows — roaring down the flank, close to the ground, at high speeds — even though they contained almost none of the fine ash found in *nuées ardentes.* It was something not yet recognized in geology: pyroclastic flows galloping along, containing only gas and bits of rock, nearly devoid of the glowing ash that customarily gives the flows their fluidity. Marta had, in effect, discovered a new kind of pyroclastic flow.

Geologists often get proprietary about the volcanoes on which they work. And if Galeras can be said to belong to anyone, it would have to be Marta. Born in 1960 in its shadow, she has spent most of her professional life studying the volcano. She has worked in the crater countless times and witnessed its many mutations, has walked every inch of the amphitheater and its outer flanks, has watched fumaroles appear and disappear all over the volcano, has become familiar with every quirk of its seismic activity, and has visited each settlement around Galeras. INGEOMINAS geologists even named one of the fumaroles Calvache — for Marta. She knows the volcano's moods, senses when it's safe to walk onto the crater and when it's not. Her mastery of Galeras, her utter familiarity with the mountain and her confidence on it, would save my life.

Marta grew up in Pasto but often visited the family's *finca* on the other side of Galeras, in Cariaco. Her father, a civil engineer, died when she was very young, leaving her mother to raise Marta and her three siblings. Galeras was quiet in the 1960s and early 1970s, so as a girl she was only vaguely aware that the mountain was volcanic. Strangely, Galeras played no role — at least not a conscious one — in her choice of a career. She went into geology because a pair of cousins had already entered the field. Marta didn't even set foot in the crater of Galeras until she was twenty-eight. But her upbringing nearby did inculcate her with one trait that would serve her well: She loved to walk in the mountains.

When she was eleven, her family moved to Bogotá, where she attended high school and graduated from the prestigious National University. She then took a job with the state hydroelectric company in Manizales, working initially on a plan to tap nearby Nevado del Ruiz for geothermal energy. In late 1984 Nevado del Ruiz stirred, an event that transformed Marta's career. Over the next year, the volcano experienced a series of earthquakes and minor eruptions. Local and international scientists quickly realized that a sizable eruption at Nevado del Ruiz could melt some of the glaciers and snow that covered the 17,457-foot summit year-round. Such a blast would unleash a torrent of water and mud that would barrel down the valley of the Lagunillas River, threatening the town of Armero. An eruption in 1845 had done just that, creating a *lahar,* or mudflow, that killed 1,000 people not far from Armero. Now, in 1985, tens of thousands of people lived in the path of such a *lahar,* most of them in Armero, 35 miles from the volcano. For those in the town, it was difficult to grasp how a distant volcano, one they couldn't even see, could pose any danger.

Trying to persuade authorities to adopt an evacuation plan, scientists drew up hazard maps showing a "100 percent probability" of mudflows sweeping through Armero if an eruption occurred. But local officials and businessmen accused the scientists of fomenting hysteria, which could hurt commerce and lower property values. Even the church expressed skepticism; the archbishop of Manizales attacked the press for propagating "volcanic terrorism." Meanwhile, Marta, often joined by Nestor García, spent more time on the volcano, measuring gases in the crater as well as monitoring gas levels in the hot springs on its flanks. On November 12, 1985, the day before the eruption, she and Nestor made the arduous descent into the crater. In volcanology, timing is everything.

The eruption of November 13, 1985, was worse than anyone had imagined. That evening, around nine o'clock, a relatively small series of pyroclastic flows melted less than 10 percent of the glaciers on Nevado del Ruiz. The water streamed down the Lagunillas and Azufrado rivers, creating a towering, rock-studded mudflow when they merged upstream of Armero. At 11:30 P.M., when the *lahar* came shooting out of the canyon near Armero, it was 100 feet high and traveling at 35 miles per hour. Dropping to a thickness of 10 to 15 feet when it reached the more open ground near the town, the mudflow swept it away, killing 23,000 people — nearly the entire population — in a few hours. Many victims drowned or were suffocated by the mud; others died from trauma inflicted by the *lahar*. Had there been a system to warn of the eruption and approaching mudflows, the people would have had ample time to walk to safety a few hundred feet up the sides of the valley.

Appalled by the loss of life and aware of how little other Colombian volcanoes had been studied, Marta resolved to devote her career to volcanology.

The day after the eruption, I left my wife and three-week-old daughter to travel to Armero and Nevado del Ruiz, beginning a stint of work in Colombia that would take me there twenty-five times in the next fifteen years. After flying over the ruined town, we circled the volcano repeatedly, using the COSPEC to measure SO_2 remotely as we tried to determine if Nevado del Ruiz had spent itself or was likely to erupt again. On a day trip to Manizales, I briefly met Marta as she worked with the dozens of foreign geologists who had come to study the volcano. She made an imposing first impression. Even in Colombia's macho culture, her energy and intellect commanded respect.

Returning to Nevado del Ruiz six weeks later, I discovered just how tough Marta could be. I had come to study the extensive network of geothermal springs that percolated out of the volcano's flanks, hoping that changes in the water's gas content might reveal something about the magma body underneath. Marta agreed to take me to a highly active spring at about 16,000 feet on Ruiz's flank. Arriving at mid-afternoon, we discovered that the dirt road to the spring had been cut by mudflows from the November 13 eruption. We left the jeep, walked 5 miles around the volcano in the thin air, then descended another mile into a canyon. Finally reaching the springs at nightfall, we sampled the water, which bubbled out at 150 degrees F.

We then hiked back uphill to the main road and headed for the jeep as thick clouds enveloped the mountain, settling in just below the track on which we were walking. The full moon cast an unsettling glow on clouds so thick, I felt as if I could step off the serpentine road and onto this gray carpet. The silence was majestic, the only sound the crunching of our feet on the path and my labored breathing. We marched on, savoring the thrill of being alone on top of the Andes, walking on the clouds.

Marta hiked briskly, easing ahead as I struggled to keep up. By the time we got back to the jeep, around eleven-thirty that night, my legs were rubber, and I was near collapse after our high-altitude, 12-mile jaunt. Marta looked ready to walk another 12 miles.

Over the next several years, Marta and I collaborated closely as I returned repeatedly to work on Nevado del Ruiz. She decided to come to America to work with me on her master's degree at Louisiana State University, where I was an assistant professor. Choosing which volcano to study was not difficult. It was right there, in her backyard, waiting for the right volcanologist: Galeras.

Marta had first set foot on the Fire Mountain in 1988. That year the volcano had come back to life, alarming policemen at the post on the scarp with its rumblings. The previous year, another geologist had been on Galeras and found no fumaroles. Descending the amphitheater scarp and climbing onto the crater, Marta was surprised, then, to discover jets of gas shooting out of three fumaroles. Every time she returned, the fumaroles grew larger, the gases hotter.

Galeras's forty-year sleep was over.

*   *   *

To understand Galeras, you have to go back to the beginning, for the fire that shot from the volcano on January 14, 1993, is a direct link to the celestial fire that formed the sun, the earth, and our entire solar system. As the American volcanologist Thomas A. Jaggar once said, a lava splash is a souvenir of the creation.

It all began some 4.6 billion years ago when clouds of dust, gas, and heavenly debris — much of it from exploded stars — congregated in a swirling cloud in space. As this cloud, or nebula, began to rotate, it flattened into a shape like a disk. Its atoms succumbed to gravity's pull, gathering in the center to form the nucleus of what would become our sun, which contains 99 percent of the mass in our solar system. Exposed to extraordinary pressure and temperatures reaching 1.8 million degrees F, the hydrogen atoms underwent nuclear fusion, a process that continues to this day and allows the sun to generate heat and light.

As our sun was forming, the swirling nebula began to cool, causing particles of heavenly matter to condense, collide, and — pulled by gravity — join to form the nucleus of Earth and the eight other planets of our solar system. These whirling protoplanets sucked more matter into their centers, eventually attaining the mass they have today. Like the sun, Earth's core — filled with naturally radioactive elements — began generating the heat that still emanates from it. This process of planetary formation ended about 4.56 billion years ago, a date we can establish because vestiges from the world's formation — meteorites — are still drifting around space, occasionally dropping to Earth like calling cards from the beginning of time. With remarkable precision, they can be dated by their remnants of radioactive elements.

Around 4.5 billion years ago the earth started to cool, and as it did a rocky crust formed. (The oldest rocks on earth, found in Greenland, are exactly that old.) Roughly 4.2 billion years ago, the earth began to separate into layers. The heavier elements, like iron, dropped to the center. Less dense elements, such as silicon and aluminum, rose toward the surface, forming igneous rock, which is cooled, hardened magma. The earth's interior maintains that differentiated structure today, with a solid, inner core — made up primarily of iron — that is about 8,000 degrees F; a molten outer core that creates our magnetism; the mantle, composed primarily of solid rock; and the crust, which contains about 95 percent igneous rock. The distance from Earth's surface to the center is 3,959 miles. The crust, with an average land thickness of just 25 miles, is, in comparative terms, no thicker than the skin on a large apple.

Volcanism began on Earth at least 2.2 billion years ago, as shown by the remains of extremely fluid, hot lava flows that once poured over South Africa and Australia. The heat created in the core and mantle, as well as the continual melting of rocks, also released vast amounts of gases — steam (H_2O), carbon dioxide, sulfur dioxide, nitrogen — that rose to the surface through volcanic vents, spewing out the primitive precursors of our atmosphere. The condensation of these gases almost certainly formed our oceans.(Some scientists believe the seas came into being when comets, which are little more than gigantic ice balls, struck the earth.) Today, when I walk into a crater and sample gases rushing out of a fumarole, I'm measuring a process that has been going on for more than 2 billion years. Indeed, the earth's volcanoes continue to release gas into the atmosphere, although far less than they once did. Today, the CO_2 streaming from volcanoes is only about 0.2 percent of the amount of CO_2 pollutants — in the form of greenhouse gases, such as auto exhaust — spewed into the atmosphere by man.

Volcanism is hardly confined to Earth. One third of the moon's surface is made up of lava plains. The largest volcano in the solar system, Olympus Mons on Mars, is 372 miles across and 16.7 miles high. That's three times as high as Mount Everest and so much larger than the biggest volcano on Earth, Mauna Loa in Hawaii, that Olympus Mons could cover all the Hawaiian Islands. Believed to be extinct, Olympus Mons was formed when a plume of magma rose from deep inside Mars, oozing onto the surface to create a gently sloping "shield" volcano, so named for its shape. Olympus Mons is believed to be made of basalt, a volcanic material that is the solar system's most common rock. Other than our planet, the only place known to have active volcanoes currently is Jupiter's moon Io, which has at least seven volcanoes that discharge clouds of sulfurous gases 300 miles into space.

The phenomenon that would eventually create Galeras and most of the earth's volcanoes can be traced back roughly 2 billion years, when the surface of the globe began to break into shifting plates. Floating on the hot, plastic-like layer of the upper mantle known as the asthenosphere (Greek for "weak sphere"), the more brittle crust fractured into great slabs. Resting on fields of near-molten rock, the plates slowly bumped and ground against each other, forming and reforming, over the course of nearly 2 billion years, into different configurations of oceans and continents. Then, around 300 million years ago, these shifting plates merged into one great landmass. That the world's seven continents had once been united, then slowly drifted apart, was brilliantly deduced in 1910 by the German meteorologist Alfred Wegener. He saw what is clear to all of us today: Africa and South America, North America and Europe, Australia and Antarctica, once fit together like pieces of a jigsaw puzzle. He called the unified landmass Pangaea ("all lands" in Latin), supporting his hypothesis with indisputable evidence: the similarities of rocks and fossils from different continents. Wegener was not sure exactly what forces were driving this continental drift, but later geologists would answer the question through the theory of plate tectonics.

Pangaea came apart long ago, and today we are left with seven continents separated by seas and oceans, the whole of it floating on top of twelve major plates. The ground on which we stand is shifting at a steady, albeit excruciatingly slow, rate. The system that drives plate tectonics and volcanoes is like a conveyor belt, slowly pushing the continents away from one another. The process begins near the center of the Pacific and Atlantic oceans, where mid-ocean ridges along plate boundaries gradually spread apart, allowing vast amounts of lava to continually spill out onto the ocean floor. (Three quarters of the surface of the globe is covered by the ocean and its lava floor.) The spreading of the sea floor means that Paris and New York are moving apart at one and a half to two inches per year, about the rate at which fingernails grow. The advancing slabs of the ocean crust are made up of heavy basalt, rich in iron and magnesium, and are relatively thin — about 4 miles deep. As these plates run into the lighter continental plates, whose average thickness is 25 miles, the submarine slabs dive down, or "subduct," under the continental plates. As the oceanic plates grind relentlessly under the continental plates, the colder oceanic slabs are heated by the surrounding mantle. That heating causes the oceanic plates to release water and other fluids, which then stimulate the melting of a small portion of the mantle itself.

The melting usually occurs at a depth of between 60 to 100 miles, although we know, by measuring the earthquakes accompanying subduction, that the ocean plates continue to shove down to a depth of at least 435 miles. The melted magma, which is lighter than the surrounding rock, gradually rises through cracks in the mantle, often at a rate of only an inch per day. When it emerges, perhaps 10,000 years after it began its journey, it builds a volcano. The word "tectonic" comes from the Greek *tekton,* which means "builder," and that's precisely what the plate tectonic process does — construct volcanoes and enlarge continents.

The subduction of oceanic plates under continental plates explains why many volcanoes, such as those in the Pacific "Ring of Fire," are found on or near a coastline. It's also why earthquakes are concentrated in the same area, since these great slabs of rock collide, then subduct. Most of the world's powerful earthquakes are related to subduction.*

The confluence of earthquake and volcanic activity was vividly illustrated in 1902, when profound tectonic forces exerted themselves on the Caribbean plate, with the Pacific plate driving in from the west and the Atlantic plate squeezing in from the east. In the space of a few months, the eastern side of the Caribbean plate experienced two large volcanic eruptions, including the disaster at Mont Pelée, and the western side was rocked by three major earthquakes and

* There are, however, notable exceptions. California's San Andreas Fault, as well as the recently active Anatolian Fault in Turkey, is rife with earthquake activity because two plates sideswipe each other, causing shallow — and often devastating — earthquakes.

four powerful eruptions in Guatemala, El Salvador, and Nicaragua — all the result of plate tectonics.

The volcanic mound on which I nearly died is a mere 5,000 years old. Its precursors in the Galeras volcanic complex date back 1.1 million years. But the range in which it sits, the Andes, was created roughly 70 million years ago. The Andes and Galeras are part of the "Ring of Fire," a string of approximately twelve hundred active volcanoes running through South America, Central America, North America, Russia, Japan, and the Philippines. In each place, the Pacific plate and related, smaller plates plunge under continental plates, or other oceanic plates, to form volcanoes and mountain ranges.

Extending 5,500 miles from Venezuela to Patagonia, the Andes contain 176 active volcanoes. In Colombia, the Andes comprise three ranges, known as *cordilleras*, or "ropes": the Occidental, Central, and Oriental. The Oriental and Central ranges came into being about 70 million years ago through classic subduction processes, with the Nazca plate — in the Pacific Ocean — wedging eastward under the South American plate. Most of the magma created by melting plates never spills out onto the surface to form volcanoes. Instead, it fights its way upward, is trapped, and then solidifies, which is how the Andes were built. That hardened subterranean rock eventually became exposed through weathering and erosion, revealing the gray blocks of the Andes today.

The western range is younger, formed about 65 million years ago through an entirely different geological process. At that time, a portion of the Nazca plate did not subduct under the Latin American plate but smacked head-on into it. The resulting collision shoved the sea floor of the Nazca plate high into the air, like the trunk of a car being crumpled upward after a rear-end crash. As a result, what was once the bottom of the Pacific Ocean now sits at 10,000 feet in the Andes, its surface stamped with marine fossils. The Himalayas are an even more dramatic example of such a collision, or "uplift," created when an ancient sea floor was forced high into the air following the convergence of two plates. John McPhee, in *Basin and*

Range, summed up the process well: "If by some fiat I had to restrict all this writing to one sentence, this is the one I would choose: 'The summit of Mt. Everest is marine limestone.'"

Colombia's active volcanoes are strung along the central *cordillera*. Galeras sits at the point where the three *cordilleras* converge, creating an area of crisscrossing faults and hyperactive volcanic and earthquake activity. While it is convenient to think of Galeras as a hole in a cone in a fixed position, what we call Galeras is really nothing more than a moving geological target and — from a volcanologist's point of view — a newborn. Galeras is the latest in a series of six volcanoes, dating back more than a million years, that make up what we call "the Galeras volcanic complex." Marta Calvache has shown that the six different embodiments of Galeras stretch across a 15-mile swath of the Andes. The chain of incarnations has slowly meandered eastward, with one volcano dying out and another being born as shifting fault lines channel magma in new directions.

Each of Galeras's predecessors has left its mark on the landscape. Coba Negra — the great-granddaddy of Galeras, centered a few miles west of the current cone — let loose with a massive blast 580,000 years ago, which buried the surrounding countryside within a 12-mile radius in pyroclastic and lava flows tens of feet thick. That blast created a 3-mile caldera whose remains form the 13,000-foot rampart that now flanks the Azufral Valley, west of Galeras. Many of the quarries that surround the volcano are composed of loose rock and pumice from Coba Negra's pyroclastic flows.

More than 45,000 years ago Jenoy, Galeras's grandfather, spit out the pyroclastic flows on which Pasto is built. Galeras's father, Urcunina, is the mountain visible from Pasto and forms the amphitheater surrounding the current cone. Active between 18,000 and perhaps 5,000 years ago, Urcunina reached a height of about 15,000 feet before experiencing a major collapse, which defines the landscape around the volcano today.

The volcano on which my colleagues would perish emerged about 5,000 years ago, formed by magma that poured out of a new opening in the earth and slowly built a cone rising 150 yards above the floor of Urcunina's amphitheater. In its brief geological life, this most recent version of Galeras has experienced six major eruptions. In the recorded history of the region, which spans a mere 500 years, the volcano has had two dozen smaller eruptions and an equal number of episodes, including earthquakes and ashfalls, that have unnerved those living around it. One of those blasts dropped ash on Quito, Ecuador, 120 miles to the south.

Professor Emiliano Diaz del Castillo Zarama has described the history of the volcano's eruptive activity. On December 7, 1580, a sizable blast occurred, which — from one contemporary account — "threw a great quantity of boiling water that burned the sides of the mountains" and ejected a huge cloud of ash that "fell with great fury." Boiling water streaming down the mountain and igniting fires? No such phenomenon is possible. But the description sounds like a pyroclastic flow. As ash blanketed Pasto, its residents were sufficiently scared to pray for protection from Saint Andrew, and they promised to erect a church in his honor.

On July 4, 1616, an eruption took place that sounded, the residents reported, like "a tempestuous sea or a raging river." In 1797 a series of eruptions culminated with a large blast on February 4. An accompanying earthquake destroyed the Ecuadorian city of Riobamba, 48 miles south.

Around 1830 an eruption disgorged a pyroclastic flow that streamed about 5 miles down the volcano's northern flank, sweeping through what is now the town of Jenoy. From 1865 to 1869, Galeras was wracked with activity. At its peak, the volcano emitted a lava flow 3.5 miles long and 90 feet deep. It oozed westward down the valley of the Rio Azufral, toward the town of Consacá.

In 1887 and 1891, eruptions occurred that were "seen far away as flames." On August 27, 1936, an enterprising photographer snapped a remarkable picture of a pyroclastic flow rumbling 2 miles down the northern flank of Galeras. Above the flow, a mushroom cloud rose several miles into a clear Andean sky.

Despite the Fire Mountain's frequent rumblings and emissions, those who live nearby are sanguine about the threat it poses, according to Diaz del Castillo.

"People look at it peacefully and without fear," he wrote.

They appreciate its majestic beauty and apparent calm. When people get away from the area, they search for the volcano's silhouette in the distance. They are not afraid of the volcano because it has no history of eruptions that have caused damage to people or towns. Its immense eruptions have always been beautiful nature shows.

Every time the inhabitants of Pasto and Nariño climb Galeras and go down into its crater, they do it with a deep feeling of admiration and respect. Peasants say that people should neither scream on the volcano nor fire any weapons. They claim that those actions get the mountain upset, that the fragile atmosphere is ripped apart and the majestic silence is broken.

To Marta Calvache and her colleagues, gathering at 13,000 feet, Galeras was a thing of beauty, to be sure, but it was also an object of study, a lump of deposits that could be read like the rings of a tree. In the early afternoon, taking a break from examining the yellow and gray strata, they sat near a wall of ancient volcanic ash and pumice and ate a lunch of ham sandwiches and the sweet, taffy-like confection *arequipa*, made locally from molasses. As the hour approached one-thirty, Marta had already roused her colleagues from their meal and was busy explaining how, thousands of years ago, pyroclastic flows had burst forth from Galeras and swept the surrounding slopes, now thick with green *frailejones*.

5

IN THE CRATER

S O MUCH of that day on Galeras was spent in the fog that, inevitably, I picture our movements through a swirl of gray. We were enveloped in a continual succession of Andean clouds as we worked in what Mike Conway called "a typical, nasty, high-altitude volcanic environment." We also had to contend with plumes of gas streaming from the fumaroles in Galeras's crater and on its flanks. The video footage from that day shows the extent of the gloom. It's all mist and obscurity, men in brightly colored jackets set against a murky backdrop. In fact, the footage makes it look worse than it actually was. I, for one, was accustomed to maneuvering in the clouds. And as we were finishing our work, the sky occasionally lightened and the wind rose, quickly dissipating the steam from the fumaroles. Then Igor Menyailov and Nestor García became plainly visible on the floor of the volcano.

On the southeastern rim of the crater, Geoff Brown and I talked for about five minutes. He wanted to walk about 200 yards to the western rim and take one or two more readings before quitting, so he set off, his gravimeter in a backpack slung over his shoulder. Fernando Cuenca and Carlos Trujillo followed Brown around the rim.

Mike Conway, Andy Macfarlane, and Luis LeMarie stood nearby on the lip of the volcano, studying the strata of rock and ash on the crater wall.

"Mike and I paused and took some more pictures," Macfarlane

remembers, "because the wind was blowing the fog out of the crater pretty well and there was a good view of the interior of the crater and the positions of the interior fumaroles, with their mineral halos."

I was itching to get off the volcano. It was one-thirty and we'd been on Galeras for more than three hours. My desire was shared by Conway, who stared at a fragment of the hardened magma dome on the bottom of the crater, imagining the forces that still might be building underneath. At the top of my voice, I yelled at Igor that it was time to clear out. He hollered back, acknowledging my words and gestures. But he was a hundred yards away, and I could scarcely make out what he was saying.

"How are the samples?" I hollered.

"Good," he yelled back. "Not *govno.*"

Govno is Russian for "shit." He had taught me the word, and he was smiling as he saw me catch the meaning.

Later, all the survivors from the crater rim remembered that smile in those final minutes. Squatting next to the fumarole, a cigarette dangling from his lips, Igor smiled as he talked with Nestor, smiled as he packed up his collection bottles, smiled as he rested before walking out of the crater. "He and Nestor looked good," recalled LeMarie, the Ecuadorian chemist. "They looked really happy. They shouted to us that they would rest a minute and Igor would smoke a cigarette, and then they would go."

For Nestor García it was a great moment, working beside Igor in the crater. Like many Colombian scientists, Nestor couldn't find a pure research position, so to continue working on volcanoes he cycled through a series of jobs. He had worked for the state hydroelectric company, as a chemist in a distillery, and as a geochemist at a sulfur factory. He was now teaching part-time at the National University in his hometown of Manizales. Over the years he had done fieldwork with several prominent volcanologists who specialized in gases. When he heard that Igor Menyailov was coming to the conference in Pasto, he was so eager to meet the Russian that he paid his own way there. Sitting with Igor, poking tubes into fumaroles, was just where he wanted to be.

Nestor and I met in Manizales in January 1986, two months after the disastrous eruption of Nevado del Ruiz. He was extraordinarily fit — five-foot-eight and with the muscular build of a judo champion. He was also quite handsome, with looks reflecting his mixed Spanish and African heritage: café-au-lait skin, dark curly hair, and a neatly trimmed mustache. Quiet, bespectacled, and intensely curious, Nestor quickly learned how to use the COSPEC, and we spent several days circling Nevado del Ruiz, measuring its emissions of sulfur dioxide.

He was working at the distillery then, studying Ruiz on his own time. I was so impressed with his passion for volcanoes that I invited him to a conference, being held in Baltimore that May, on the Nevado del Ruiz eruption. Later, visiting me in Baton Rouge, he walked into my backyard to get some exercise. I watched in amazement as he performed a spectacular gymnastic routine that included flips and handsprings. Back in Colombia, we often worked together on volcanoes, and when the time came to invite people to our 1993 conference, Nestor was at the top of my list.

He was born in 1954 into a middle-class family in Manizales, a picturesque town at 7,270 feet in the heart of the lush coffee-growing country of western Colombia. A quiet and disciplined child, he began practicing meditation and judo around age eleven. He went on to found the town's judo league, and it was in the judo academy, at age eighteen, that he met his wife, Dolores. They were married in 1973, when Nestor graduated from high school. Fourteen months later their first child, Paula, was born. Dolores describes him in terms that could easily have been applied to Igor Menyailov: "Respectful, shy, quiet, discreet, a man of very few words."

Nestor studied chemical engineering at the National University in Manizales and continued to compete in judo, winning, among other honors, a gold medal at a championship of the Andean countries. During the day he studied, and at night, to support his family, he taught judo.

From Manizales, on a clear day you can see to the east the snow-covered peaks of Nevado del Ruiz and other volcanoes of the central *cordillera*. To anyone with a love of the mountains, Ruiz is a magnet, and Nestor felt its pull. During his university years, he and his friends often climbed to its crater. After graduating in 1979, he began working for the hydroelectric company in Manizales, a job that took him to Ruiz frequently to study the volcano's potential as a source of geothermal energy. Like all of us who wind up in the thrall of volcanoes, Nestor was drawn to the power and spectacle of the crater.

The hydroelectric company sent Nestor to New Zealand for a year to study its volcano-powered geothermal plants. On his return, he worked on Ruiz with, among others, Werner Giggenbach, a German-born New Zealander whom Nestor had met on his sabbatical. Arguably the world's foremost specialist on volcanic gases, Giggenbach took Marta Calvache and Nestor under his wing, and spent several days with them at Ruiz, helping them gather reliable gas samples inside the crater. Working with a man of Giggenbach's caliber was a pivotal experience for both Nestor and Marta, introducing them to a new way of taking a volcano's pulse.

In the fall of 1985, as Nevado del Ruiz became increasingly active, Nestor visited it repeatedly, often accompanied by Marta and Adela Londoño, a friend who had been his professor at the National University in Manizales. Using Giggenbach's methods and equipment, they sampled fumarolic gases. The pressure inside Ruiz was clearly building. More gases were escaping from the volcano, and their temperatures were rising, indicating an active magma body. In the two months before the eruption, the appearance of the crater began to change, with new fumaroles opening up. Yet despite these signs, Nestor, Marta, and Adela continued to hike into the crater. It was a taxing climb that involved a tricky ascent up its 17,457-foot glaciated flank followed by an extremely steep descent — along treacherous and often slippery paths — into the crater itself. Ruiz's crater was large and deep, filled with roaring fumaroles that released billowing clouds of bright yellow, sulfur-rich gas. I tried to hike into the crater of Ruiz six times but was thwarted on every occasion, either by bad weather, eruptive activity, or car trouble on the way up the mountain.

Nestor risked his life at Ruiz because he, like many other geologists, believed it posed a danger to Armero and the nearby towns. More than any other Colombian volcanologist I knew, Nestor struggled to persuade the civil authorities to adopt a warning system and evacuation plan.

But by November 1985 his frustration was growing. Politicians wouldn't heed scientists' warnings, in part because volcanologists couldn't say definitively if and when an eruption would occur. When the volcano blew on November 13, Nestor was shocked at the massive death toll and the failure of science to force the authorities to act. Feeling personally responsible, he vowed to learn more about volcanoes.

The trauma of Ruiz came at a difficult time for Nestor. Two years before, finding it hard to support his family on his salary from the hydroelectric company, he had become a chemist at a distillery. In 1986, to keep his hand in volcanology, he also took a part-time job teaching geology and chemical engineering at the National University in Manizales. That same year, his marriage ended in a permanent separation, caused largely by his extramarital affairs.

In addition to their daughter, Dolores and Nestor also had a son, Marcello. Nestor remained a strict and dedicated father, but because he was so busy — at work and on volcanoes — he did not see his children as often as he would have liked, Dolores said. "He was," she said, "a workaholic."

On December 31, 1992, less than ten days before leaving for Pasto, Nestor had a long conversation with his wife. Recuperating from an eight-day bout with kidney stones, he was in a pensive mood.

"He told me things he had never said in all of our life together," his wife recalled. "He thanked me for being his wife and for the wonderful children we had together. He also thanked me because the children were white. He said that to be dark-skinned was difficult, and I felt he was referring to the experience he had in New

Zealand, where he ran into a lot of discrimination because of his dark skin and curly hair. He told me, 'You are my wife and you will be my wife until our deaths.'

"He felt very good about meeting the international scientists, but he did have a strong fear that something was going to happen. When he said these things to me I saw a deep sadness in his eyes. I asked, 'Why are you telling me these things?' and he said, 'I don't know. I have to tell you. I need to tell you.'"

A week before going to Pasto, Nestor and his sister, María Elena García Parra, drove around Manizales, visiting places they had haunted as children.

"We went where we learned to ride bicycles, where we learned to roller-skate, where we played soccer," she said. "He even played soccer with some of his childhood friends. And after that trip I remember walking into our kitchen with a lot of sentimental feeling and saying to my mother, 'Who of us is going to die?' Because people say that before a person dies he goes to all his old favorite places."

Standing next to me on the crater rim, checking in regularly by radio with the observatory in Pasto, was one of my closest associates at INGEOMINAS, José Arlés Zapata Granada. Wearing a bright yellow parka, José Arlés — a good-looking, baby-faced thirty-five-year-old with large dark eyes and black hair that fell over his forehead — had been helping me keep track of our large group all day. Whenever I climbed onto Galeras with José Arlés, he was in charge of the radio. That morning, as we stood near the Deformes fumarole, he had talked with a friend in Pasto, optimistically predicting we would be back in town by two for lunch. Now, we'd be lucky to make it by four.

I liked having José Arlés by my side. He was a quick study who had rapidly mastered the COSPEC and was becoming a specialist on Galeras's gases. He had been on Galeras countless times and knew the volcano better than anyone else on the summit that day. I was reassured by his ritual of communicating with the observatory. Time and again, the staff there told us that the six seismic stations around Galeras showed no hint of unusual activity.

I met José Arlés in 1986, after the Ruiz eruption, when he was a student volunteer at INGEOMINAS in Manizales. Then, in December 1989, we hiked together into the crater of Galeras. While sampling gases at Deformes, the fumarole spit molten sulfur into my face. My gas mask took the brunt of the liquid, although I did receive a quarter-size burn on my forehead. Seeing I was all right, José Arlés laughed, and I joined in. Galeras had just welcomed me with a kiss.

Of all the Colombian geologists I knew, José Arlés's story was the most remarkable. He was one of twelve children — six girls, six boys — born into a campesino family in the state of Valle, not far from Cali. His father helped run a coffee plantation and farmed his own land, growing beans, plantains, rice, sugarcane, yucca, and other vegetables. When José Arlés was fifteen, his parents sent him to live in Manizales with his brother Rigoberto, who worked in a match factory. José Arlés found a job in a textile factory, and at night he took high school courses. He quickly became a valued employee, and after high school the factory helped pay his tuition to a night trade school. But he dreamed of attending college, and at the age of twenty-six entered the University of Caldas in Manizales.

Intrigued by Nevado del Ruiz and the other volcanoes in his backyard, José Arlés took geology courses. On the day Nevado del Ruiz blew, he was supposed to have gone to Armero on a field trip with his fellow students, but his sister forgot to wake him and he missed the bus. As it turned out, nearly a dozen of his classmates died in the mudflow. The next day he traveled to Armero to help rescue his friends; most of their bodies were never found. As for Nestor García, Marta Calvache, and a generation of Colombian geologists, Ruiz was a watershed event for José Arlés.

He visited the crater a half-dozen times as a volunteer with INGEOMINAS scientists. Graduating from the University of Caldas in 1989, he immediately was hired by INGEOMINAS. Galeras had come alive the year before, prompting his superiors to send him to the new observatory in Pasto.

In 1990 José Arlés met a striking Pastusa named Monica Gonzales Vallejo, then twenty years old, and the two fell wildly in love. He was drawn to her exuberant personality and striking looks. She was attracted to his quiet confidence and ambition. Pursued by many suitors, Monica chose someone her parents initially considered beneath their middle-class station.

Married eight months after they met, José Arlés and Monica settled into newlywed nirvana in Pasto. He was the organized, low-key member of the marriage, she the flamboyant partner who had to drag him onto the dance floor at parties. Their only disappointment was an early miscarriage. Recognizing José Arlés's passion for volcanoes, Monica also fretted every time he walked onto Galeras. The volcano was regularly experiencing small eruptions, as he and an INGEOMINAS colleague, Milton Ivan Ordóñez, learned one day in 1991 when they were working near the crater.

"Suddenly there was an explosion and we hid behind a big boulder," said Ordóñez. "Ash was falling on our backs. And as we crouched under the rock, José Arlés looked at me, smiled, and said, 'If we don't die here, we'll never die in an eruption.'"

Monica tried to dissuade José Arlés from working on volcanoes, even going so far as to pull strings to get him hired as a geologist at an oil company. But as she quickly learned, such a scheme was fruitless. The one thing not in her power was keeping José Arlés off Galeras.

"We always talked about volcanoes," said Monica. "Whenever there was a problem at a volcano, he'd go there. He was crazy about volcanoes. I told him I thought he was playing with his life, and he replied that volcanoes *were* his life."

In 1992 his superiors at INGEOMINAS chose José Arlés to attend a one-month course on volcanoes in the Canary Islands, an archipelago formed by volcanic activity. The INGEOMINAS officials thought so much of him that they put him in charge of the Pasto observatory when the director was out of town. José Arlés was advancing steadily toward his dream. Already a rising star at INGEOMINAS, he planned to pursue a graduate degree, perhaps in America, and he and Monica were hoping again to have a baby.

In a country beset with problems, José Arlés had risen from poor beginnings and carved out an impressive niche for himself. He had a terrific wife, many close friends, and a rewarding job. His future had never looked brighter.

My surviving colleagues from the crater rim vividly remember the last time they saw Geoff Brown, Fernando Cuenca, and Carlos Trujillo. It was around one-thirty that afternoon; clouds were once again bumping across the top of Galeras, and Brown and the two Colombians were walking clockwise around the crater's lip, headed for the western rim.

"Geoff left us and the last time any survivor saw Geoff he was . . . climbing into the fog up a high section of the crater rim, walking right along its sharp edge with Fernando Cuenca struggling unsuccessfully to keep up," Andy Macfarlane wrote to a friend in February 1993. "The inside crater wall fell very steeply from the rim to the crater floor in this area."

The image of the slight, youthful Cuenca puffing along the crater rim, vainly attempting to catch the middle-aged Geoff Brown, is not one Fernando would like etched in the public's mind. Of all the geologists on the volcano that day, Fernando was the youngest — just twenty-seven — and by far the least experienced. It was only his second time on a volcano. His first had been the year before, also on Galeras, when he and a colleague had made it as far as the amphitheater before stopping because they feared a possible eruption. I had just met Fernando at the Pasto conference and knew him not at all. But I learned later that he was a sweet man, even a soft man, who was deeply in love with his young Russian bride. He was a promising geophysicist, too, but had only just embarked on his career after six years of study in the Soviet Union.

Fernando Augusto Cuenca Sanchez was born in southwestern Colombia in a small town near the headwaters of the Magdalena River, the country's main waterway. His father worked in a bank in the city of Neiva, where Fernando grew up playing the guitar and exploring the nearby creeks and rivers with his friends. He considered becoming a priest and spent two years at a seminary in Manizales. Ultimately, however, he returned to Neiva, where he earned a bachelor of science degree with honors. Inducted into the Colombian army, he served with a United Nations peacekeeping force in the Sinai. That experience gave him a love of travel and, returning to Colombia, he won a competition to study abroad. He chose the Soviet Union, arriving there in 1985, the first year of Gorbachev's perestroika.

At a disco near the central Russian city of Tula, where he was studying, he met a willowy, attractive, nineteen-year-old woman, Larissa Gorbatova. It was love at first sight. They courted for five years, and Larissa soon followed Fernando to Moscow, where he continued his studies at a geophysical engineering institute.

The couple was married in Moscow in 1991, and after receiving their degrees — Fernando's was the rough equivalent of a master's in geophysics — he brought his bride back to Colombia. In mid-1992 he landed a job at INGEOMINAS in Bogotá, where he impressed people with his easygoing manner, sincerity, and intelligence. Unlike Nestor or José Arlés, Fernando Cuenca was not stricken with a passion for volcanoes. In fact, he was even considering looking for work with one of the multinational mining companies in Colombia. He was honored to have been chosen by his superiors to attend the conference in Pasto and, as a geophysicist, was looking forward to watching Geoff Brown work with the gravimeter. But Fernando Cuenca was unformed, a man taking the first step on his professional road.

The man trailing behind Cuenca and Brown, obscured by the fog, was not a even a geologist. But he loved volcanoes.

Carlos Enrique Trujillo, a native of Pasto, was a thirty-six-year-old professor of civil engineering at CESMAG, a university in the city. His field of interest was topography, and in addition to his teaching duties he had taken a keen interest in the volcano that loomed over him. He was particularly fascinated by a developing field of study called deformation, in which lasers and tiltmeters — sophisticated levels — are used to measure changes precisely on the surface of a volcano. By determining if a volcano's flank had risen or fallen a fraction of an inch, scientists hoped to know if a magma body was rising inside a mountain such as Galeras. Trujillo's work was related to Brown's, and the Colombian leapt at the chance to help the English gravity specialist on Galeras.

In 1992 INGEOMINAS had contracted Trujillo to perform deformation studies at Galeras, and he was in the midst of that work in January 1993. Sometimes he would go to Galeras twice a week. During the school year, he regularly took students to the volcano to study its topography, sometimes observing Galeras from the amphitheater scarp, sometimes walking onto the volcano itself.

Trujillo — a slim, bespectacled man with a full head of black hair and a dark mustache — had an impressive collection of books and literature on volcanoes, especially considering it was his avocation. The day before our excursion, he accompanied Geoff Brown on an initial foray onto Galeras. On the morning of January 14 Trujillo woke up early and dropped his only child — a son, Mauricio, then six — at school. Mauricio had asked his father that morning if he could accompany him to Galeras, a place that had acquired mythical stature in the boy's mind. No, replied the father. But he promised to return early and take Mauricio for a swim.

The three men materialized out of the clouds. One moment I was standing at the edge of the crater, looking at Igor Menyailov and Nestor García, and the next moment I turned around and saw a middle-aged man and two boys in their late teens talking with José Arlés. I said hello, and they smiled and greeted me. The older man was short and stocky with thick, wavy, black hair. The boys were taller, and one had a wispy mustache that traced a faint line above his upper lip. What struck — and concerned — me was that, in contrast to our Gore-Tex jackets, high-tech boots, and other fancy gear, the three wore only light street clothes, and the boys were wearing sneakers.

The man was courteous and intensely curious, asking us about the state of the volcano, the gases venting from the fumaroles, the work being done by the men in the crater. I tried to be polite, but I'm afraid my answers were brusque. I was much more concerned about herding my group off the volcano. We were just minutes from leaving.

Later, I learned that as the trio was walking onto the volcano they met an INGEOMINAS driver and assistant, Carlos Alberto Estrada, who was preparing to hike up the amphitheater scarp. Carlos urged them not to go to the crater, saying that the scientists were just about to leave. But curiosity got the best of the man, and they continued up the cone.

I later found out that the man was Efrain Armando Guerrero Zamboni, a forty-five-year-old dean of academics and a social sciences teacher at the University of San Felipe in Pasto. The boy with the faint mustache was his eighteen-year-old son, Yovany Alexander Guerrero Benavides, who was in his first semester at CESMAG University. The second boy was a close friend of Yovany's, Henri Vasquez. He was also eighteen.

The Guerreros lived in a small, neat, two-story stucco house in a middle-class neighborhood. Their home sat literally at the foot of Galeras, and its summit was visible on cloudless days. Efrain's wife, Gloria Benavides, was a homemaker. The couple also had a daughter, Paula, who was fourteen at the time.

Efrain Guerrero liked to play soccer and took his students and children to soccer games. He was a nature lover and an amateur photographer. And he was no stranger to Galeras, having hiked up the mountain five times before.

Yovany shared his father's passion for soccer. He was a good student and, according to his mother, "a very formal person, very respectful, very friendly." He was too young to know yet where he was headed in life. His friend Henri had finished high school and was trying to figure out his next move.

The three men had planned to hike to the volcano the week before, but Efrain had been too busy and the trip was postponed. Then he heard about the scientists working on the mountain and decided to walk to Galeras with Yovany and Henri on Thursday, January 14. He was particularly interested in the instruments the volcanologists would be using to measure Galeras's gases.

The night before, over dinner, the family had discussed the excursion. Efrain asked his daughter to come with them, but his wife forbade it.

"I was very worried because I knew the volcano was active and dangerous," said Gloria. "I told him I didn't think he should go to the volcano. But he said no, he was going, because it was a good opportunity to talk with the scientists. Yovany was very curious. He really wanted to go with his father."

The men set out sometime after 7 A.M., embarking on what must have been a 10-mile hike, given the many switchbacks on the bumpy road to Galeras and the 5,000-foot rise in elevation. Other than being winded, they seemed in fine shape by the time they encountered our group. As we prepared to leave, they decided to walk off the volcano with us.

That rocks tumbled off the crater's inner wall in the final minutes before the eruption, there is no doubt. But when they fell, and what we interpreted the rockfall to mean, is a matter of disagreement.

Luis LeMarie, the Ecuadorian, does not remember a rockfall per se. He recalls walking up to José Arlés on the rim of the crater, where the two of them made "a very interesting observation." Looking at the floor of the volcano, they saw what he described as a column of yellowish ash or smoke rising about 10 feet into the air. It looked drastically different, he said, from the steam rising out of the nearby fumaroles. The smoke appeared just about the time the three tourists showed up, Luis said, and it concerned him enough that he asked me what it was.

"Do you think this is important, this ash?" According to him, I replied, "No, no. It's a normal thing."

I don't remember this exchange, although it very well may have taken place. If Luis did indeed see something that wasn't coming from a fumarole, it could have been a cloud of dust kicked up by falling boulders.

Andy Macfarlane, also standing on the edge of the crater, described in a letter his recollection of the cascading rocks:

There were three moderate-sized rockslides within the space of a minute or so. They were clearly audible, but I couldn't see where they had taken place. I asked Stan about them, and he said he thought there might be some microseismic activity, but he didn't seem really alarmed. Based on my own experience with rockslides on dormant volcanoes in the Cascades, I was not either. José Arlés, who was also with us, reported that there was no seismicity recorded at the observatory (he was chattering back and forth with the observatory frequently), so we didn't worry about it.

Much later Andy said, "It was a little nerve-wracking, but we didn't hear the slides and start running. It's not like we thought it was blowing."

Mike Conway, who had had considerable experience on volcanoes, remembers a scenario that in some ways resembles my own. He recollects that the rockfalls continued, and as they did, he — and I — felt a greater sense of urgency to get down from the crater rim.

"There were two or three rockfalls going on, and Stan said that we ought to go," recalled Conway. "We were on the rim. We could hear the rockfalls, but we couldn't see them. It was hazy, with a lot of fumarolic gases. There were a lot of rockfalls going on, and at first it didn't concern me at all. I don't think they were necessarily precursors to the eruption at all. Rockfalls are very common. I wouldn't doubt that Stan yelled at Igor and Nestor to get out of the crater. Stan did gesture. Stan was waving and trying to get them to come out. You know, you see the dome popping up and I just felt it was time to get out of there. It was spooky. You hear the rockfalls and you wonder, 'Is this something I should be worried about?'"

It was now between 1:35 and 1:40 P.M. Mike, Andy, and Luis all agree that at this point we began walking off the volcano. As Mike remembers it, the tourists went first, walking diagonally down and across the cone, following the well-worn path in the scree that leads to the amphitheater floor. José Arlés was next, followed by me, Andy, Luis, and finally Mike himself. We made it, according to Mike, about one quarter to one third of the way down the cone, a distance of perhaps 25 yards.

As Andy remembers it, the three tourists went first, followed by Andy and me. Behind us, perhaps 10 yards above, Mike and Luis brought up the rear. "As we started down, I was talking to Stan," Macfarlane wrote later. "He remarked that sometimes he felt silly going up onto these volcanoes wearing $1,000 worth of mountaineering gear, while the locals climb up in whatever jeans and sneakers they have." He and I, according to his recollection, had descended about 20 yards vertically from the crater rim.

As Luis LeMarie remembers it, the tourists went first down the cone, followed by José Arlés and me. Then, highest up, came Luis, Andy, and Mike. Luis estimates that the three of them had walked to a point roughly 20 to 30 yards down the trail.

In my mind, the rockfall and the eruption are inextricably linked, one quickly following the other. I had asked the tourists to start down, had told Luis, Mike, and Andy to go, and was preparing — with José Arlés at my side — to leave myself. Then rocks started tumbling off the inside wall of the crater — first one, then a handful, then a cascade. In my mind, there was no doubt that this was either a prelude to an earthquake or an eruption. In Spanish and English I shouted, "Hurry up! Get out!" I vaguely remember seeing Geoff Brown on the opposite rim of the crater and gesturing at him to flee. I distinctly remember looking down and seeing Igor and Nestor García scrambling to get out of the crater — an image my colleagues say I could not possibly have seen since I was already at least 10 yards below the lip.

After that I remember turning. I remember the volcano shaking. I remember dashing madly downhill, the world around me a jouncing tableau of boulders and scree. I had no idea where my colleagues were, saw nothing but the charcoal universe of the cone.

Then there was a hellish, ear-shattering *Boom!* as the earth blew apart and Galeras disgorged its contents.

I was all adrenaline.

6

....

THE VOLCANO LOVERS

KNEW, of course, that my luck might run out one day. But even though I accepted that possibility, I never actually *believed* it would happen to me. People in high-risk professions are confident they can beat the odds. I always felt the same way. Otherwise, I'd never have gone near a crater.

Entering the profession, the first threshold a volcanologist must cross is a willingness to take risks. Meeting with prospective graduate students, I always spend an hour or two talking about the job's inherent dangers. Are they prepared to work on ground that might, at any moment, blow up beneath them? If a student seems too apprehensive, I suggest another line of work.

From the beginning, the pleasures of working on volcanoes so overshadowed the prospective perils that I never considered working in a less hazardous realm of geology. Initially, like most of my colleagues, I was drawn to the profession because of the very spectacle of volcanoes. How mesmerizing to watch Stromboli shoot out streams of lava, Pacaya lift massive blocks of volcanic rock into the air, or Mount St. Helens blow up like a balloon before finally unleashing a devastating eruption. The awesome power of volcanoes fascinates us all, but it exerts a special pull on volcanologists — a pull that overrides the fear we all feel near the crater. Whenever I have gone into the field with the best in our business, people like Igor Menyailov and Geoff Brown, I have noticed that they share a common trait: They never seem to fret about the danger. It is an accepted part of their job, and, after concluding a volcano is reasonably safe on a particular day, they go about their business with a remarkable air of tranquility.

I suppose that, to varying degrees, all volcanologists are thrill seekers. I never feel so alive as when I'm clambering on a volcano. Katia and Maurice Krafft took things to extremes, but Katia's reflections on risk-taking capture the heady intensity of our work.

"I would always like to be near craters, drunk with fire, gas, my face burned by the heat," Katia once said. "It's not that I flirt with my death, but at this point I don't care about it, because there is the pleasure of approaching the beast and not knowing if he is going to catch you."

There are geologists, and then there are volcanologists. Only a few hundred scientists work on active volcanoes worldwide, and we share a strong esprit de corps. Within this community there are those who study dead volcanoes and those who climb on living volcanoes. My colleagues who've never set foot on an active volcano have made great contributions, but the best work, I believe, comes from those of us who walk into the crater. Haroun Tazieff, a flamboyant French volcanologist, put it this way: "Studying dormant volcanoes is of no more profit to the volcanologist who is attempting to make forecasts than is the study of healthy people for the practicing physician."

The public understands that volcanologists are a different breed. When I'm on an airplane and my seatmate asks me what I do, my answer depends on my mood. If I'm not feeling talkative, I'll tell him I'm a geologist, a response that usually brings the conversation to a halt. But if I'm feeling garrulous, I'll say that I'm a volcanologist. After that, the questions never cease.

The bond among members of our profession is strengthened by the rigors and dangers of fieldwork. Sharing hardships and memorable experiences, we develop a soldierly camaraderie. Dick Stoiber and I have slept on smoldering peaks. We've been detained by gunmen en route to volcanoes. We've been in car accidents coming down from volcanoes and survived a few close calls during eruptions. Our profession is not for those who prize a secure, sedentary life. Perhaps that's why so many of our marriages fail.

Ultimately, however, volcanologists are united by something greater than the kick we get from riding the beast's back. The science is in its infancy, and today's researchers are pioneers in an endeavor that could eventually save tens of thousands of lives. For people like Igor Menyailov, the science always came first, but in the back of his mind — of all our minds — was the understanding that our work was humanitarian.

Over the years, as I studied the people who have advanced our understanding of volcanoes, I realize that we have much in common. We have all been fascinated by the majesty of volcanoes. We have been intensely curious about their inner workings, grasping the link between volcanism and the origins of the planet. And we have always wanted to get closer, not because we're suicidal, but because being close is often the best way to observe and to measure. In A.D. 79, the Roman scholar Pliny the Elder, seeing from afar the great column form over Vesuvius, sailed toward Pompeii to observe the eruption and rescue his friends. He paid with his life. Seventeen hundred years later an English gentleman and scholar, Sir William Hamilton, repeatedly charged up the erupting Vesuvius at considerable risk, knowing that only through close observation could he fathom the volcano's workings. Just a decade ago my colleagues Katia and Maurice Krafft, learning that the Japanese volcano Unzen was unleashing spectacular pyroclastic flows, flew halfway around the world to photograph them. They wanted to get closer, hoping their record of the deadly phenomenon could help warn people of volcanic dangers. They, too, paid with their lives.

Pliny the Elder was the first scientist known to have perished in an eruption. On the morning of August 24, A.D. 79, he was at his seaside villa in Cape Misenum, 20 miles due west of the crater of Vesuvius on the Bay of Naples, where he commanded the Roman fleet. The fifty-six-year-old aristocrat had been up before dawn, engaging in his customary study, after which he sunned himself in the warm

Neapolitan air, took a cold bath, lunched in a supine position, then returned to his studies.

Born Gaius Plinius Secundus, Pliny the Elder is remembered today not for his military exploits, but for the wide-ranging studies that made him, along with Aristotle and Virgil, one of the most learned men of the classical era. He is known chiefly for his thirty-seven-volume *Natural History,* a compendium of, among other subjects, geography, botany, zoology, anthropology, and astronomy that contained, Pliny boasted, 20,000 facts. He was curious about everything and spent many of his waking hours — an average of twenty a day — devouring books and treatises.

"Before daybreak he would visit the Emperor Vespasian and then go to attend his official duties," wrote his nephew Pliny the Younger, who was staying with him that summer. "On returning home he devoted any spare time to his work . . . He made extracts of everything he read, and always said that there was no book so bad that some good could not be got out of it."

At one that afternoon, Pliny the Elder's sister told him of a towering cloud "of odd size and appearance" rising from the direction of Vesuvius. The scholar walked with his sister and nephew to a small hill, which gave them a clear view of the cloud, mushrooming ever upward over the Bay of Naples. Eventually reaching 16 miles into the sky, this cloud was an ideal example of what came to be known as a Plinian eruption column, a tower of ash and gas propelled into the stratosphere by a series of magmatic explosions so closely spaced that they become a continuous, deafening roar.

"It was not clear at that distance from which mountain the cloud was rising," wrote Pliny the Younger.

> Its general appearance can best be expressed as being like an umbrella pine, for it rose to a great height on a sort of trunk and then split off into branches . . . Sometimes it looked white, sometimes blotched and dirty, according to the amount of soil and ashes it carried with it. My uncle's scholarly acumen saw at once that it was important enough for a closer inspection, and he ordered a boat to be made ready, telling me I could come with him if I wished. I replied that I preferred to go on with my studies . . .

The elder Pliny exhibited a true volcanologist's instincts: get closer. His nephew's initiative left something to be desired, but the younger Pliny redeemed himself with two remarkably descriptive letters about the eruption.

Soon enough, Pliny the Elder's scientific mission also turned into a humanitarian one. As he was preparing to leave in a single galley, a messenger arrived by boat with a note from Rectina, the wife of Tascus and a friend of Pliny the Elder's. She lived near Vesuvius and, as the younger Pliny put it, "was terrified by the threatening danger and begged him to rescue her." Immediately, Pliny the Elder ordered the large galleys in his fleet at the ready and, around 2 P.M., set off toward Vesuvius.

After several hours of rowing, they approached the shore near Pompeii. A hellish scene greeted them. The pillar of ash and gas was rising ever higher. The sky was hazy with hot ash, incandescent stones fell on the ships, and the sea was clogged with chunks of floating pumice. Terrified residents were escaping in small boats. All the while Pliny the Elder, "entirely fearless," made detailed notes on the eruption — observations that have, unfortunately, never been found.

"The ash that was already falling became hotter and thicker as the ships approached the coast, and it was soon superceded by pumice and blackened burnt stones shattered by the fire," Pliny the Younger wrote to Tacitus, reconstructing the scene from interviews with witnesses. But as they neared the shore, so much pumice was strewn across the water that the galleys could go no further. "He wondered whether to turn back, as the captain advised, but decided instead to go on. 'Fortune favors the brave,' he said. 'Take me to Pomponianus.'"

Pomponianus lived at Stabiae, about 5 miles from their present location and directly across the Bay of Naples from Misenum. Arriving around nightfall, they found the situation only marginally better and getting rapidly worse. Ash and pumice rained from the sky. Fires blazed on the flanks of Vesuvius. Pomponianus and the other residents of Stabiae were terrified. Vesuvius had been dormant for so long that no one imagined it capable of such fury.

Pliny the Elder did his best to allay their fears. He even ate a meal as volcanic debris continued to bury the town. Then, remarkably, he went to sleep. The eruption intensified.

"By this time," his nephew wrote, "the courtyard giving access to his room was full of ashes mixed with pumice stones, so that its level had risen, and if he had stayed in the room any longer, he would never have got out . . . The buildings were now shaking with violent shocks, and seemed to be swaying to and fro as if they were torn from their foundations."

Waking the snoring Pliny the Elder around dawn, Pomponianus and his household urged him to join them outside. As protection against falling debris, they tied pillows to their heads, then fled through the ash and pumice, already several feet deep. It was daytime, but Stabiae was plunged into darkness; residents needed torches to find their way. Pliny the Elder walked to the shore to see if he could escape by boat. But the wind was against them and the sea churning with "wild and dangerous" waves, according to the younger Pliny — a disturbance probably caused by volcano-induced tsunamis. Soon, the stress and the unceasing inhalation of ash overcame the learned Roman.

"A [sail] sheet was spread on the ground for him to lie down," according to Pliny the Younger,

> and he repeatedly asked for cold water to drink. Then the flames and smell of sulfur, which gave warning of the approaching fire, drove the others to take flight and roused him to stand up. He stood leaning on two slaves and then suddenly collapsed, I imagine because the dense fumes choked his breathing by blocking his windpipe, which was constitutionally weak and narrow and often inflamed. When daylight returned on the 26th — two days after the last day he had seen — his body was found intact and uninjured, still fully clothed and looking more like sleep than death.

How, exactly, Pliny the Elder died remains a mystery. It is possible, though unlikely, that he was suffocated by sulfurous gases, as his nephew states. The flames, the smell of sulfur, and the "approaching fire" that Pliny the Younger claims killed his uncle were actually the leading edge of a pyroclastic flow that had rolled 10 miles over land and sea to Stabiae. But if Pliny the Elder succumbed to the *nuée ardente,* why didn't others around him die as well? It's also possible that his chronically weakened airways became so inflamed from inhaling the hot ash that he suffocated. And it's entirely possible that the overweight, ailing scholar died from a heart attack.

At about the time Pliny the Elder expired, the eruption reached its paroxysmal phase. The accounts of Pliny the Younger and others, coupled with the extensive geological and archaeological records at Pompeii and Herculaneum, make it possible to reconstruct the eruption accurately. These sources reveal a tremendous cataclysm — eight times the magnitude of the one at Mount St. Helens — that buried a 115-square-mile area in ash and pumice. But what made this eruption especially lethal was the collapse of its 16-mile-high pillar of ash and gas, which, as it began to fall back to Earth, created a half-dozen pyroclastic flows that killed at least 3,500 people and roared over the Bay of Naples all the way to Misenum.

Herculaneum, with a population of about 5,000, sat 4 miles west of Vesuvius on the Bay of Naples. Not long after midnight on August 25, the gas-fed Plinian eruption began to lose some of its power, and particles of ash and gas fell out of the column, forming waves of pyroclastic flows that roared down Vesuvius's flanks at up to 60 miles per hour. These glowing avalanches devastated Herculaneum, killing hundreds, possibly thousands, as they waited on the shore for boats. The town was buried under 75 feet of pumice and ash.*

The 20,000 residents of Pompeii, a thriving town 6 miles southeast of Vesuvius, suffered even more. Ever since the eruption began on the morning of the twenty-fourth, ash, pumice, and *lapilli* — the Italian word for "small stones" — had been sifting and clattering down on the homes, shops, temples, public baths, amphitheaters, and cobblestone streets of Pompeii. Roofs collapsed, claiming many victims. Amid perpetual darkness and continual earthquakes, residents fled to the east. Around 7:30 A.M. on August 25, with the

---

*Examining the deposits blanketing Herculaneum, some geologists have argued that mudflows, rather than pyroclastic flows, devastated the town.

city already buried in 7 feet of pumice and ash, a pyroclastic flow charged down the slopes of Vesuvius. The cloud roared through Pompeii, asphyxiating and burning to death at least 2,000 people. Ashfalls and at least one additional pyroclastic flow entombed these residents, covering the city in 13 feet of volcanic debris.

Preserved under a layer of stone and ash, the town and its victims lay buried for 1,700 years. Scattered excavations took place in the eighteenth century. But it was the Italian archaeologist Giuseppe Fiorelli who — in the mid-nineteenth century — made the discovery that, in the minds of most people, defines Pompeii today. Buried in fine ash that eventually hardened, the bodies of the victims decayed, leaving hollow casings. Fiorelli poured liquid plaster into the casings, removed the shell of ash, and made haunting, realistic casts of the victims. At Pompeii today, the agony of death by pyroclastic flow is everywhere apparent: two boys holding hands, a dog straining at a leash, a woman with a handkerchief crammed into her mouth, a family of eighteen strewn about a villa.

The other testimony to the terror of that early eruption comes from Pliny the Younger. Far from the crater of Vesuvius, he, his mother, and the people of Misenum thought the world was coming to an end as a pyroclastic flow glided 20 miles across the Bay of Naples to their town. He begins his description of this cataclysm at dawn on August 25, with Misenum enshrouded in a murky cloud of ash, earthquakes rocking the teetering houses, and terrified residents fleeing to the northwest. His letter to Tacitus is one of the most descriptive pieces of writing in the history of volcanology. The seventeen-year-old coolly offers the earliest eyewitness account of a pyroclastic flow as well as a brief description of the sea being pushed and pulled by tsunamis:

We saw the sea sucked away and apparently forced back by the earthquake: at any rate it receded from the shore so that many sea creatures were left stranded on the dry sand.

On the landward side, a fearful black cloud was rent by forked and quivering bursts of flame, and parted to reveal great tongues of fire, like flashes of lightning magnified in size . . . Soon afterward the cloud sank down to earth and covered the sea. Then my mother implored . . . me to escape as best I could . . . I refused to save myself without her and, grasping her hand, forced her to quicken her pace . . . I looked around: a dense, black cloud was coming up behind us, spreading over the earth like a flood.

We had scarcely sat down to rest when darkness fell, not the dark of a moonless or cloudy night, but as if the lamp had been put out in a closed room. You could hear the shrieks of women, the wailing of infants, and the shouting of men. Some were calling their parents, others their children or their wives, trying to recognize them by their voices . . . Many begged for the help of the gods, but even more imagined that there were no gods left, and that the universe was being plunged into eternal darkness forever more . . .

Ashes began to fall again, this time in heavy showers. We rose from time to time and shook them off, otherwise we should have been buried and crushed beneath their weight. I could boast that not a groan or cry of fear escaped me in these perils, but I was only kept going by some poor consolation in my mortal lot from the belief that the whole world was dying with me and I with it.

Pliny the Younger and his mother survived. So did most of the people of Misenum, spared because the pyroclastic flow had lost its punch in its 20-mile journey from Vesuvius. The younger Pliny's uncle had expired a few hours before, on the far shore of the Bay of Naples.

In the nearly two millennia since the destruction of Pompeii, Vesuvius has continued to hold more fascination for the Western world than any other volcano. Its prominent location in Europe, its frequent, often spectacular, eruptions, its picturesque cone rising serenely over the Bay of Naples, its inclusion in the eighteenth- and nineteenth-century "Grand Tour" of the Continent, and, not least, the constant threat it poses to this heavily populated region have all combined to rivet popular attention.

All volcanologists should make a pilgrimage to Vesuvius. In 1986 I made mine, spending a month performing gas studies in the recently reactivated Phlegraean Fields, or Campi Phlegraei, the zone of fumaroles close to Vesuvius. I was impressed by the volcano's beauty but never considered studying it; I knew I could contribute more by working on less scrutinized volcanoes in countries like Colombia.

Many scholars have spent their careers investigating Vesuvius. But few, if any, have been as dedicated and passionate in their work as an eighteenth-century English aristocrat who spent thirty-five years chronicling the moods and facets of the volcano. Sir William Hamilton was many things — the British ambassador to the Court of Naples, an inveterate collector of Greek and Roman antiquities, the cuckolded husband in one of history's most infamous love triangles. But I like to think of him as, above all, a volcanologist. He was fascinated by the titanic processes that threw Vesuvius into eruption. He had a profoundly scientific bent, analyzing the changes in Vesuvius's rocks, its fumaroles, its crater. He was a keen observer, offering some of the best descriptions ever of erupting volcanoes. But above all he loved the volcano, loved to watch it as it chuffed ash, oozed lava, or shot fire and rock.

"Vesuvius held no terror for Hamilton; it fascinated him," wrote his biographer Brian Fothergill. "Any sign of activity would find him on its slopes taking notes, making sketches, digging up samples of earth, venturing near as he dared to the smoking crater or to the streams of molten lava, often at the risk of his life."

Born in 1730 in Scotland to a noble family, Sir William served as an officer in the British army for ten years and saw action in the Seven Years' War in Holland and Belgium. He then became a member of Parliament until the poor health of his first wife prompted him to take a posting abroad. Through his connections, which included a close friendship with King George III, Sir William wrangled an appointment as "envoy extraordinary and plenipotentiary" at the Court of Naples and the Kingdom of the Two Sicilies. Many men in his position might have whiled away their years in the indolent splendor of southern Italy. But Hamilton was a man of the Enlightenment, with an enormous and restless curiosity, and in his thirty-five years in Naples he mastered many realms, two above all. The first was Greek and Roman antiquities. The second was volcanology.

Arriving in Naples in 1764, Sir William knew little about volcanoes and the processes that shaped the earth. But at just that time, Vesuvius entered one of its most active periods in recent centuries. He was immediately riveted by the power of the mountain that hovered over the Bay of Naples and terrified residents with its earthquakes and eruptions. Although nominally an amateur, he became one of the first true field geologists, climbing to Vesuvius's crater seventy times in three and a half decades and studying its lower regions on dozens more occasions. He witnessed three major eruptions and many minor ones.

Within a year of his arrival, ash and gas began pouring forth from Vesuvius's crater. Hamilton — described by a contemporary as a man "of spare figure and of great muscular power and energy" — could not stay away. In November 1765, on one of his first visits to the crater, Vesuvius fired a warning shot in his direction, a small eruption that showered him with stones and forced him to "retire with some precipitation." On March 28, 1766, as lava began pouring out of the crater and earthquakes shook the villages near Vesuvius, Sir William headed for the source of the commotion.

"I approached the mouth of the volcano as near as I could with prudence," he wrote to the Royal Society of London, the foremost scientific organization of his day. "The lava had the appearance of a river of red hot and liquid metal, such as we see in the glass-houses, on which were large floating cinders, half-lighted, and rolling one over another with great precipitation down the side of the mountain, forming a most beautiful and uncommon cascade."

He spent many more days and nights on the mountain during its 1766–67 eruptions, conducting small experiments and pushing to see how close he could safely get to his subject. He stood so near a fast lava stream that he could remark how its passage left "the adjacent ground quivering like the timbers of a water-mill." He poked a stick into the stream and saw that its surface was difficult to penetrate. He tossed in large stones and noted that they didn't sink. He marveled as the streams wove in and out of one another, creating at night "a sheet of fire, four miles in length, and in some parts near two in breadth. Your lordship may imagine the glorious appearance of the uncommon scene, such as passes all description."

Indeed, His Lordship could.

Sir Joseph Banks, the renowned botanist and head of the Royal Society, wrote to Hamilton: "I read your letters with that kind of fidgety anxiety which continually upbraids me for not being in a similar situation. I envy you, I pity myself..."

Finally, in October 1767, the eruptions peaked. Sir William was there, close to the crater:

> The mountain split and with such noise, from this new mouth a fountain of liquid fire shot up many feet high, and then like a torrent, rolled on directly toward us. The earth shook at the same time that a volley of pumice stones fell thick upon us; in an instant clouds of black smoke and ashes caused almost a total darkness; the explosions from the top of the mountain were much louder than any thunder I had ever heard, and the smell of the sulfur was very offensive. My guide, alarmed, took to his heels; and I must confess that I was not at my ease. I followed close, and we ran near three miles without stopping . . . The pumice stones, falling upon us like hail, were of such a size as to cause a disagreeable sensation upon the part which they fell. After having taken breath, as the earth still trembled greatly, I thought it most prudent to leave the mountain, and return to my villa, where I found my family in a great alarm at the continual and violent explosions of the volcano, which shook our house to its very foundations, the doors and windows swinging upon the hinges.

Thanks to countless hours of firsthand observation, Hamilton advanced volcanological knowledge on many fronts. He lived in an era when many scientists believed that the earth was only 5,700 years old, yet he deduced that the planet was far older and that wherever one found basalt, there had once been volcanoes. He surmised that much of Italy's, and the world's, landscape was shaped by volcanic activity and that the multilayered strata of rock, pumice, and ash around Naples was a record of eruptions going far back in time. Observing the formation of a new cone in the center of Vesuvius, he remarked, "I make no doubt but that the whole of Mount Vesuvius has been formed in the same manner." Watching this process, and examining Mount Somma — the high rampart that half-encircled the cone of Vesuvius — he was one of the first to surmise correctly that Somma was the precursor of Vesuvius and the volcano that erupted in A.D. 79. (Today, Somma is a standard term to denote the collapsed crater walls of an older volcano that surround a younger, active cone.) He also understood that the fuel that fired volcanoes came from deep inside the earth, and he argued that volcanoes should be seen not only as destructive but also as constructive forces that built the landscape, covering it in fertile soils and transporting valuable minerals to the surface from deep underground.

Sir William observed the excavations at Pompeii and collected thousands of volcanic rocks, which he sent to England for analysis. One hundred and twenty-two of them can be found today in the Natural History Museum in London. He and his first wife also entertained a constant stream of visitors, including European royalty eager to see Vesuvius in the company of Sir William, whose reputation as a connoisseur of volcanoes grew as the years passed. He became, as one friend remarked, "the delight and ornament of the Court of Naples."

In 1779 and 1794 Hamilton witnessed major eruptions of Vesuvius. Both times he found himself in tight spots, only to be extracted by cool thinking on his own part and that of his guides. In May 1779, at the start of five months of eruptive activity, Sir William, a friend, and their Italian guide — probably the one-eyed Bartolomeo Puma, whom Hamilton called the Cyclops of Vesuvius — spent the night on the volcano. The next day, wandering around the flanks as they studied lava streams weaving down the mountain, they found themselves sandwiched between two flows. Sizing up the situation, the guide decided to walk across one of them, which was about 50 feet wide.

"We followed him without hesitation," Sir William wrote, "having felt no other inconvenience than what proceeded from the violence of the heat on our legs and feet; the crust of the lava was so tough; besides being loaded with cinders and scoria, that our weight made not the least impression on it, and its motion was so slow, that we were not in any danger of losing our balance, and falling on it, however this experiment should not be tried except in cases of real necessity."

In 1794, at the age of sixty-four, Hamilton observed his last great eruption at Vesuvius. After seven months of slumber, the volcano came alive in early June with a series of premonitory earthquakes. Then, on Sunday, June 15, Vesuvius blew, shooting a fountain of fire high into the air. A black ash cloud filled the sky as lava poured down the mountain. It was probably the most powerful eruption at Vesuvius since 1631, when an estimated 18,000 people perished.

"Fresh fountains succeeded one another hastily, and all in a direct line tending, for about a mile and a half down, towards the towns of Resina and Torre del Greco," Hamilton wrote in his last letter to the Royal Society of London.

> I could count 15 of them, but I believe there were others obscured by the smoke . . . It is impossible that any description can give an idea of this fiery scene, or of the horrid noises that attended this great operation of nature. It was a mixture of the loudest thunder, with incessant reports, like those from numerous heavy artillery, accompanied by a continued hollow murmur, like that of the roaring of the ocean during a violent storm; and added to these there was another blowing noise, like that of the going up of a large flight of sky rockets . . . The frequent falling of the huge stones and scoria, which were thrown up to an incredible height from some of the new mouths . . . contributed undoubtedly to the concussion of the earth and air, which kept all the houses at Naples for several hours in a constant tremor, every door and window shaking and rattling incessantly, and the bells ringing. This was an awful moment! . . . The murmur of the prayers and lamentations of a numerous populace forming various processions, and parading in the streets, added likewise to the horror.

The eruption continued for more than a week, the clouds of ash turning day into night. Roofs and buildings collapsed under the weight of the ash, which is composed of small stone fragments that are far heavier than most people imagine. A river of lava 1,200 feet wide advanced to the sea, destroying most of Torre del Greco and Resina and forming a jetty that extended 626 feet into the Bay of Naples. On June 17 Hamilton hopped into a boat to have a look. Once again, he ran into trouble.

"I observed that the sea water was boiling as in a cauldron, where it washed the foot of this new formed promontory," he wrote, "and although I was at least a hundred yards from it, observing that the sea smoked near my boat, I put my hand into the water, which was literally scalded; and by this time my oarsmen observed that the pitch from the bottom of the boat was melting fast, and floating on the surface of the sea, and that the boat began to leak; we therefore retired hastily from this spot, and landed at some distance from the hot lava."

Of the 1,800 inhabitants of Torre del Greco, only 15 perished. The old and the sick whom inhabitants didn't have time to evacuate were burned alive in the lava flow, which had buried the cathedral to a depth of 40 feet.

On June 30 Hamilton decided to visit the crater with his guide, Puma, trudging through a blanket of hot ash marked by the tracks of foxes and lizards. It was his sixty-eighth ascent to the top of Vesuvius in the course of thirty years. Unable to make it all the way to the crater because the eruption had ripped open chasms in the volcano's flanks, he was stunned by the havoc that the eruption had wrought on the landscape, which was buried in ash and dotted with steaming fumaroles. Where the volcano had opened up and spewed lava, more than a half-dozen new cones had formed. Holding two handkerchiefs over his mouth and nostrils to cut the power of the acidic fumes, Hamilton surveyed the scene.

"In short, nothing but ruin and desolation was to be seen," he wrote in one of his letters, several of which were later compiled into his classic book, *Campi Phlegraei.* "Ten thousand men, in as many years, could not, surely, make such an alteration on the face of Vesuvius, as has been made by nature in the short space of five hours."

Farther below, volcano-induced mudslides had carried away

homes, trees, stone walls, and more than 4,000 sheep and cattle. Near Torre del Greco, vineyards and fields were scorched, homes buried in lava. Yet, to Hamilton's amazement, the displaced residents of the town were back within a few weeks, rebuilding their homes. Over the next two centuries, many volcanologists, including myself, would be similarly astounded by people's cavalier attitude toward volcanoes.

"Such is the attachment of the inhabitants to their native spot, although attended with such imminent danger, that of 18,000 not one gave his vote to abandon it," wrote Hamilton.

In his later years, Hamilton's tranquil domestic life grew stormy. Six years after his wife died in 1782, the former mistress of his nephew showed up in Naples on the Grand Tour. The daughter of a blacksmith, Emma Hart was a gorgeous and sensuous young woman who had slept her way into the English aristocracy. Hamilton, then fifty-six, was — like most men — smitten with the twenty-one-year-old beauty and took her as his mistress. They married in 1791, and soon Emma became famous throughout Europe for her "attitudes" — a performance in which, dressed in classical gowns, she assumed the poses found on her husband's vases. Visitors swooned at her loveliness, with Goethe describing her poses as "like nothing you have ever seen." Hamilton's enemies took him to task.

"Sir William has actually married his gallery of statues," remarked Horace Walpole.

In 1798 the dashing admiral Horatio Nelson showed up at the Hamiltons', fresh from a victory over the French at the Battle of the Nile, and promptly took Lady Hamilton as his mistress. Their ménage à trois became one of England's great scandals, and when Sir William was recalled to London in 1800 he was a laughingstock. In early 1801 Emma gave birth to Nelson's daughter, Horatia. Accepting the relationship between his wife and Nelson, Hamilton inhabited the same houses as they did until his death in 1803. Nelson was killed in the Battle of Trafalgar in 1805, and Emma, fleeing her creditors, eventually died a pauper in France, her daughter at her side.

Two centuries later, Susan Sontag wrote of these events in her novel *The Volcano Lover*. And that, for me, is what endures from Hamilton — his ardor for volcanoes. A connoisseur of erupting mountains, a chronicler of fumaroles and flame, he was a true volcanologist.

Two of the greatest volcano lovers of all times lived in our era, and I was fortunate to know them. Maurice and Katia Krafft visited more erupting volcanoes than anyone else in history, witnessing 175 eruptions in dozens of countries. Katia took nearly 250,000 slides and Maurice made four long films, numerous short ones, and left behind thousands of hours of 16mm footage, enough to fill 709 boxes. Chances are good that any photograph or film clip you've seen of an erupting volcano was taken by Maurice or Katia. The French couple published twenty books and made a film about volcanic hazards that is credited with saving many lives. They amassed the most extensive collection of volcano-related books, art, and artifacts anywhere in the world. Far more exhaustive than even the Smithsonian's holdings, it contained 5,000 books, more than 4,000 paintings and gravures, and thousands of relics, stamps, and postcards. Their house, basement, and garage in Alsace were crammed floor to ceiling with things volcanic, from 4-foot-long basalt bombs to melted silverware salvaged from the 1902 eruption that destroyed St. Pierre. Their abode was, according to one friend, "a volcano temple."

Having no family — "the volcanoes are our children," said Katia — they spent nine months a year photographing and studying volcanoes around the world, dropping everything if they received news of an eruption. Their life *was* volcanoes, their goal to convey the wonder — and the danger — of "these formidable geological machines," as Maurice called them. But such a passion had its price.

"Little by little, we and the Kraffts [Maurice's parents] realized that we had lost them," said Katia's mother, Madeleine Conrad. "The volcanoes had stolen them from us."

When I embarked on my career, Maurice and Katia were a fixture on the international volcanological scene, attending all the major conferences and showing up — usually before anyone else — at every eruption of note. Like Hamilton, they were not traditional

A pyroclastic flow rolls down Galeras's northeastern flank on August 27, 1936. This photo appeared on the front page of Pasto's newspaper.
Studio Herrera, Pasto

In May 1989, Galeras became active once again, sending a plume of ash over Pasto. *Studio Herrera, Pasto*

A *tornillo*, or screw-shaped seismic signal, registered at Galeras before the January 14, 1993, eruption and subsequent blasts. Only afterward did we learn that on Galeras even a few *tornillos* can presage an eruption. *Stanley Williams*

Patty Mothes at Ecuador's Guagua Pichincha volcano, which she has studied extensively. With Marta Calvache, Patty raced to my rescue after the Galeras eruption.
Stanley Williams

My student Marta Lucía Calvache stands next to a boulder thrown out by the July 1992 eruption.
Stanley Williams

The active cone at Galeras is ringed by an amphitheater, a remnant of an earlier incarnation of the volcano. At lower left, on the rim of the amphitheater, is the police post, the staging point for exploration of the volcano. *José Arlés Zapata*

English gravimetry expert Geoff Brown. *Hazel Rymer*

Carlos Trujillo with his son, Mauricio, and his wife, Anna Lucía Torres, several years before the eruption. *Courtesy of Anna Lucía Torres*

Efrain Armando Guerrero Zamboni (left) and his son, Yovanny, were two of the tourists who joined us on the volcano just before the eruption. Guerrero's wife, Gloria Benavides, is at right. *Courtesy of Gloria Benavides*

Members of our group pose before climbing onto the cone of Galeras on January 14, 1993. Standing, left to right: Alfredo Roldan, Stan Williams, Nestor García, and José Arlés Zapata. Squatting: Fabio García (left) and Igor Menyailov. *Fabio García*

Left to right: Stan Williams, Igor Menyailov, and José Arlés Zapata on the cone of Galeras shortly before the eruption. *Noticieras de las 24 Horas*

Working on the cone before the eruption are Menyailov, García, Williams, and Zapata. *Noticieras de las 24 Horas*

Igor Menyailov sampling gases at the Deformes fumarole about two hours before the eruption. *Eduardo Cruz/Volcan Galeras*

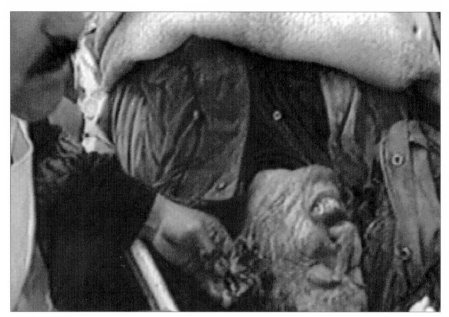

A rescue worker treats me before my evacuation from Galeras. *QAP Noticias*

Rescue workers loading me onto an army helicopter, which flew me to the provincial hospital in Pasto. *QAP Noticias*

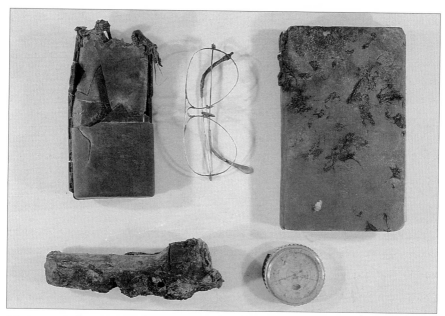

My burned glasses case, glasses, field notebook, flashlight, and altimeter.
Daniel Ball

The police station on top of Galeras, damaged and abandoned after the eruptions of 1992 and 1993. The windows in the foreground were blown out by volcanic bombs. *Stanley Williams*

Dr. Porfirio Muñoz (right) and I in front of the hospital in Pasto in 1999. Muñoz, fresh from his surgical residency in Bogotá, performed the surgery that saved my life. *Fen Montaigne*

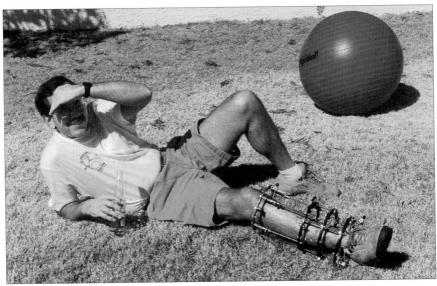

The Russian "birdcage" device used to repair my shattered right leg. *Lynda Williams*

Katia Krafft (left) and her husband, Maurice, in Chile in 1983. The Kraffts probably visited more erupting volcanoes than any other individuals in history. *André Demaison*

A pyroclastic flow moving away from the Soufriere Hills volcano on Montserrat in the West Indies, February 1977. A similar flow at Unzen volcano in Japan killed the Kraffts on June 3, 1991. *Courtesy of Montserrat Volcano Observatory*

In Rabaul, Papua New Guinea, ashfalls from a series of eruptions in September 1994 denuded trees and destroyed buildings, but smooth evacuation procedures kept the number of casualties to a minimum. *Stanley Williams*

Mount Vesuvius, seen from the ruins of Pompeii. One of the world's most active volcanoes, Vesuvius threatens more than half a million people in the Naples area. *Stanley Williams*

Marta Calvache and I working on Galeras in 1999 with two of her Colombian colleagues. *Fen Montaigne*

volcanologists with doctorates or government titles. Maurice had a master's degree in geology and Katia a bachelor's in geochemistry. They had never worked in a university or on a geological survey and supported themselves through photography and lectures.

Though I never spent time with them in a crater, I met them at numerous volcanoes and meetings from Indonesia to Mount St. Helens. At first glance, they made an odd couple. Maurice's boisterous, forceful personality, his booming laugh, and his six-foot, 240-pound frame filled a room. With his large hands, bulbous nose, and blocky head topped with thick, curly brown hair, he looked more like an Alsatian peasant than a world-renowned volcanologist. Physically, Katia was everything he wasn't: short, retiring, and waifish, with close-cropped, brown hair and birdlike features. But they shared great physical stamina, courage, and an iron will. We always spoke of them as a single entity, Maurice-and-Katia. She stayed in the background and took care of the finances and the day-to-day running of their affairs. He was the great talker, the one who conceptualized and planned their unceasing expeditions. "I am the whale and Katia is the pilot fish," Maurice once said.

Both of them felt the pull of volcanoes from an early age, their fascination forged by family visits to the Italian volcanoes that had mesmerized Hamilton, including Vesuvius and Mount Etna. Maurice's parents were physicians with a deep interest in the natural world, and when the boy was ten they took him and his brother on the grand volcano tour.

"We climbed Stromboli at night," Maurice's father, Raymond Krafft, wrote in a memorial book, *The Fire of the Earth*, "and it was there, in front of the fascinating night eruptions, where red and black mixed, silence and the muted sound of the explosions, the atmosphere both bewitching and impressive, it was there that the virus of volcanology bit Maurice."

He was bitten badly, collecting volcanic rocks, making volcanoes out of sand and fireworks in his garden, and joining the Geological Society of France at the age of fourteen. As a high school student, he traveled through France and Germany, studying extinct volcanoes.

Katia made the same Italian tour with her parents as a teenager, spellbound by the regularly fountaining lava at Stromboli and the ruins at Pompeii and Herculaneum. Returning to Alsace, she saw a film, *Rendezvous with the Devil*, by France's best-known volcanologist, Haroun Tazieff, and she was hooked. She told her parents she was going to be a volcanologist.

She met Maurice at the University of Strasbourg in the late 1960s, and they were married in 1971. Maurice had already made a prize-winning documentary film about the ancient volcanoes of the Auvergne region of France. With that money he financed his first full-length film, on the volcanoes of Iceland. Katia began taking still photographs, and the Krafft team was born.

They struggled financially in the 1970s but still managed — through corporate sponsorship and the growing revenue from their photography — to visit dozens of volcanoes. But by 1980 they were well on their way to becoming the Cousteaus of French volcanology. For those traveling with them, their expeditions were a blend of torture and exhilaration. Typical of their trips was the one made to 9,481-foot Oldoinyo Lengai, a remote volcano in Tanzania where extremely fluid lavas — never observed anywhere else — gush out of the crater at unusually high speeds.

Katia and Maurice raced from France to photograph the new lava lake on top of Oldoinyo and the jets of liquid magma squirting out. During a weeklong stint near the bubbling crater with the German volcanologist Jörg Keller and local guides, Maurice was like a man possessed.

"I saw him filming until he had blisters on his hands," recalled Keller. "He could be really nasty. He'd say, 'Katia, go there! Jörg, go there!' He was so focused that he would growl at anyone who got in his way. While he was working he was two hundred percent into it. I think Katia accepted that while Maurice was filming he was so devoted that he could be insupportable for everyone around him."

André Demaison, a writer who became a close friend and traveling companion of the Kraffts, was also there. He said that the workday at Oldoinyo — as at all volcanoes with Maurice — was "terrible." They arose at 4 A.M., worked until well past dark, and finally collapsed into bed at midnight. It was not uncommon for Maurice to lose six pounds a day.

"He had an obsession for perfection," said Demaison, who is now writing a biography of the Kraffts. "Maurice demanded a lot when he worked. He was anxious, brooding. He was like a storm, like a volcano in eruption."

But the reward came at Oldoinyo Lengai. It always did with Maurice and Katia.

"We were at the summit at the end of the day," recalled Demaison. "Maurice and Katia had put down their cameras, we had eaten dinner, and we were relaxing. We were looking at the lava lake and the stars. The night was black; there was silence except for the gurgling of the lava. It was like a noise from the beginning of the earth. We were in communion with the volcano, the origins of the earth, the universe. At one point Maurice pointed out Mars and said, 'I have a dream to walk one day on Olympus Mons on Mars.'

"It was a beautiful moment. It was like time stopped. You are in the universe and you are nothing. Maurice and Katia used to say that volcanoes are the school of humility. You are nothing, and when you go to volcanoes, your mask falls off and you see the real person."

Maurice and Katia became famous for their photographs and movies of spectacular lava flows in places like Iceland and Hawaii. In some of the photographs, either Maurice or Katia — usually wearing a shiny, aluminum-colored hard hat and fire-retardant suit — stands before a fountaining wall of incandescent lava. But in the later stages of their career the Kraffts became primarily interested in explosive volcanoes — "hard" volcanoes, they called them — and in using their photography to help prevent deaths from eruptions. In one of the many lectures he gave each year, Maurice talked about their fascination and the risks it entailed:

The last time I came, I presented the volcanoes of Africa, that is to say the nice ones, the beautiful ones. Today, I've got the hard ones. Like there is hard rock, there are hard volcanoes, killer volcanoes. By

the way, of the 350 professional volcanologists, there are about 300 —
and they are right — who specialize in the nice ones. In other words,
red lava flows, fountains of molten lava, boiling lava lakes. It's spectacular, it's scary, but frankly, to get killed in that type of eruption
you have to make a big mistake or have very bad luck.

But there are some 50 other volcanologists, of which I am a part,
who specialize in explosive volcanoes, which is more exciting to me.
There is nothing red. Rather, there are 20-, 30-, 40-kilometer ash
clouds that move at 1,000 kilometers per hour and that sweep 20, 30
or 40 kilometers away from the volcano. It's the bomb with a lit fuse,
and we don't know how long the fuse is. In five years, I've had five
colleagues killed by eruptions — that's 10 percent. You may say that
leaves a spot for youth, and that's true, promotions are often rapid. I
would say that if one truly specializes in explosive volcanoes then it's
not worth contributing towards retirement, and that if one makes it
to retirement it's a little suspicious. It means that he really didn't do
his job conscientiously.

Maurice was well known for such bravado. The French press
was fond of repeating his bons mots, such as "With all the risks we
take, it would be a real shame to die in our beds" and "When we
know everything about volcanoes, we'll throw ourselves into the
first crater that comes along." Asked once how he felt right before
an eruption, Maurice replied, "The same way you feel right before
an erection!" Sometimes he referred to himself as "Lucifer Boom
Boom!" But behind such bluster was a great deal of anxiety, not
so much about dying on a volcano as about gaining the respect of
the scientific establishment and continuing to do first-rate photography.

Maurice and Katia were eager — some would say obsessed — to
take pictures of pyroclastic flows at close range. Few people had succeeded in capturing a series of *nuées ardentes* in still pictures, let
alone on film. In August 1986 Jürgen Kienle, a volcanologist at the
University of Alaska at Fairbanks, called Maurice and Katia to tell
them that the Augustine volcano in Alaska was emitting pyroclastic
flows. Two days later the Kraffts were there. Kienle, a German friend

of the Kraffts, was about to get a lesson in just how far the couple was willing to push the envelope.

The Kraffts rented a helicopter to take them from Homer, Alaska, to Augustine, which was on an island southwest of Anchorage. Landing near the volcano, they could see pyroclastic flows sweeping down its flanks at twenty-minute intervals. At first ecstatic, Maurice soon announced that they were too far away. He asked the pilot to take him closer, next to an area of older stone and ash deposits known as "the door to hell." It was only 100 yards from the edges of the *nuées ardentes* whooshing down Augustine. Maurice tried to coax the pilot and Kienle to move nearer, saying he had been that close to dozens of pyroclastic flows at Galunggung volcano in Indonesia in 1982 and assuring them it was safe.

"His proposition was dangerous, but I didn't have a voice since they had rented the helicopter and my role was that of guide," Kienle wrote in the memorial volume about the Kraffts.

The pilot said he would drop Maurice and Katia off at "the door to hell," but he refused to stay there with his helicopter. After the pair hopped out, Kienle and the pilot flew 500 yards lower on the flank. But seeing the Kraffts struggle with their mounds of equipment, Kienle and the pilot set out on foot to help them.

"It was a fantastic scene — hypnotic," wrote Kienle. "The electric charge was such that my hair stood on end and the clouds seemed to be lit up by a neon halo. The *nuées* traveled like cats — slowing down and then suddenly springing forward. A few times the *nuées* were coming toward us, and once extinguished they left at our feet a residual layer so hot that it burned our special boots . . . Maurice and Katia were in heaven, but I didn't have the confidence in the regularity of the flow. What if a larger *nuée* came toward us?"

Just as Kienle feared, a pyroclastic flow bigger than the previous ones soon crested the crater and headed their way. The main body of it passed a few hundred yards to the side, but its cooler edge engulfed the group.

"Almost immediately we found ourselves prisoners in a mass of sulfuric air that to our surprise didn't burn," recalled Kienle. "A fine ash, like flour, covered the equipment and us. For a few minutes there was zero visibility. Then suddenly it lifted. Maurice exclaimed, 'That's enough!' We quickly got down to the helicopter . . . The incident had shaken us, and even Maurice showed signs of being nervous." Before flying back to Homer, Maurice scribbled in a shack on Augustine, "To see a pyroclastic flow from 50 meters — that's an experience you should have!"

That night, over dinner and wine, they experienced the exhilaration — known to war correspondents and other danger junkies — that comes from surviving a close call. But the next day Kienle became angry with the Kraffts. Had Maurice really been that close to a *nuée ardente* at Galunggung? No, he confessed, he'd never seen one at that range. Then he confided to Kienle that as he considered approaching "the door to hell," he figured the odds of being engulfed in a pyroclastic flow, and probably dying, were as high as 50–50.

"As a father of a family, I felt that I had taken too great a risk," he wrote. "That day I begged them to be more prudent if they didn't want to be transformed into human fries in the devil's basin. I asked them to do it for me and for the many others who loved them."

Maurice's footage was, indeed, spectacular, and it is often used in films demonstrating the dangers of *nuées ardentes*. But over time, as Kienle ruminated on the recklessness of the Kraffts, he grew increasingly incensed. He stopped speaking to Maurice and Katia. The rift persisted for several years until Jörg Keller invited them all to a dinner of reconciliation at his house in Freiburg, Germany.

In his final years Maurice worked on a video for UNESCO, "Understanding Volcanic Hazards," designed to be shown to citizens and officials living near active volcanoes. Pulling together two decades of his remarkable footage, he made a simple yet powerful film that outlined the seven main volcanic hazards, from tsunamis to *nuées ardentes*. He finished a rough cut in early 1991.

In late May the Kraffts were in Martinique, at the site of the 1902 Mont Pelée eruption, when they received a fax from one of their many contacts around the world. It was from Harry Glicken, the young American geologist who — by one day — avoided death in the 1980 eruption of Mount St. Helens. He informed the Kraffts that

Mount Unzen, in southern Japan, was emitting large pyroclastic flows. Jettisoning their work in Martinique, Maurice and Katia flew home to pick up more equipment, then continued on to Japan.

Glicken, then thirty-three, was a bright, absent-minded, likable volcanologist whose career had been sputtering after he failed to land a job with the USGS. In 1990 he began doing postdoctoral research at Tokyo Metropolitan University. At that time Unzen, on the southern island of Kyushu, spat out a series of pyroclastic flows, attracting the attention of Japan's highly competitive media. Glicken seemed of two minds about heading to Unzen with the Kraffts, understandable in the face of such danger. To one friend he wrote, "I can watch real pyroclastic flows at Unzen — that will be great!" But to another he complained, "I'm mulling about going, but I have a feeling that it would just be a colossal waste of time that I can ill afford." But by the time the unstoppable Maurice arrived, Glicken was no doubt swept up in the excitement, and Harry, Maurice, and Katia quickly headed for Kyushu.

At 4,458 feet, Unzen is not a big volcano, but it has a deadly history. In 1792 a volcanic landslide there collapsed into the sea, creating a tsunami that killed 15,000 people. In May 1991 pyroclastic flows began rushing eastward down the valley of the Mizunashi River, forcing the evacuation of 3,500 people near the towns of Fukae and Shimabara. When the Kraffts and Glicken arrived on May 29, a large crowd of photographers and newsmen had gathered in the evacuated area, hoping to glimpse Unzen's *nuées ardentes*. But the weather was abysmal, foggy and overcast, and all the milling crowd of newsmen could do was listen to the ominous rumbles of the eruptions and landslides. The Kraffts and Glicken joined the waiting throng.

Maurice became increasingly restless as the days passed and the poor weather continued. Further, Maurice always liked to get a "global" view of a new volcano by first flying over it, and he was upset that the Japanese media had reserved every available helicopter. The atmosphere in the abandoned suburb of Shimabara was tense. Mike Lyvers, a geologist, visited the spot the day before the June 3 eruption. He found a pack of reporters, their cameras aimed at the cloud-shrouded volcano. Occasionally, through the murk, he glimpsed pyroclastic flows rolling down Unzen — glowing, red-orange clouds crackling with sparks.

"The noise was terrible, a cacophony of avalanching and exploding rocks," Lyvers wrote to Richard V. Fisher, Glicken's faculty adviser at the University of California at Santa Barbara. "Between eruptions it was strangely silent until the terrified dogs started barking again — the evacuees had all left their pets behind . . . It was obvious that a large flow could emerge from the canyon mouth and engulf us. I had a terrible feeling of dread and decided to drive out of the area."

The weather cleared the next morning, and the local officials gave the swarm of reporters permission to drive closer to the Mizunashi Valley and observe the *nuées ardentes*. The Kraffts and Glicken joined them. The group totaled more than forty people, including some policemen and a handful of taxi drivers ferrying the journalists into position. Maurice, Katia, and Harry walked past the abandoned village, with its temple honoring the victims of the 1792 tsunami, and took up a position a couple of hundred yards from the Mizunashi River and no more than 20 or 30 yards above the valley floor. They could clearly see the light gray, ash-covered zones of devastation where earlier pyroclastic flows had swept down the Mizunashi.

Moving away from the main body of Japanese journalists, the Kraffts set up their equipment. Then they waited, hoping to get footage of a *nuée ardente* even more spectacular than their film of Augustine. Two miles away, at the volcano's summit, a hardened spine of lava teetered over the lip of Unzen's crater. Suddenly the fragile spine crumbled, uncorking pent-up gas and magma that exploded into millions of tiny ash particles. A pyroclastic flow formed instantly and advanced down the Mizunashi Valley at speeds of up to 60 miles an hour. It was several times larger than any of the recent *nuées ardentes* Unzen disgorged. At first Maurice and Katia must have been thrilled with the sight. Very quickly, however, they must have sensed the danger.

Videotape from that day shows a boiling, dark gray mass advancing at astonishing speed, its billowing cells towering hundreds of feet in the air. The main body of the pyroclastic flow hugged the Mizunashi, but a glowing ash cloud — reaching 840 degrees F — engulfed Maurice, Katia, Harry, and the nearby journalists and drivers. The Kraffts, Glicken, and many of the journalists were killed in seconds, their lungs scorched and robbed of air by plugs of ash and mucus, their bodies flash-burned by the heat. Peter Baxter said the victims' clothing and hair immediately burst into flames. At the same time their bodies were "carbonized," the heat so intense that it burned the flesh off their fingers. Death would have come almost simultaneously from the heat and from their inhaling clouds of superheated ash. The pyroclastic flow surged on for another mile, leaving 179 burned houses, charred and crumpled cars, and a bleak, ash-covered landscape in its wake.

In all, forty-three people died. Seventeen victims on the outer edge of the pyroclastic flow lived for a while before enduring agonizing deaths. Some slowly suffocated from the ash that had lodged in their windpipes and lungs, while others died at the Shimabara Hospital from burns to their flesh and lungs.

At the site of the pyroclastic flow, the authorities were unable to recover all of the victims because of the continuing danger. Police finally retrieved the remains of the Kraffts and Glicken three days later, identifying them through dental records. The Kraffts — she was forty-nine, he forty-five — lay next to each other, covered by 3 inches of pyroclastic ash. The French press, perhaps in an apocryphal flourish, said they were stretching out their hands to each other.

Though badly shaken by the news, the world's volcanologists were not entirely surprised. Maurice and Katia had always taken risks. But their contributions were enormous, as shown by events elsewhere in Asia at the time of their deaths. At that very moment, Maurice's UNESCO video was being shown to thousands of people near the highly active Mount Pinatubo in the Philippines. Two weeks later, Pinatubo experienced a massive eruption. But nearly all the residents had been evacuated, thanks, in part, to the film.

In addition to their films and pictures, Maurice and Katia's dream of teaching the public about volcanoes lives on in other ways. Their collection of books and artwork is in the National Museum of Natural History in Paris. Many of their artifacts are displayed at the Center of European Volcanism in Clermont-Ferrand, a museum they helped create.

By their early deaths, Maurice and Katia escaped what his brother, Bertrand, called their greatest fear: being unable to work on volcanoes because of age or infirmity. Katia had said many times that if she could choose her death, it would be on a volcano, beside Maurice. I will give Maurice the last word.

"You may say to me that I should be afraid of these volcanoes," he told the audience at one of his lectures. "Not at all. In the last fifteen years I've seen so many beautiful eruptions that I've been complete for a while now."

7

·····················

THE ERUPTION

A T 1:41 P.M., the sound of the earth's crust shattering was replaced by a thunderous roar as the pressure of gases blew off
Galeras's dome and the volcano ejected tons of rocks and ash. Instantly, a fusillade of red- and white-hot stones — some the size of
tennis balls, some the size of large TV sets — sizzled through the air.
Protecting my head with my backpack, I raced down the rugged
gray flank of the volcano.

I have heard that time slows down in a disaster, that for some it
even seems to stand still. For me, nothing could have been farther from the truth in the opening moments of the eruption. Everything seemed to move at warp speed. The crater was roaring, the
volcano throbbing, and the air crackling with volcanic shrapnel.
Racing frantically, overloaded by sensations and emotions, my
mind seemed to blow a fuse. After a few seconds, however, something instinctual took charge. I flew down the slope, my only im-
pulse to put as much distance between me and the crater as possible.

Then the rock hit me. It was as if someone had taken a swing at
my head with a baseball bat, rudely interrupting my progress down
the cone. The projectile, probably no bigger than an orange, struck
with such force that I was knocked a few feet sideways and crumpled on the flanks of Galeras. The blow, just above my left ear, caved
in my skull, driving several bone fragments into my brain. Stunned,
feeling little pain, I lay on the slope for a minute, my head ringing,

the air filled with the bellowing of the eruption and the *Zzzzip! Zzzzip! Zzzzip!* of incandescent chunks of Galeras whizzing past. Bomblets from the volcano, many more than a yard in diameter, shattered when they hit the earth, flinging out fragments of red-hot, hissing shrapnel.

I had made it no more than 20 yards below the crater's lip. Pulling myself to my feet, I looked to the side and noticed, just a few yards away, a vivid patch of yellow set against the lead gray flank of the volcano. It was, I realized, José Arlés Zapata. His head was bloody, his body contorted. His radio lay smashed beside him. Not far away, the three tourists were splayed across the field of scree. Bloodied and disfigured, caught in positions of grotesque repose, they, too, were clearly dead.

The sight of their bodies caused neither sadness nor shock. I merely took it as further proof of what I already knew: something awful was happening, and I needed to get away.

Stumbling forward on the 40-degree slope, I was pelted by more rocks, several of which slammed into my backpack, which by now was on fire. I managed to run a few more yards before a barrage of rocks cut me off at the legs, knocking me once more to the ground. Rolling on my side, I looked down. A bone protruded from my lower left leg, poking through my torn, smoldering pants. Another projectile had nearly severed my right foot at the ankle; my boot dangled by a skein of tendons and flesh. I stared at my mangled legs and thought it odd that I didn't feel more pain. As I lay there, with rocks exploding around me, I felt as if I were gazing at myself from afar, almost as if I had floated into the air and was observing, with an odd detachment, this badly injured man lying on Galeras's flank.

I had experienced several small eruptions and realized that my best chance of surviving this blast — much larger than anything I had ever been caught in — was probably to stay put and dodge the volcanic bombs. But I had no idea what might be coming next, and I was hell-bent to get clear of Galeras's cone. All I wanted to do was stand up and keep running. There was no hope of supporting any weight on my right leg, so I tried to pull myself up on my left, which still had one intact bone. Wobbling as I rose to a crouch, I glanced again at my right foot, incredulous that it was still somehow attached to my leg. As I teetered there, bent in two, I lifted my eyes toward the cone and saw a roiling, black plume of ash and debris ascending into the sky. Looming over me, its billowing form only heightened the scene's dreamlike quality.

In seconds I fell on my face once more. This time I knew I was down for good. I lay there, the nearly severed foot bleeding steadily. The wounds scarcely hurt. I noticed, however, that my back, arms, and legs had been burned by the fiery rocks that had pelted me.

Realizing I had to take shelter, I dragged myself several yards across the scree and hunkered behind a dark boulder the size of a desk. My pants and jacket were on fire, and I rolled around to extinguish the flames. The largest blaze was on my back, where my knapsack was now consumed by flames, melting my flashlight and glasses case, incinerating some clothes and $7,500 in traveler's checks, and causing third-degree burns on a 10-inch swath of my back. I slipped off the backpack, then patted out the flames on my pants. Strangely, given all that was happening, I was worried about the money. Feeling the $10,000 bankroll in my pocket and fearing it would burn, I stuffed it into the front of my shirt, the only part of me that wasn't smoldering.

The eruption, only a few minutes old, was still going full bore. The ground beneath me shook continuously as Galeras underwent what turned out to be the most powerful eruption in the previous five years. The black column was now rising high above the volcano, darkening the sky and sifting ash down on the mountain. The stench of sulfur filled the air. With the boulder shielding me from horizontal projectiles, I turned onto my back and scanned the sky for rocks that were dropping out of the eruption column and heading my way — a difficult task, especially considering that my glasses had been shattered. The largest chunks of debris had been expelled in the first several minutes, and now glowing red, orange, and white rocks — ranging from the size of a marble to that of a softball — whistled out of the sky. I struggled to concentrate on these fragments, and when one looked as if it would fall directly on me, I rolled out of the way.

Although I had no idea at the time, Mike Conway and Luis LeMarie were huddled not far from me, perhaps 30 yards to one side. In my memory they were below me. In theirs I was below them. We were all caught in the same eruption, but each survivor holds a different disaster in his mind. This is what they remember.

Mike and Luis were walking down the same side of the cone as I, the south-southeast side, which faces the escarpment where the police station is perched. Mike remembers walking about a quarter to a third of the way down the cone, perhaps 75 to 100 feet. In Mike and Luis's version, they are the highest on the flank, with Andy Macfarlane and me walking a little below them. José Arlés and the three tourists are even lower on the cone. Mike remembers hearing a thunderous explosion. He remembers somebody — probably me — yelling, "It's the volcano! Run!" Then he looked over his shoulder and saw a dark gray plume shoot out of the crater.

"Projectiles began landing all about us," he later wrote. "We all began to run downslope. The number of projectiles flying about us was increasing, so I dove behind rock debris about ⅓ meter [one foot] high and yelled to Luis LeMarie to get down. Luis dove into a small depression right next to me. At this time I lost track of everyone else in the group. My impression is that others continued to run downslope."

Luis remembers the shock of the blast and then seeing José Arlés and me streaking down the cone. With little experience on volcanoes, the Ecuadorian obeyed Conway's command and dove into the scree. Mike, curled into a "fetal ball," pulled his knapsack over his head and neck to shield himself from the volcanic bombs. Luis did the same, using his hands as protection. No sooner had they burrowed into the loose stones than Mike began raising his head to steal glances at the crater. He was worried about large blocks rolling down and crushing them. But being a volcanologist, he was most concerned about pyroclastic flows — although had one crested the crater lip and *whooshed* downslope there is little he could have done.

Lying half to two thirds of the way down the slope, he and Luis were bombarded with scorching rocks that broke their bones, burned their skin, and set their clothes on fire. Mike suffered a broken right hand, a burn the size of a softball on his back, and smaller burns on his arms, hands, and buttocks. Luis fared even worse. Striking him like hammer blows, several sizable rocks broke a small bone in the back of each of his legs. Another rock broke a finger, and yet another fractured his collarbone. Falling debris scorched his arms, hands, and head. Luis also remembers something no one else does — a small ash cloud rolling over them.

"This flow of ash we felt over our heads," Luis told me later. "We could feel our heads burning slowly. It felt like we were put inside an oven. It was terrible."

Conway saw rocks 5 feet in diameter shooting from the volcano and crashing on Galeras's flanks. Every fifteen seconds he lifted his head, straining to see what more the volcano had in store. Ever the volcanologist, his powers of observation were keen.

"It was a classic Vulcanian eruption characterized by a single large explosive blast directed vertically," he wrote to a friend. "As I glanced up at the south rim I could see tongues of the convecting plume jetting 5 to 15 meters onto the flanks of the cone. These tongues probably consisted of hot, magmatic gases and numerous dense particles . . . I thought that I could see an incandescent flame within the body of the plume, behind a veil of colder outer plume. The incandescent part of the plume appeared quite narrow, with a diameter of 5 to 10 meters."

Again and again, Conway checked for pyroclastic flows. "I had every intention of surviving," he said later. "I knew people didn't survive pyroclastic flows. But I thought that if one comes I'll lay there, cover my head, not breathe, jump up and take a breath, and then get back down. I had to feel I had some control. I had to have a plan."

Luis wanted to scramble farther down the cone. But Conway

could still hear the sizzling missiles and see dark bombs streaking against the cloudy sky. "No, wait," he told Luis. "At least another thirty seconds."

Andy Macfarlane recalls the two of us descending from the rim of the crater together, following the path that moves diagonally across the cone. The Colombian tourists, he recalls, were ahead of us. Luis and Mike were about 40 feet above us. José Arlés was about 10 feet below us on the flank.

We had made it about 70 feet down the slope, Macfarlane remembers, when the volcano blew. "The sound was loud but not ear shattering — it was reminiscent of close thunder or a sonic boom, and for a split second it was not clear to everyone what was going on," he wrote a month later. "I turned and looked back up the cone and saw a black cloud going up over the crater. In that instant I realized what was happening, and almost before we could start running, blocks of hot rock started falling all around us."

As Macfarlane turned to run downhill, a rock nicked him above the left eye, cutting him and causing a hairline fracture to his skull. He remembers bolting down the slope, passing me.

From this point on, my perception of time is quite unreliable because instants seemed to last forever. Large blocks, some of them more than a meter across, were falling all around us, with many smaller pieces. The violence of the impacts was incredible, and when the falling rocks hit boulders on the ground, they shattered and sprayed hot, sharp shrapnel. When the blocks split open, they were glowing hot inside, and fragments would just lie there and hiss.

Continuing to run, he saw a volcanic bomb cut down one of the tourists. Macfarlane took a "sprawling, cartwheeling fall" over some boulders. He passed José Arlés, in his distinctive yellow parka, sprawled face down on the scree with blood streaming down his face. The Colombian geologist was clearly dead. Macfarlane kept running. "I was sure," he wrote, "we would all be killed."

As he dashed down the volcano, he did his best — with limited success — to avoid the large volcanic bombs that had crashed onto the crater. "The big blocks made wide, shallow pits where they landed on soft ash, and when I lost my footing I tended to roll into these pits on top of the hot rock and then be impelled to get up and keep going."

Someone — probably Mike Conway — yelled at him to hide behind a boulder, so he threw himself behind a 20-inch rock. As he did so, Conway came tearing down the slope, searching for a boulder to protect him. Looking skyward, Macfarlane rolled out of the way of the volcanic blocks falling down, his vision blurred by the blood pooling in his left eye.

"While I was looking up," he wrote, "I heard three or four big impacts right around me; from that I realized I had no chance of seeing them coming so it didn't matter whether I looked up or not. It also seemed to me that the blocks were falling much more vertically than horizontally, so that hiding behind a low boulder did not offer much protection. By then, I fully expected to die at any moment, and I decided to just keep going rather than hide and wait and hope that somehow I would be missed by the bombardment . . ."

Continuing his scramble down the cone, he remembered Peter Baxter's words from the previous day: the mortality rate of those caught in an eruption is about 50 percent.

> This, perversely, was a source of great encouragement for me, because I was repeating to myself, "We won't all die," over and over, trying to convince myself that if I kept moving I might possibly have a chance. I also remember collecting many burns on my hands from putting them on hot rocks as I was crawling over boulders or getting to my feet. There were hot rock fragments all over the ground on the side of the cone. I thought to myself that the burns didn't matter so long as I was still alive . . .
>
> I didn't get far before I fell again over another boulder and landed below it. Behind this boulder was Stan, a little higher up and right behind the boulder. He was conscious and appeared at that time to have a head wound — at least there was blood all over his face. He shouted at me, "My leg is broken! My leg is broken! It's severed!" and

he lifted his left leg. I could see that both bones in his lower left leg were broken cleanly at about the same place, so his booted foot was hanging limply . . .

I have no recollection of seeing or talking with Macfarlane as I lay on the volcano.

Andy Adams had left the crater rim an hour before, accompanied by Alfredo Roldan, a Guatemalan chemical engineer. Seeing that Adams was tired and winded, I had suggested he head down the cone and begin the taxing climb up the steep face of the amphitheater. By 1:41 P.M., Roldan had made it to the top of the scarp. Lagging behind, Adams had managed to walk off the cone, cross the moat, and begin the hike up the scarp. Pausing every couple of minutes to catch his breath, he had ascended the more gradual slope of the lower escarpment and was poised to begin the climb up the sheer upper section when Galeras blew.

"I dived against the caldera wall behind some boulders and tried to crawl under my hard hat," Adams wrote that evening.

Hunched into a ball, Adams — who was about 1,200 feet from the crater — was bombarded with rocks ranging from the size of a pea to that of a softball. An army veteran, he said the projectiles sounded like bullets or shrapnel, streaking in with a *Zzzing!* that tore the air, then exploding against the scarp wall. At least five rocks crashed into his hard hat, and Adams is convinced he would have been killed or seriously injured without it. Hot fragments struck his coveralls but did not burn through the fire-resistant cloth.

"I had been on Pacaya when it was erupting, but this was much larger than anything I had seen before," he said. "I just hit the dirt. I didn't panic. I had had survival training in the army and at the lab, and knew the best thing was to get down and get covered."

Looking up after a minute or two, he saw the black ash cloud streaming out of the crater into the sky. He reached for his gas mask, unsure, like the rest of us, whether the eruption had peaked or worse things were to come.

*   *   *

On top of the scarp — 800 yards from the crater — several men crouched low behind boulders. Stones pattered on clothing and rocks. A television reporter in a blue windbreaker grasped for a microphone and looked into the camera with wide-eyed alarm. Breathless, he repeated, "Stones are falling now! Stones are falling now." Then, as if unsure whether the volcano had really erupted, he asked, "Why was there this explosion?"

Someone switched off the camera. Soon the operator turned it back on, focusing on the cone. Billows of dark gray smoke tinged with brown streamed from the volcano.

Farther up the ridge on top of the amphitheater, volcanic bombs crashed through the roof and peppered the wall of the police post. Scores of rocks smashed into an INGEOMINAS Nissan Patrol, knocking out its windows and ripping holes in the steel body. A soldier was at the post. At some point he peeked around the corner of the concrete structure, only to be driven back by the fusillade. His hand was still sticking out beyond the wall. A volcanic bomb tore it off.

All around Galeras — on its flanks, in the river valleys running off the mountain, in nearby towns — roughly seventy-five scientists were in the midst of field trips, studying the volcano. In the valley of the Rio Azufral, on the western side, Peter Baxter was with a group investigating civil preparedness. The day before he had been tempted to join me and his friend Geoff Brown on Galeras. "I do think about, to some extent, the danger," Peter told me later. "And I asked myself, have I really got a good reason for going down?" He concluded he hadn't and went instead with the civil defense group.

At 1:41 P.M., a geologist in Peter's group was explaining how the valley had for thousands of years been a natural conduit for pyroclastic flows. The summit of the volcano, about a mile up the valley, was shrouded in heavy clouds. The Azufral is a narrow, swift river that forms below Galeras's peak and slices down to the Rio Guiatara, 9,000 feet below. Where Baxter was standing, at about 8,000 feet, the valley is lush with coffee bushes, banana plants, purple bougainvillea, orange trees, and wide-canopied balsa trees.

Near the river is a trout farm, where a businessman raises fish in concrete pens and sells them to nearby restaurants. Paralleling the river is a bumpy dirt road, flanked by the stucco and brick homes of campesinos. Just about every material that goes into making one of those houses is volcanic in origin.

Pointing at a cross section of the landscape, a geologist showed Peter and the fifteen other members of his group the strata of pyroclastic and lava flows. As Baxter raised his camera to take a picture, he heard a loud noise, "like a peal of thunder." The sound turned into a loud rumbling that continued for at least thirty seconds — "not very long," recalled Baxter, "but long enough to make you realize that there was something very strange." The members of the group looked at one another, not saying anything at first. Someone suggested it was thunder. Just then a campesino emerged from his house and said, "It's not thunder. It's the volcano." At that point, said Peter, "we all realized something ghastly had happened."

He looked at his watch. It was one forty-five. He realized that this was precisely when Geoff Brown had said he'd be in the crater. His second thought was that he was standing in a perfect conduit for pyroclastic flows. He stared up the valley toward Galeras, but the green landscape melted into the clouds, revealing nothing of the volcano. Someone suggested driving to a nearby village on the river, but Baxter — who the day before had shown grisly slides of pyroclastic flow victims — said they should stay put. He figured that if a *nuée ardente* came sweeping down through the clouds, they might at least stand a small chance of running up the sides of the valley to safety. Several minutes later, the group climbed into jeeps and sped off to Pasto. As Baxter fretted about Geoff Brown, me, and the dozen others who had gone to the crater, the enormity of what had happened began to sink in.

No more than a mile or two downstream, the members of the geology field trip had been studying the debris avalanches that had settled in the Azufral Valley over the last few hundred thousand years. Headed by John Stix, an organizer of the conference, the group numbered about twenty people. Not far from the town of Consacá — where red arrows on stucco walls indicate evacuation routes in case of an eruption — the scientists stood on the north side of the valley, examining some avalanche deposits. It was warm, with temperatures in the sixties, and the group was nearing the end of its day. Suddenly, a loud explosion boomed down the Azufral.

"It echoed down the valley and rolled right past us," said Fraser Goff, of the Los Alamos National Laboratory. "It was deafening. It froze some people, but two or three of us, including me, took off running uphill. We didn't know if a landslide was coming down or not."

Someone suggested that the blast may have been men dynamiting a quarry. But when the rumble kept echoing down the valley, the scientists realized that Galeras was erupting.

Pete Hall, from Quito, recalls the group's scraping away at deposits when "suddenly there was this tremendous roar up above." At first he thought it was thunder and, having heard so much thunder in the Andes, he wasn't concerned. But when the rumbling continued, several scientists wondered aloud if it was an eruption. Nearby sat some Colombians, watching the geologists. Pete approached them.

"Do you think it's thunder?" he asked.

Shaking his head, one man replied, "That was not thunder."

Hall's first thought was of his wife, who he realized was near the summit. Fearing the worst, the scientists decided to hike out of the canyon, which they knew was a natural path for *nuées ardentes*. Ash began drifting down from the clouds. Hustling back to their small bus, they radioed the INGEOMINAS observatory, which confirmed their fears. Galeras had erupted. The group set off for Pasto.

In downtown Pasto, the scene at the observatory was mayhem. The seismographs from the six stations around Galeras were registering a continuing series of earthquakes, the needles on the drums etching wild swings on the black surface. A staff member called the police and civil defense, explaining that there had been an eruption and asking them to dispatch rescue teams to the volcano. Though everyone on the flank of Galeras heard the eruption, many people in Pasto had no idea it had occurred. An observatory employee tried to rouse José Arlés on his radio but got no response. A reporter and an INGEOMINAS worker on top of Galeras's amphitheater had radioed to report what the observatory already knew: the volcano had erupted.

Indeed, all the observatory staff had to do was look out the window. Soaring above Galeras's mantle of light gray clouds was a charcoal gray column of ash that eventually rose 2 miles into the sky. Chuck Connor, in bed with the flu, was resting when a hotel employee burst in and announced that the volcano had erupted.

Connor, who had not heard the explosion, looked out the window. "It was a very cloudy day, but you could see clearly the gray ash plume contrasting with the clouds," he said. "It was like a thunderhead, and there was a dramatic contrast with the clouds around it. It was bulbous, had a tight roll to it, and it was already several kilometers up. I got dressed and went downstairs, and someone from the observatory confirmed that there had been an eruption."

His team of Mike Conway, Andy Macfarlane, and Luis LeMarie was supposed to be in the crater. "At that point I thought that everyone was dead," he recalled. "I thought that people were not going to live through it."

Marta Calvache, the director of the observatory, stood on the overgrown track of the old Camino Real, chipping away at volcanic deposits on Galeras's northeastern slope. She stopped to point out to her ten colleagues a gray layer of pyroclastic ash no more than 3,000 years old. Patty Mothes remembers Marta's mentioning the threat to Pasto and the towns on the northern slopes of the volcano. "If a pyroclastic flow comes this way," Marta told the scientists, "there's no reason it's going to stop here. Obviously it's going to go a lot farther down."

Marta's group was the closest to the volcano, perhaps 500 to 800 yards below the top of the mountain. When Galeras blew, no one mistook it for thunder. Some, like Marta, knew instantly that it was an eruption. She remembers hearing two explosions. Momentarily, Patty Mothes — who has probably spent more time on Andean volcanoes than any other American except her husband —

thought at first it might be a jet fighter. "It was like a big jet sound, like WOOOOOOOOO," she recalled. "It got louder and louder. A tremendous upwelling of sound is coming out and everybody just stops and says, 'What's the noise?'"

When pumice and ash began falling, they knew. Then, Marta recalled, "there was a noise like something was coming." She wondered: Could it be a pyroclastic flow? The same thought flashed through Patty's mind. She remembered Peter Baxter's advice from the previous day: If a *nuée ardente* is headed your way, find a depression in the ground, dive into it, and cover your head.

Suddenly, the scientists started bolting in all directions. "No one said run, and no one said anything about the volcano," recalled Marta. "But people just started to run." Marta did, too, heading away from a nearby canyon that could channel a pyroclastic flow. Patty stayed put, examining some of the pumice that had sprinkled onto the ground. It was older rock, which had been altered by acids inside the volcano. Then she thought to herself: If a pyroclastic flow is coming, it will probably arrive soon.

Ash continued falling. The scientists regrouped. One of them, a Canadian graduate student, began crying, afraid of what might come next and worried about her fiancé, who was on a separate field trip. Patty tried to console her, saying he was probably on the lower slopes of the volcano, far from danger. Gradually the group's panic subsided, to be replaced by concern about the men actually in the crater.

Marta and Patty led the scientists along the Camino Real to the jeeps, about a half mile down the trail. The pair had one thought in mind: rescue. Between the two of them, they knew all the scientists who had walked onto the volcano, and they wanted to get to the top of the scarp as quickly as possible. Sizing up the group, Patty concluded that they were underdressed, rattled, and too inexperienced to participate in a rescue. "I just didn't see that they would be that useful, to tell the truth," Patty told me later. "We didn't want anybody along who wasn't going to go for it."

Arriving at the jeeps, Marta sent her group on its way down the mountain. "I told the people, 'You go to Pasto and I will go see what happened.' Patty said, 'No, I'll go with you.' And I said, 'Okay, let's go.'"

Rocks continued to hurtle from the volcano and crash around me. It seemed as if the most violent phase of the eruption, with its deadly barrage of volcanic bombs, lasted for at least fifteen minutes But the other survivors insist it was more like five or ten. I dodged projectiles until the eruption slowed, when gravel-sized particles rattled down. Then, strangely, it began to rain, almost as if the blast had altered the climate in this corner of the Andes. Drizzle mingled with the ash, coating my head with a gray paste. Galeras's violent shaking finally eased, and the adrenaline quit coursing through my system. Exhausted, I put my head down on the craggy slope.

I began to grasp what had transpired. José Arlés and the three sightseers were dead. Of this I was sure. I didn't know what had happened to Igor and Nestor García, but given the force of the blast, I couldn't imagine that they had made it out of the crater alive. As for Geoff Brown, Fernando Cuenca, and Carlos Trujillo, I had no idea whether they had perished or were lying injured on the opposite flank of Galeras. I vaguely recalled seeing Mike Conway, Andy Macfarlane, and Luis LeMarie around the time of the eruption, but I had no idea of their fate.

Over and over I told myself that I had to remain conscious. Though I knew I had suffered a bad blow to the head, I had no idea it was a life-threatening injury. Nor was I aware that the rock — or rocks — that hit me in the head had also broken my jaw, destroyed the hearing in my left ear, and caused the retinas in both eyes to become partially detached. I also didn't realize that the rocks that had smashed into my spine had caused hairline fractures in two vertebrae — injuries that could have been far worse, even crippling, had I not been wearing a backpack.

What really concerned me was my right leg and foot. Wrenched grotesquely out of position and dangling from the lower leg, the foot looked as if it had been all but amputated. The entire leg was starting to hurt, and I realized that with such an injury I would eventually go into shock. I began thinking about my family — my wife, Lynda, my eight-year-old daughter, Christine, and my five-year-old son, Nick. I told myself that I didn't want to die, that I wasn't going to die, and that I was going to make it off the mountain and return home to Phoenix. I tried hard to think about my family, but it was difficult to stay focused for very long. My mind repeatedly returned to my friends — José Arlés, Geoff, Igor, and Nestor — and the rest of our group. I became furious that something so trivial as a power blackout had brought us to Galeras on this day. How could it have happened? How could we not have seen signs that the volcano was going to blow?

My thoughts were interrupted by what I am certain was a second eruption. I'm not sure when it occurred — perhaps 15 minutes after the first one, perhaps an hour — but I heard another loud explosion followed by a brief shower of larger stones. The volcano shook more intensely, an unmistakable and terrifying sensation if you happened to be lying on its flank. At that point Galeras seemed as if it were alive, a large beast that was toying with me. I felt helpless, vulnerable, inconsequential. Unable to move, I was at the volcano's mercy. I hated that feeling. I despised having lost control of the situation.

I was not the only person who remembered a second eruption. Carlos Alberto Estrada, an INGEOMINAS driver and field assistant, was climbing up the amphitheater scarp when Galeras first blew. He clearly remembers a second explosion but says it occurred only minutes after the first. Andy Macfarlane doesn't specifically recall a second eruption but contends that Galeras began to spew out noticeably more gas and ash about a half hour after the initial blast.

Later, I learned that what we all had feared most was pyroclastic flows. Although the general public remains largely unaware of *nuées ardentes* — whenever they think of a volcano, it's lava, lava, lava — the members of the volcanological tribe know there is nothing more deadly than these glowing clouds. And for those of us at the conference, our respect for pyroclastic flows had been transformed into horror after seeing Peter Baxter's photographs of the *nuée ardente* victims at Unzen and Mont Pelée.

After the second blast, I began thinking about the volcano's pattern of eruption. Marta had done a brilliant job of establishing the sequence. First Galeras cleared its throat, as it had in that afternoon's initial eruption. We knew this from the rocky yellow deposits on the mountainside. Then it typically cut loose with a pyroclastic flow, as shown by the gray deposits lying on top of the yellow ones. Was that what was in store today? Were the first and second eruptions mere preludes to a much larger blast that would kill all of us still alive in the amphitheater?

Twisting my head toward the crater, I studied the upper cone for signs of a *nuée ardente*. But all I could see was the black pillar of ash towering into the clouds. Gradually, the volcano's tremors subsided. My relief was tempered by indescribable fatigue. Stay awake, I kept telling myself. Stay awake.

Earlier, as the initial blast spent itself, Mike Conway lifted his head off the rubble and scanned the sky. The ash column was still there and pebbles continued to fall, but the volcano was firing out far fewer shrapnel-like projectiles. He decided it was time to go. He had his hands full. Of the three walking wounded, he himself was the least injured. The other two, Andy Macfarlane and Luis LeMarie, could not possibly make it out on their own.

Mike urged Luis to get up. By his reckoning, only five or six minutes had passed since the volcano had erupted. The Ecuadorian tried to struggle to his feet, but the fractured clavicle, the broken bones in both of his legs, and multiple burns had left him debilitated. "I have a problem with my legs," said LeMarie. "I don't know if I can walk."

Helping Luis to his feet, Mike tried to lead him down the cone. But both of them kept stumbling and falling on the rugged slope strewn with boulders. Breaking their falls with their hands, they touched burning-hot ejecta, forcing them to scramble rapidly to their feet again, which often — in Luis's case — led to another fall.

"I was kind of numb," said Conway. "But we didn't have any idea of how injured we were until we kept falling down a lot."

Andy Macfarlane recalled lying near me and asking about my injuries: "Clearly, he [Stan] couldn't move on his own, and I couldn't tell how serious his head wound was. The only thing that I could think of that could help him would be to pick him up and carry him, and I reached out to him from below and tried to grab his hand, but we couldn't quite reach each other. My legs had been badly bruised in my earlier falls and were weak and not responding very well, and I realized that if I couldn't even reach him from downhill and was having serious trouble walking myself that I had no chance of carrying him. At that point I had to leave him and just hope that he could ride out the blockfall there and be rescued. I felt terribly guilty at the time and for weeks afterward, but realistically there was nothing else for me to do."

Stunned, disoriented, and entering a state of shock, Macfarlane rose and wandered around the lower half of the cone. As Conway and LeMarie were lurching down the flank, they ran into him meandering uphill.

"No! No! Andrew!" yelled Conway. "The other way!"

Gathering Macfarlane into their group, Conway herded the pair down the cone. Macfarlane remembers the three of them lying down behind a large boulder to rest. Andy told Mike that he had seen me and that I was badly injured. But in his dazed condition he didn't remember where I was. Neither did Mike, but his concern was getting the three of them off the cone and on top of the scarp.

"We're all injured," Conway told LeMarie and Macfarlane. "We've got to get ourselves off of this vent."

Mike could see that both Luis and Macfarlane were rattled and nearing the limits of their endurance. Both were breathing heavily in the thin air. He tried to reassure them.

"This is a classic Vulcanian blast," Conway told the pair, their faces streaked with ash and blood. "It's a discrete blast. It's going to be a long time before gas pressure builds up and it blows again. The vent is degassing now. This is a situation we can survive. Stay calm. We'll find our way out of this."

The volcano emitted a loud, jetlike sound. Macfarlane remained thoroughly unsettled. "There was, through all of this," he wrote later, "the terrible tension of not knowing whether the volcano was just coughing a little bit or was clearing its throat in preparation for a major eruption. It was a debilitating sense of dread, and we were all listening very closely to hear whether there was going to be another big roar. As we lay there, Mike got me to hold my pack over my head to ward off the flying fragments, and we rested a few minutes."

Rocks the size of peas and marbles continued to fall. Then the rain came, mixed with ash. Luis remembers how refreshing the cool drops felt on his burns. But Macfarlane, his clothes pocked with rips and burn holes, began to get uncomfortably wet.

Mike roused his colleagues for a final push off the cone. As they struggled downhill in the fog, they passed the bodies of José Arlés and the three tourists. Mike could see that some of their skulls had been crushed. The clothing of one of the tourists was on fire. The scientists continued walking.

Finally, perhaps a half hour after the first eruption, they made it to the floor of the amphitheater, where they once again took shelter behind a boulder. The cloud cover was denser now, and as he looked toward the scarp, all Conway could see was fog. He had no clue where to find the path to the top. But the fog soon dispersed, revealing the way. As they blundered across the moat, which is about 50 yards wide, Conway yelled for help. From the top of the escarpment, 200 yards away, someone hollered back.

Andy Adams — caught in mid-ascent by the eruption — was close to making his escape from the horseshoe-shaped amphitheater. He had remained hunkered down behind a rock until the barrage of volcanic bombs let up. Peering over a rock, he saw a large plume boiling out of the crater. "My impression," he said, "was that everyone behind me was dead." Fearing that the column of ash and gas would waft his way, Adams, who was then forty-four, was ready to put on his gas mask. But suddenly a wind rose and blew the plume away from the scarp, toward the west.

"That's when I said, 'Hey, I'm getting out of here,'" recalled Adams.

Ascending the upper portion of the escarpment is difficult under tranquil circumstances. It's steep, the footing is tricky, and a slip could send a climber hurtling 150 yards down the precipitous face. Most climbers use yellow, nylon rope, which is about 75 feet long and anchored to a spike on top of the scarp. Adams grabbed the line, pulling his large frame slowly up the mountain, stopping frequently to catch his breath. At one point, looking down as he rested, he saw — between a break in the clouds — three people moving slowly across the moat: Mike, Luis, and Andy Macfarlane. Adams was greatly relieved that they were alive, but he quickly abandoned the idea of going back down to help them. He was too exhausted. Resuming his climb, small rocks kept striking him, some burning his neck. At last he pitched over the rim of the scarp and onto the ridge on top of the amphitheater. He was utterly spent and indescribably relieved to be out of the cauldron.

Conway, Macfarlane, and LeMarie had made it across the moat to the bottom of the scarp, using their backpacks to shield themselves from falling rocks. Macfarlane was beginning to shiver from shock and hypothermia. Although the temperature was probably in the high forties, the light rain had soaked Andy's clothes and hastened his loss of body heat. Luis was in terrible pain. Mike realized the pair couldn't make the ascent on their own, but he also knew that, given his injured hand and his burns, he couldn't help them further. "Wait here behind these boulders," he told them. "I'm going to go get help."

The climb to the rope seemed to take forever. Conway snaked up the path, occasionally tripping on a rock or sliding backward on scree. He stopped often to rest. When he finally reached the line, he tried to grab it with his right hand. "I'd put my hand on the rope and it would slide down, and then I'd put it there again and it would slide down again," he said. "And that's when I said to myself, 'Hey, something's wrong.'"

Using his left hand, he began to haul himself upward.

Meanwhile, LeMarie and Macfarlane had no intention of remaining in the moat. As Macfarlane said later, "The main thing driving us up the slope was the fear that there might be a pyroclastic flow in our direction, and we thought that the higher up the wall we were, the better our chances of surviving such an event. It seemed all important to get as high on the caldera wall as we could."

Macfarlane struggled up the scarp. Collapsing again and again, he would lie on his back and look at the ash column churning out of the cone, its lower portion streaked with incandescence. He tried to watch where he fell, as fiery, football-size stones littered the path. On several occasions, however, he crumpled on the trail and lay his head on a hot chunk of ejecta, burning his scalp.

"The feeling of fatigue was so total that if a pyroclastic flow were to come my way, I wouldn't have been able to lift a hand to do anything about it," Macfarlane wrote later. His entire body trembling from hypothermia and shock, he could not take another step and began calling for help. Although no one responded from above, he was relieved to hear me screaming for assistance from somewhere on the cone. "But there was no one else calling from over there," he wrote, "and that confirmed my fears."

One third of the way up the scarp, still many yards from the rope, Macfarlane gave out, lay down, and waited to be rescued.

Despite his broken legs and collarbone, Luis crawled, dragged, and hobbled up the escarpment, testimony to how intensely he dreaded another eruption or pyroclastic flow. He passed Macfarlane and somehow made it all the way to the rope. Grabbing the line with his right hand, he could do little more than swing from side to side as he tried to pull himself higher. He, too, could go no farther on his own. As Luis lay down, Andy could faintly hear me calling from the cone in Spanish, "¡Ayúdame! ¡Ayúdame!" — "Help me! Help me!"

Marta and Patty sped up the mountain in their jeep, plowing through puddles and bouncing over boulders. As they negotiated the sharp turns, several cars and jeeps came racing down the mountain, nearly running them off the road. They were filled with terrified national park employees and soldiers — including the man with the severed hand — fleeing the eruption. Knowing they would need help, Marta and Patty flagged down an army truck and asked the soldiers to join in the rescue. Shamed, perhaps, by the sight of the

two women heading into the teeth of danger, the soldiers reluctantly complied.

Marta had a radio, and all the while she was getting reports from the observatory, which was in contact with the journalists on top of the mountain. The news was sketchy. The gas group and the gravity group had both been on the cone when the volcano blew. Some people had been killed. Some were injured. Some were missing.

On the ridge above the amphitheater, Andy Adams walked to the police station, where a Colombian television crew frantically sought news from the crater. Its camera rolling, the crew followed Adams, whose face was smeared with ash. Walking away from the camera, Adams finally waved off the reporter, saying, "I don't want to do this. I don't want to do this."

The reporter turned to Alfredo Roldan, the Guatemalan chemical engineer. "What happened?" the reporter asked.

"An explosion can happen at any time," answered Roldan. "It just happened now. It could have been yesterday or tomorrow or in a year . . . All volcanoes are unpredictable anywhere in the world."

Mike Conway was 10 yards from the crest of the scarp, fighting to make it up the last stretch. In English and Spanish, he shouted for help. It arrived in the form of Carlos Estrada, the INGEOMINAS field assistant, who grabbed Mike and pulled him to the top. Walking 75 yards to the police post, Mike was also approached by the TV crew. He looked awful. His yellow parka was shot through with burn holes. Beneath his blue knit cap, the left side of his face was caked with blood, and he was coated in ash. He walked into the post, followed by the camera, and spoke with Adams.

"Luis, with help, and Andy Macfarlane, with help, can make it up," said Mike.

Adams, looking drained, responded, "We got to send somebody down there."

The camera closed in. Mike lost his patience, thrusting his hand toward the lens and barking, "No! No!"

Mike, the first survivor from the cone, got on the radio with the observatory in Pasto and urged them to get rescue teams to the volcano immediately. "I told them that Andy and Luis were hurt and needed help," he recalled. "I didn't tell them that I saw dead people. I was worried that they would learn people had died and would be afraid to go down. I told them people were alive. I accentuated the positive. There are people alive. They can get out. But they need help."

Every few minutes, I cried out in English and Spanish. I yelled to see if anyone else was alive. I yelled for help. I yelled because that was all I could do and because the sound of my own voice offered a certain reassurance that I was still there, that I hadn't given up. No one replied.

It felt as if I had been sprawled on the cone for hours, although only about one hour had passed since the eruption. Rain had penetrated the many holes in my jacket and pants, and I was chilled to the bone. I began to shiver — as much, I knew, from shock as from the cold. I knew that I was not going to die from my injuries and, as time passed, I became less worried about a second eruption. But I feared going into shock and was terrified of being left on the volcano after dark. It was mid-afternoon. (I was wearing a watch but don't remember ever looking at it.) I knew that at our equatorial latitude it would get dark — swiftly, without a lingering dusk — around 6 P.M. The rescue teams had three hours to find me and any other survivors.

I was no longer sure I would get home alive. I began to cry, thinking I would never see Lynda, Christine, or Nick again. To die on Galeras, I thought, would be to fail my family. I worried that my wife would not only be sad but angry that my irresistible attraction to volcanoes had been my undoing. I had to get home. In my dazed state, this thought drifted again and again through my mind. Whenever it did, I cried out, "*Ayuda me!* Help me!"

Galeras was still chuffing, still sending a column of ash into the sky. Would rescue teams be reluctant, I wondered, to descend onto this volcano, which looked far from spent? As I fretted over who might show up and when, the answer soon came to me.

Marta.

8

·····················

WARNINGS

W HAT HAD HAPPENED? As I lay on Galeras's cone, I had ample time to think about that question. My first concern, however, was whether the volcano was going to belch out a pyroclastic flow. As close as I was to the crater, I knew that even a minuscule *nuée ardente* would kill me. Gruesome images from Peter Baxter's presentation the day before flashed through my mind. Fifteen years of study had also left me with a clear understanding that pyroclastic flows — with their combination of high heat, suffocating ash clouds, and speeds reaching 100 miles per hour — were the deadliest volcanic phenomena. There was no worse way to die in an eruption.

I had read the accounts of those who had survived pyroclastic flows, and they all described similar sensations: the roar of the flow as it nears, a feeling of excruciating heat, the stench of sulfur, a descent into darkness as ash pours into the nose and mouth, and, finally, a feeling of complete suffocation as the cloud displaces all the oxygen from the air. A survivor of the 1902 Mont Pelée eruption called it "swallowing the fire." Another survivor, Charles Alexander, offered a detailed description of the 1902 *nuée ardente* on the Caribbean island of St. Vincent that killed 1,680 people. Working 3 miles from the crater of the Soufrière volcano in a sugarcane field, the forty-year-old laborer began to head home as ash rained down. Suddenly he heard a "great noise" like a "rushing river."

"With many others I run into Victor Sutherland's shop . . . ," he said later. "About two o'clock great darkness come on, and we shut the doors and windows. After this a great heat come with hot ashes through the chinks of the doors and windows, and through the holes in the roof. The hot ashes get into our mouths, and stop our mouths as fast as we try to breathe. We toss backwards and forwards for about two seconds, then everyone fall down. I did not lose my senses, but cannot tell exactly what happened after I fall. I feel choked with the hot stuff going down my belly, and smell plenty sulfur. This did not last long, only two or three minutes, then I try to get up, but two people both dead lie across me, and after a struggle I get on my feet."

Lying on the cone, I remembered Peter's telling the conference that while the odds of living through a direct hit from a pyroclastic flow were not good, people could take steps to improve their chance of survival. He spoke of sealing oneself in a house, boarding up windows and doors just as coastal residents try to protect themselves in a hurricane. Peter also advised us that if we were ever caught in the open, we should find a depression in the ground, cover ourselves with whatever was available, and try to hold our breath until the *nuée* passed. Those who panic or exert themselves are more likely to gulp great drafts of ash and gaseous air, quickly clogging their airways and rendering them unconscious after a few breaths. Those who completely cover their mouths until the worst of the *nuée ardente* passes have a better prognosis. Baxter's advice echoed faintly in my head, but looking around the volcano's boulder-strewn flank, I saw no refuge. If a pyroclastic flow rolled out of the crater, there was nothing I could do.

Fortunately, the *nuée ardente* never materialized. Twenty minutes went by, then a half hour, and soon I was reasonably sure that the worst of the eruption was over. Still lucid, I was left to wonder what had happened to my colleagues, to fret about whether I'd be rescued, and to ask myself again and again: How could Galeras have blown with no warning?

Walking into a crater is never a sure thing, but all the signs had indicated that Galeras was in a quiet phase. Gas emissions were low.

Seismic activity was negligible. The temperature of fumarolic gases was stable. Deformation measurements did not show the cone swelling. Had we missed something? Had Galeras sent us a signal that we ignored?

After the eruption, many colleagues assured me I had done nothing wrong, that there was no way to have foreseen the eruption. What I didn't know was that for several years a few of my colleagues had been saying quite the opposite behind my back. Their allegations came down to this: I had missed subtle seismic signs of an eruption and had recklessly led my colleagues to their deaths. When I first heard these accusations, I was too stunned to react. Now I shake my head in wonder. How easy it is to snipe after the fact, to apply the knowledge we have now to the events of 1993. But for me, Marta, and the other scientists in Pasto that January, there was no such twenty-twenty vision. We studied the best available data. We made what looked like a sound decision. And just when we were on the cone, Galeras behaved capriciously, as natural forces are wont to do. I was fooled, and for that I will take responsibility. But I do not feel guilty about the deaths of my colleagues. There is no guilt. There was only an eruption.

On the scale of great eruptions, Galeras was a nonevent. The word "hiccup" even assigns too much power to the blast when it is compared with massive eruptions from the past. In terms of rock and ash ejected, the January 14 eruption was a mere .003 percent of the volume of the blast at Mount St. Helens. And the Mount St. Helens eruption was tiny compared to a monstrous volcanic blast like Tambora in 1815, which spewed out an estimated 100 to 150 times more material than the Cascades peak. Eruptions on the scale of Tambora occur on average once every thousand years. Eruptions such as Mount St. Helens occur on average every ten years somewhere around the world. And eruptions such as Galeras happen every other day. (In any given year, sixty volcanoes erupt worldwide.) Had thirteen people not been standing in and around the crater of Galeras, no one would ever have heard of this inconsequential geological event.

Yet despite its puny size, the January 14 eruption was driven by the very same forces that produced Tambora. As always at volcanoes, it was the gas that sparked the cataclysm. If the chunks of rock that killed my colleagues were the lead slugs, then the gas was the gunpowder.

The gas-rich magma that fed the Galeras eruption came into existence about 80 miles beneath the Andes as a result of one plate subducting beneath another. It took that magma roughly 5,000 to 10,000 years to squeeze up through the mantle and the solid crust, rising about 1.5 inches per year. The magma finally came to rest in a series of underground chambers 3 to 7 miles beneath Galeras's cone. From those larger pools of magma, molten rock slowly migrated to the surface in tear-shaped globs. Those globs were channeled together into a column that extended from the floor of the crater to about 400 yards underground.

For nearly fifty years, since the last active period in the 1930s, the plug of magma and gas beneath Galeras remained relatively stable. Then, in 1988, something happened. Maybe an earthquake shook up the volcano's innards, opening new pathways for the magma to rise to the surface. More likely, after a half century of quiescence, pressure in the magma chambers built to the point where it needed to escape, either by venting gases, blowing its top, or both. From 1988 to 1993 Galeras saw all manner of such activity.

In 1988 there was no volcano observatory in Pasto, so it fell to the policemen and soldiers stationed on top of the amphitheater scarp to notify the world that Galeras had come alive. Rumbles, foul smells, clattering rocks — these and other messages from inside the earth put everyone on notice. Marta arrived in late 1988, sampling gases and studying the fumaroles that had opened up on the cone. Over the next five years, the appearance of the cone and the crater changed frequently as powerful jets of acidic gas forced open new vents all over Galeras. At different times, a dozen fumaroles were spewing gas on the volcano, and Colombian geologists gave them names like Deformes, Bernardo, Besolima, Adela, and Calvache. These fumaroles were escape valves for the mounting gas pressure, and for science they served as windows into the earth, a direct pipeline to the magma body. From late 1988 to July 1992, Galeras's fumaroles were venting variable amounts of gas, but one thing was clear: The volcano had reached a new plateau of activity.

In May 1989 a five-day series of blasts propelled an ash column 2 miles into the air and ejected 523,000 cubic yards of ash and rock — more than ten times the amount that would be emitted during the January 14, 1993, eruption. (Though the January 1993 eruption coughed out far less material, it had much more power, according to seismographic evidence.) These eruptions, the first in five decades, cut into Nariño's limited tourism, prompted some national banks to stop making loans to the area, brought on a recession in Pasto's construction industry, and rattled the region's business and political leaders.

As Galeras became steadily more active over the next two years, the people of Pasto and the Department of Nariño were whipsawed by a series of confusing — and sometimes alarmist — statements from politicians, the press, and scientists. Unsure of how active Galeras might become, Marta and other geologists — including myself — rightly warned that the volcano must be watched and might well pose a threat to the surrounding communities. But the press, with the disaster at Nevado del Ruiz fresh in its mind, hyped the threat. The politicians, fearful of being accused of negligence in case of a fatal eruption, overreacted.

The mayor of Pasto ordered a series of "voluntary preventative evacuations" that served merely to confuse the populace. The National Emergency Committee, meeting in Pasto shortly after the first eruption, recommended that the city be evacuated — a decision that was, thankfully, overruled in Bogotá. Inevitably, when no major eruption occurred, local officials and businessmen reacted angrily. In 1990 the new mayor of Pasto urged the "de-Galerasization" of the region, which meant that everyone should quit making a fuss about the volcano. Since then, politicians and civil defense officials have tried to play down the threat while simultaneously working on emergency evacuation procedures.

Meanwhile, the volcano kept rumbling. After the May 1989 eruption, seismographs began showing large numbers of a particular type of tremor that indicates magmatic fluids and gases are on the rise. These tremors, called "long-period" earthquakes, bear virtually no resemblance to the classic earthquakes in which tectonic plates strike or grind against one another, causing rocks to break. (Such fracturing registers as a sharp jump on a seismograph.) Rather, long-period earthquakes occur when magmatic gases and fluids force their way through cracks in the rock under the volcano, causing a mild, vibrating tremor — similar to air passing through an organ pipe. Transmitted through the volcano's surface, long-period quakes etch a gentle, uniform, slowly developing pattern on the seismograph.

After the May 1989 eruption, INGEOMINAS seismographs were registering fifty long-period earthquakes a day, a sign that Galeras was increasingly active. Meanwhile, our COSPEC readings showed that it was sometimes venting several thousand tons of sulfur dioxide a day — a high figure that confirmed its new level of activity. Those statistical diagnoses were further confirmed by visits to the volcano, where new fumaroles and craters were appearing on the cone. Galeras also was experiencing numerous tiny explosions that tossed out small amounts of rock. Several times in 1990 and 1991, Marta and I rode up to sample gases in and around the crater. But we had to content ourselves with standing on the edge of the amphitheater, watching as the volcano sputtered and coughed. It was too dangerous to go any farther. On the days we did venture onto the cone, gases shot out of Deformes fumarole in a constant, deafening roar.

In August 1991 our team experienced one of those satisfying moments in volcanology, when several methods of taking the measure of a volcano all point to the same conclusion. The number of long-period earthquakes increased dramatically, to 300 per day, indicating that a lot of magma was moving beneath the volcano. At the same time, using the COSPEC, we saw a jump in the release of SO_2 — to about 1,000 tons per day. This was a very high number — at the time, only five other volcanoes worldwide were pouring out that much SO_2 — and offered further proof that a magma body was on the rise. Finally, deformation studies showed that the volcano's flank had distended 2 feet, the result of growing pressure from magma and gases. What made this data particularly intriguing was that just two months earlier, at Pinatubo in the Philippines, a sharp rise in long-period earthquakes and SO_2 emissions had preceded a massive eruption. It was clear that Galeras had entered a new and dangerous phase.

Finally, in October 1991, we saw what all the fuss was about. INGEOMINAS volcanologists noticed that a plug of lava was being squeezed out onto the floor of the volcano. Magma, driven by gases, was escaping and its cooler upper edges were forming a hardened dome in the crater. The dome eventually rose 150 feet above the crater floor and reached a diameter longer than that of a football field. Specialists estimated that the dome contained 458,000 cubic yards of material, which capped an underground magma body of 3.7 million cubic yards. Extruded magma domes are notoriously unstable, and the growth of the dome — coupled with hundreds of long-period earthquakes per day — clearly showed that Galeras had reached a precarious state.

In November 1991 Bernard Chouet of the USGS, an expert on long-period earthquakes, came to Galeras and did some superb research correlating the long-period events with the volcano coughing out ash and gas. As Galeras experienced 300 long-period earthquakes a day, Chouet and the INGEOMINAS seismologist Fernando Gíl Cruz stood on the crater rim and watched a 150-yard fissure periodically open slightly, releasing puffs of ash and gas. Those releases corresponded with the long-period earthquakes. In effect, Chouet and Gil had witnessed the volcano exhaling, with the long-period events registering the flow of Galeras's breath as it rumbled through the earth and into the atmosphere.

A few months later, Chouet wrote a report for INGEOMINAS about his findings, saying there was little danger of an eruption as long as the volcano kept regularly degassing, or breathing. If the long-period events and degassing stopped, he said, it could mean that the volcano was entering a dormant phase. However, he wrote that an end to the degassing, accompanied by the appearance of deeper long-period events, could also mean that the volcano was becoming sealed and might erupt. Unfortunately, Chouet — with whom I did not get along — never sent me a copy of his report, nor did anyone from INGEOMINAS.

As Chouet had warned, the dome soon became sealed. In early July 1992, a special long-period earthquake — known as a *tornillo,* or screw, because of its long, screwlike appearance on the seismographs — occurred on Galeras. Nine *tornillos,* some lasting two minutes, took place in about a week. At the same time, the Pasto observatory's seismographs were registering other long-period earthquakes, sometimes as many as thirty per day. All the while, little gas was escaping. Then the cracking of the dome's surface caused dozens of high-frequency, short-lived earthquakes to ripple through the volcano; these were called *mariposas* because of the butterfly shape they scrawled on the seismographs' drums.

On July 16, 1992, several days after the appearance of the *mariposas,* Galeras erupted, destroying 80 percent of the lava dome. A plume of ash rose 3.5 miles into the air before falling between the towns of Sandoná and Consacá. The volcano propelled 12-inch blocks of rock 1.5 miles from the crater and launched 12-foot boulders into the amphitheater. Twenty-four hours later, one such boulder — after sitting in the cold air at 14,000 feet — still had a surface temperature of 610 degrees F. Sixteen days later, when Marta and I climbed onto the cone to sample gases, some of the ejected rocks were still hot to the touch.

Galeras seemed to have spent itself in that eruption — a typical pattern with many volcanoes. As the weeks passed, we measured only trace amounts of sulfur dioxide. Using lasers and reflective mirrors, Colombian scientists detected no swelling of the flank. And in the coming months, seismic activity was extremely low, with almost no long-period earthquakes. By the time we convened in Pasto in early January, it looked as if Galeras had passed through this latest eruptive episode.

In the first two weeks of January, geologists at the INGEOMINAS observatory counted seventeen *tornillos.* As our conference got under way, INGEOMINAS and foreign seismologists were not alarmed by this desultory pattern of *tornillos;* at the time, such small numbers were considered benign. (Before the eruption of the Redoubt volcano in Alaska, for example, seismographs picked up 4,000 long-period earthquakes in one day.) Only after further eruptions in 1993 did we finally come to understand that small numbers of *tornillos* at Galeras — even as few as one or two per day — *might* presage an eruption. But there was no such understanding then. In the days before our trip into the crater, no one brought the *tornillos* to my attention or warned that the volcano might be poised to blow. Seismologists at the observatory also saw no clusters of other long-period earthquakes and no *mariposas*, all of which had preceded the July eruption. Based on all available evidence, the consensus at the observatory was that Galeras was safe. Indeed, in the days before we climbed Galeras, other scientists worked on the volcano.

So what *did* happen? In July 1992, Galeras had dissipated much of its pent-up energy. Immediately afterward, large amounts of sulfur dioxide and other gases poured out of the crater, then gradually tapered off, much as champagne at first spurts out of a bottle, then settles down. But sometime in late 1992 the cracks that let the gases escape began to seal. The highly acidic gases altered the rock within the volcano, essentially gluing shut many of its fissures. We detected so little gas from the volcano not because there was no gas but because it couldn't escape. In effect, by January 1993 Galeras was like a pressure cooker with a clogged safety valve. Gas pressure was increasing and heat was rising, but sitting above the cauldron we saw no sign of intensifying activity. Galeras fooled us.*

In retrospect — and with the insight provided by four more eruptions in 1993 — Galeras may have been sending us a subtle signal that it was preparing to blow. In the three weeks before the fatal eruption, the duration and power of the long-period earthquakes were increasing, with some lasting nearly three minutes. Then, in the three or four days before the eruption, these quakes, which had been occurring twice a day, dropped to once a day or less. We later realized that the volcano had become so plugged that magmatic

* Later research also showed that a new magma body may have taken up a position 8 miles beneath the cone, producing gas that added to the growing pressure under Galeras.

gas and fluids simply stopped rising beneath the crater, hence the decrease in long-period events. The final long-period earthquake, with its *tornillo* signature, took place four hours before the eruption, just as we were hiking into Galeras's amphitheater.

José Arlés was in constant contact with the observatory, and no one mentioned the *tornillo* that had shown up on the seismograph at 9:47 A.M. They didn't mention it because no one in the observatory would have seen long-period earthquakes — especially just one — as a premonition of disaster. As we worked in and around the volcano that day, it was stable — as stable as a balloon just before it pops. At 1:41 P.M., the rocks plugging the vent at the bottom of the crater could contain the growing gas pressure no longer and Galeras blew. Though only a relatively small amount of ash and rock was ejected, the eruption was four times as powerful as the July 1992 eruption, which had destroyed the dome.

One eruption does not make a pattern. But the three subsequent blasts at Galeras in 1993 — in March, April, and June — enabled American and Colombian scientists to spot the *tornillo* trend. My graduate student Tobias Fischer added a crucial piece to the puzzle when — after months of work at Galeras in 1993 — he correlated the release of SO_2 with long-period earthquakes. As the tremors decreased just before an eruption, the quantity of sulfur dioxide streaming from the crater also plummeted. After an eruption, when the pent-up gases were being released, the SO_2 flux climbed dramatically.

But even after discovering this apparent pattern, we couldn't reliably forecast every eruption at Galeras. One blast in April 1993 was preceded by *no* long-period *tornillo* earthquakes. In June, observing a series of *tornillos*, INGEOMINAS geologists successfully predicted an eruption. But on at least two occasions later that year, a series of *tornillos* appeared on the observatory's seismographs, yet no eruption followed.

We did learn that Galeras had a special pattern of behavior, often experiencing relatively few long-period earthquakes before an eruption rather than the thousands experienced by other volcanoes. But as John Stix and five Colombians wrote after studying long-period earthquakes at Galeras, "The presence of . . . long-period signals by itself is problematic when trying to accurately forecast activity."

Steve McNutt, a professor at the University of Alaska and an authority on long-period earthquakes, said later, "With one event per day, you would not think anything was happening. That didn't portend evil. Galeras is the first volcano in the world where we'd seen only *tornillos* and in such low numbers. The *tornillos* would have caught my interest because they are unusual events. But would I have thought there would be an eruption? I don't think so . . . Most of what we do is retrospective. Hindsight is better than foresight."

Chouet, however, believes that I — or someone at the conference — should have seen the eruption coming and never taken a group onto the volcano. He contends that because a handful of *tornillos* preceded the July 1992 eruption, the alarm should have been raised at the observatory when a smattering of *tornillos* showed up in early January of 1993.

"You have a sequence prior to the previous explosion and now you see another sequence," Chouet said later. "That should get your attention immediately." And because I was the "chief honcho" at the conference, Chouet argues that I should have aggressively questioned the local seismologists about any suspicious activity.

"From my perspective," said Chouet, "there was no need for people to have died on that mountain . . . My feeling is that something went awfully wrong at some point with the communication, or some messages were not heard."

The problem is that no one ever sounded an alarm, which is understandable given the state of our knowledge at the time. Fernando Gíl Cruz, Chouet's Colombian collaborator, told me recently, "No one saw the significance then of so few *tornillos*. We could not understand that pattern until after [later] eruptions. In January, no one saw any danger." Even Chouet himself wrote that, unlike a volcano such as Redoubt, the Colombian volcano was "an example of a leaky system with subtle precursory activity."

The eruption of January 14 taught us much about how Galeras

behaves. Regrettably, people died in the process. It sickens me that we had to pay such a price. But in volcanology, progress often comes on the heels of disaster.

Huddled on the slopes of the volcano, growing increasingly cold as I waited to be rescued, the word *tornillo* never entered my mind. Nor did I fathom that there could have been any seismic warning of the eruption. Now José Arlés lay just a few yards away, dead, and when I thought of Igor and Nestor in the crater I was overwhelmed with grief and confusion. How could they have survived? How could Geoff have survived? How could anyone have survived?

9

....

RESCUE

A SH DRIFTED DOWN on the windshield of the jeep carrying Marta Calvache and Patty Mothes to the top of Galeras. As they passed the cluster of antennas and neared the top of the mountain, their driver was afraid to go closer to the volcano. In the back of the jeep, the two soldiers Marta had enlisted were equally frightened. Marta and Patty were scared, too, and on the way up had discussed the dangers. Patty offered the reassuring prognosis that, in her experience in Ecuador, once a volcano like Galeras had blown its top and expelled its gases, it usually did not erupt again immediately.

That said, racing into the mouth of an erupting volcano ran counter to common sense, and few would question the caution of these men. Later, I would relish the irony of the situation: In macho Colombia, a pair of women led the effort to rescue the injured on Galeras.

Pulling in behind the concrete police post on the amphitheater scarp, Marta and Patty confronted a grim scene. Volcanic bombs had smashed the windows of the white Nissan Patrol and knocked holes in the post's roof and walls. White-hot, angular rocks littered the ground. When Patty spat on one, it hissed back at her. The volcano still thrummed and emitted an eerie sound, like the howl of a strong wind. When the swirling clouds over the ridge occasionally parted, Marta and Patty glimpsed a column of ash — thinner than before, the color closer to white than gray — emanating from the crater. Patty spoke with Andy Adams, who told her that several men were alive below and that the fate of the others was unknown.

Perched on the scarp, the two women strained to see or hear signs of life in the amphitheater. Marta heard nothing, but Patty caught the sound of my yelling for help. We had been good friends for years, and she knew my voice.

"In the fog I heard Stan saying, 'Help me! Help me!'" recalled Patty. "It sent a chill through me. I had just seen him that morning, and I could tell he was really bad off because of his voice. And I yelled out, 'Yeah, we're coming, Stan! We're coming!'"

I never heard her. I vaguely remember hearing Marta, but I'm not sure when the sound of her voice first came my way. As Patty yelled from the top of the escarpment around 3 P.M. — probably 500 yards in a straight line from where I lay — I had been prostrate on the volcano for more than an hour, and as time passed I became colder and less lucid. The cold was the worst part — a chill that emanated from my very core and spread outward until my entire body shook in an effort to warm itself. Soon, my mind focused solely on getting warm, and I fantasized about being in bed under a pile of blankets.

Rescue teams had not yet arrived. Carlos Estrada, the INGEO-MINAS driver and field assistant who had been with us on the volcano, had just made it to the top of the scarp and was ready to help. Driving madly up the mountain was Milton Ordóñez, an INGEO-MINAS volcanologist who had been at home in Pasto when he heard the eruption. The two soldiers with Marta and Patty agreed to stay on the lip of the scarp and assist them, but they refused to climb down onto the cone.

Estrada spied Luis LeMarie, who was about halfway up the scarp and unable to climb higher because of his broken legs and clavicle. Scrambling down the steep parapet, he grabbed LeMarie and half-carried, half-dragged him to the top.

With Estrada's help, LeMarie made it to the police post, where he collapsed on a chair. Pale, his face splotchy with ash, his hand bloodied, he drank some water. Someone helped him unzip his yellow jacket. He was out of breath and in pain but still tried to answer questions from the Colombian TV crew that had been with us on the volcano earlier in the day.

"I believe at the crater . . . went down the Russian, Igor, Stanley . . . No, Nestor. Then Andrew and Mike and I and Stanley and José Arlés we were coming in front . . . It caught us on the way down and there were three others from Pasto, young people, and they looked very bad. I believe they're dead. I saw the blows to their skulls . . . I believe that they were hit by very large rocks.

"And Mike and Andrew and I were able to get headfirst behind a rock and so that saved us. But we were hit on our legs by many rocks, and I believe my legs are fractured. I don't know how I was able to climb up . . . I don't know any more." Then he shut his eyes, and the TV crew left him alone.

By this time, around 3:15 P.M., Milton Ordóñez of INGEOMINAS had arrived, as well as a handful of policemen and Red Cross workers. Grabbing ropes, blankets, and a stretcher, a half-dozen people began backing down the scarp. As she held on to the rope and eased down the andesite ramparts, Patty told herself that the volcano was spent, that it would be hours before it could recharge and erupt again. "I just felt it was my destiny to go and get Stan and the others out of there," she said later.

The first person they found was Andy Macfarlane, who had collapsed on the lower fringes of the scarp about 150 yards from the top. He had a hairline skull fracture and burns on his hands, arms, and legs. Though his injuries were far from life threatening, he was going into shock. When Patty and the others found him, his entire body was shaking, his teeth chattering. Blood covered the left side of his face and had dried on his bright red hair and beard. He was pale, his eyelids fluttering at half-mast, and he could only mumble when Patty spoke to him. His blue jacket was pocked with burn marks. As Patty and the others were checking his wounds, they exposed the ardent fly-fisherman's T-shirt, which read, FISH WORSHIP: IS IT WRONG?

"He was really immobilized," recalled Patty. "But I couldn't determine what was immobilizing him, because he didn't seem to have any broken legs. I think he was just in shock. All he talked about was how he was really, really cold. He was in kind of a delirium."

Patty and a Red Cross worker put a blanket over Macfarlane, gave him a drink of water, and held a bandage over his wound. Patty took off her alpaca scarf and wrapped it around his head. Then Patty, Marta, Milton Ordóñez, and a Red Cross worker tried to carry him toward the rope, 50 yards higher on the steep slope. It was tough going. Macfarlane was dead weight, and hauling him over the scree and boulders seemed to take forever. Soon, however, more rescue workers arrived with a metal stretcher. Someone attached a rope to one end — it may have been the rope permanently affixed to the upper part of the scarp — and a growing cadre of rescuers hauled him up as others guided the gurney.

Macfarlane's recollections did not jibe entirely with those of the people who helped him. But his recall was still surprisingly good, given his bewildered and exhausted state. "The first people to reach me were two Red Cross (?) workers who gave me water and tried to help me walk, one on each side," he wrote later.

They were obviously afraid and shouting frantically to others who were on the way down. I felt like asking them what they were doing there so soon, because it was still dangerous. I got another 8 or 10 steps before collapsing completely, and from then on I couldn't move under my own power. Patty got there shortly after and began talking to me and encouraging me and rubbing me to get my circulation going, and encouraging the others to do likewise . . . She was an absolute, flesh-and-blood angel of mercy.

I remember looking up and seeing the helicopter sweep briefly out from the caldera [amphitheater] rim before it landed. After a while a metal mountaineering stretcher arrived and I was strapped into it, the stretcher tied to the nylon rope at the base of the cliffy stretch of caldera wall, and I was hauled bodily out of there. I was so drained that my legs couldn't support me in the stretcher and I slid to the bottom, but the pain probably kept me awake.

From the top of the scarp, Andy Adams watched the intensifying rescue effort. Fresh from the chaos below, he marveled at how many people were descending willingly onto the still-quaking volcano to retrieve the injured.

Once Macfarlane was pulled out of the amphitheater, I was the last survivor on the volcano, although no one knew that at the time. Strangely, I didn't hear the commotion as Marta, Patty, and the rescue teams found Macfarlane. I vaguely remember hearing the *whomp, whomp, whomp* of helicopter blades, a sound that gave me some hope of rescue. But, I wondered, would people really venture onto the cone?

After leaving Macfarlane with the rescuers from the Red Cross, Marta and Patty clambered back down the scarp to look for me and any other survivors. They were joined by Milton Ordóñez, Carlos Estrada, and Ricardo Villota, a young INGEOMINAS field assistant. As Marta scurried across the moat and onto the cone, she spoke by radio with the observatory in Pasto. Fernando Muñoz, a volcanologist there, warned her that the volcano was being rocked by earthquake activity. Everyone should get out immediately. But Marta, determined that no survivors would be left on Galeras, brushed aside the warning.

"People were expecting new eruptions," she said. "But I didn't worry about that. Or I was not thinking about it. I was thinking about the injured people, not that there was going to be another eruption."

Reaching the cone, the INGEOMINAS workers split up. The smell of sulfur filled the air, and as my colleagues searched for me they dodged boulders hissing on the ground. I had stopped yelling for help, and Marta darted across the lower slopes, trying to find me in the monochromatic universe of the cone. Fresh ash had covered everything in a thin blanket of gray, and large boulders — some old, some new and white-hot — made finding a prone body that much harder. Ricardo Villota ran to Marta. He had just found the corpse of José Arlés, his skull cracked wide open. As he started to tell Marta about it, she looked to the side and spied an ash-covered figure lying crossways on the flank of the volcano — me.

I heard Marta calling my name and looked up to see her hovering over me. My relief was indescribable. Once I saw her, I knew I was going to get off the volcano. No one remembers the precise time, least of all me. The consensus among those on the cone is that I was found around three forty-five, about two hours after the eruption. No one agrees, either, on exactly where I was lying, although it was somewhere on the lower half of the cone, probably about 75 yards down from the crater.

I was a dreadful sight — sprawled on my side, caked in ash and blood, wet from the rain, bones protruding from my burned clothes, my jaw hanging slackly. I remember very little but recall that once the sense of relief passed, I began to feel the cold — and pain — more intensely. According to Marta I didn't complain about my head wound, only about my shattered right leg. Looking down, she could see it was bent at a grotesque angle. She gave me some water and covered me with some lightweight blankets from her knapsack.

Patty Mothes arrived, which I scarcely recollect. "I held your hand and I said, 'Stanley, it's Patty and I'm here to help you. We're here now.' And you had a lot of blood coming out of your ear and your head. I put a bandanna there or something to stop the blood." Patty remembers me muttering, "I want to see Lynda, I want to see my children, I want to live." At times I seemed coherent, at times I was out of it.

"You were on a distant plane," she told me later. "You were just thinking about the essential things. There wasn't any chitchat of any kind. I think you knew you were on the outskirts of death. You were already so cold. Your body temperature was quite low."

A Red Cross worker showed up and, seeing my shattered ankle and leg, tried to remove my boot. When I shrieked in pain, Patty yelled at the worker to leave the leg alone.

Milton Ordóñez saw a foam cooler lying next to José Arlés, whose body lay nearby. Cutting a piece from it, Milton fashioned a splint and tied it to my lower right leg with shoelaces. Marta, Milton, Patty, and Ricardo then placed me on the stretcher Marta had carried down from the police post. Picking me up, they trudged across the broken terrain. I continued mumbling how cold I was. At one point someone stumbled, and I let out a cry of pain. It took about a half hour to get me to the bottom of the scarp, where more rescuers arrived with an aluminum mountaineering stretcher. The Red Cross workers, many wearing bright orange vests, transferred me to the new litter and began the arduous ascent up the amphitheater wall. Patty, Marta, and several INGEOMINAS workers fanned out on the cone to look for other survivors. They found the three tourists, all plainly dead. Then Milton approached the body of his colleague José Arlés.

"I hugged him," recalled Milton. "I was crying. I didn't believe he was dead. I thought maybe he was just sleeping, but he was stiff and cold."

Ricardo ran up to José Arlés's body. Turning it over, he saw that the back of his friend's head had been severed, exposing his brain. According to Milton, Ricardo started screaming. Milton slapped him in the face to calm him down, then sent him back up the scarp. Milton continued to comb the flanks of the volcano and saw what he thought was the body of Carlos Trujillo near the top of the cone. Ricardo Villota thought that he, too, had seen Trujillo's body. What they saw remains a mystery, but it almost certainly wasn't Trujillo's corpse. What was left of Trujillo was eventually found on the opposite side of the volcano, hundreds of yards away.

Chaos prevailed on the cone. The volcano rumbled like a giant bellows, and the rescuers dashed across the flanks, wondering if Galeras might blow again. Evidence of its effects on the human body was there for all to see. The very presence of the three tourists was confusing. Were they volcanologists? People from the area? Marta and the other INGEOMINAS workers didn't recognize them, although the condition of the corpses made quick identification difficult.

Having found me, Marta and Patty searched for any other survivors. There was no trace of Igor Menyailov, Nestor García, Geoff Brown, Fernando Cuenca, or Carlos Trujillo. Patty ran 100 yards to the top of the cone. It was a grim trip. She was alone, she had no radio for communication with the observatory, and as she moved higher the scorching blocks tossed out by the volcano increased in size. Ascending the flank, she kicked ash off the scree and weaved in and out of the hot ejecta. She soon saw José Arlés. Then a little higher, about 50 yards from the top of the cone, she saw the three tourists, their brains spilling out on the ground. Somehow, she had the presence of mind to photograph them. They are haunting pictures, the bodies coated with slate-gray ash, their faces pale. They blended in with the flank, almost as if they had merged with the volcano. Their tennis shoes were plainly visible. Patty briefly contemplated organizing the retrieval of the bodies but quickly dismissed that idea. The living were top priority.

Reaching the lip of the crater, she was drained by exertion, altitude, and fear. Gas and steam poured out of the volcano in a white column, filling the air with an oppressive stench of sulfur. Large, red-hot boulders dotted the crater floor. Frantically, she looked for signs of life, for bodies, but the landscape was nothing but boulders, scree, and ash. Then, after hours of gloom and heavy overcast, the clouds suddenly parted to reveal the brilliant blue Andean sky. Shafts of sunlight fell on the volcano.

Patty began moving west around the crater rim. She confronted a radically changed landscape on the edge of the crater, for much of the western lip had been blown away. Moving farther west, she found herself perched on an unstable promontory completely exposed to the volcano. A tiny cough from Galeras would probably have been enough to kill her.

"I got too nervous," Patty told me later. "I mean, I'm thinking about my husband and kind of praying that nothing would happen to me at this point because I didn't know that part of the volcano. I was looking for rocks to dive under in case it should blow again."

A Red Cross worker came running up the flank toward Patty. He, too, was winded and wide-eyed with fear. Looking around, Patty told him, "*Todos estan muertos. Y me voy.* Everyone's dead. And I'm leaving."

She took one last look, then dashed down the cone.

On top of the scarp, the Colombian TV crew was filming the rescue effort. The crew focused on the cone, a gray monolith under a blue sky. As the camera closed in on the upper part of the cone, several dots of color became visible. Knapsacks? Bodies? It was impossible to tell. A little while later, the camera followed a man as he sprinted down the volcano, a speck on the flank of Galeras.

At the bottom of the scarp, a team of rescue workers began hauling me up in the stretcher. They had attached one or two ropes to the litter, and at the top of the wall of volcanic rock — more than 100 yards above me — a dozen men pulled in unison.

"Give it all you've got!" a rescuer shouted as the TV camera rolled.

"Hit it! . . . Let's go!" others yelled.

Below, rescuers held the stretcher and guided me upward. It was excruciatingly slow. I remember little other than the pain that shot up my right leg as the stretcher lurched with each pull. Marta and Patty were by my side, and Marta remembers me asking again and again: "When are we going to arrive at the top? . . . Why is it taking so long? . . . Are we close?"

At the same time, Red Cross workers were evacuating Luis LeMarie, Andy Macfarlane, and Mike Conway by ambulance.

Patty recalls that it took about fifteen minutes to carry me to the top, possibly a little more. Marta thinks it took an hour. Others say it took more. To me it seemed interminable.

A tiny, olive green army helicopter swooped in like an insect and landed precariously on a narrow, rocky strip crowning the scarp. The helicopter dislodged some rocks, which tumbled down the cliff not far from the group carrying my stretcher. Sometime around 5 P.M., more than three hours after the eruption and with an hour of daylight remaining, a crowd of workers on the lip of the scarp finally grabbed my stretcher and deposited me on safe ground. Amid the hubbub and shouts of the rescuers, I felt a vague sense of relief. But mostly I felt cold, colder than I'd ever been in my life.

The rescuers loaded me aboard the helicopter. I vividly remember Patty coming with me on the chopper and telling the pilot to turn on the heat as we took off. The sensation of hot air enveloping me was one of the most sublime I've ever experienced.

My memory of the heater is no doubt correct. But about Patty I was all wrong. She asked to ride with me, but the helicopter was too small. For years I was sure that Patty had been at my side. Only later did I learn that she and Marta had stood on the ridge on top of Galeras, watching as the helicopter lifted off and banked toward Pasto, 5,000 feet below.

Returning from their field trips, the other scientists gathered at the observatory and the Hotel Cuellar. Both places were awash in rumors, anxiety, misinformation, and grief. My old friend Chuck Connor sloughed off his flu symptoms, got dressed, and went down to the hotel lobby, where the volcanologists were beginning to congregate. He tried to get someone from INGEOMINAS to take him up to Galeras, but everyone refused, saying no more rescuers were needed. So Chuck went to the observatory instead, where more than a dozen staff workers and conference participants had gathered. As he walked through the door, the receptionist stared at him in disbelief. She'd heard he had been killed on Galeras.

Already, the people at INGEOMINAS knew that José Arlés was dead, and many were in tears over the loss of one of their most beloved colleagues. But much of the rest of the information flying about was wrong. I was variously reported to be dead or uninjured. Someone said that Andy Macfarlane was dead and that Mike Conway, who had minor injuries, was seriously hurt. People scurried around the small offices, stopping to scrutinize the soot-covered drums of the seismographs, which were still registering major tremors under the volcano. Someone said the injured were being taken to the central hospital, and Connor, realizing there was little he could do at the observatory, went to check on those who had been hurt.

The Department of Nariño's government hospital is an off-white, five-story, concrete structure in southeast Pasto. It is equipped for standard operations like appendectomies, not sophisticated procedures like heart bypass operations. In 1993 the hospital lacked a CAT scan machine and all but the most basic medications. It did have a dedicated, well-trained staff, and as the injured scientists trickled in, they were well cared for by a cadre of doctors and nurses.

By five-thirty that afternoon, Luis LeMarie, Andy Macfarlane, and Mike Conway were all in the emergency unit, a series of rooms with beige walls, gray stone composite floors, and brown examining tables. They were variously being treated for burns, broken bones, and shock, with Luis receiving the most attention because of his fractured collarbone. After racing back from the field trip in the Azufral Valley, Pete Hall — who was fluent in Spanish — went to the hospital and helped oversee the treatment of his colleagues. I was flown to a sports stadium downtown, then taken by ambulance to the hospital around 6 P.M. Pete was standing in the emergency room when I was wheeled in. He saw a figure covered in wet ash, his face caked with blood, his parka burned, his right foot flopping around the gurney, held on by a tendon or two. The figure was moaning and crying. Pete had no idea who it was.

"What's your name?" he hollered.

I opened my eyes and, according to Pete, shot back, "I'm Stanley Williams!"

I remember almost nothing from that evening. Pete informs me that the doctors and nurses spent the first half hour or so removing my clothes and cleaning off the ash that covered me from head to toe. As they worked, the $10,000 I had stuffed in my shirt came tumbling out. A nurse put the money in a black plastic bag and carried it out of the room. Slowly, as they washed off the layers of ash, the extent of my injuries became clear. The right leg was obviously a mess, but someone realized that beneath the caked blood and ash on my head was an exposed skull fracture.

As I look back on that day, I'm amazed at the good fortune that helped me survive. I still have no idea how I managed to escape with a skull fracture while the four people closest to me on the volcano all had their heads split open. The second stroke of luck came at the hospital. I badly needed a neurosurgeon, and had the eruption occurred ten days earlier, there would have been none at this provincial hospital. But on January 6 — just eight days before the eruption — a highly competent neurosurgeon reported for duty in Pasto. On the evening of January 14 the hospital called him. Galeras had erupted. One of the scientists had been struck in the head by a volcanic missile. Could he come immediately?

Dr. Porfirio Muñoz Bermeo was just thirty-one years old at the time. A stocky, well-dressed man with a large round face and thinning brown hair, he had completed his specialization in neurosurgery at the National University in Bogotá less than two weeks earlier.

"I saw a man who was very sleepy and in a stupor," recalled Dr. Muñoz. "He was very groggy but at the same time he was restless. He couldn't communicate well. The fact that he wasn't alert indicated major trauma to the brain. He had multiple traumas and had an exposed fracture of the temporal [temple] bone. He was leaking brain fluid."

Dr. Muñoz could see that a quarter-size section of my head above the left ear had been staved in. He could see exposed brain tissue. He could see skull fragments in the tissue. But he wanted to see details that only a CAT scan could reveal, and he ordered an ambulance to take me to a clinic downtown, where one was available. In the meantime, just before dark, Patty and Marta flew off the volcano in a helicopter. Arriving at the sports stadium, they rushed to the hospital just as I was about to be taken to the CAT scan. Pete Hall was elated to see his wife, but their reunion was brief. Patty volunteered to accompany me to the clinic. As I waited to be rolled into the cylindrical machine, I was groggy and complained about being so cold.

Realizing the nurse was doing little to raise my body temperature, Patty said to her, "Look, I want you to heat up some warm water right away and I want you to give his feet a bath because he is freezing. And put a hot compress on his face." Then Patty put her arms around me. Her warmth was divine.

Peter Baxter had arrived at the hospital after trying to hitch a ride to the volcano, only to be told he should help care for the wounded already in Pasto. When I returned, he was consulting with Dr. Muñoz about my injuries. The results of the CAT scan were not encouraging. The doctor could see that skull fragments had been driven into my brain, narrowly missing the sigmoid sinus, an area about one centimeter square that drains venous blood from the brain. Without an operation, there was a danger of infection, hemorrhaging, and swelling of the brain.

"Clearly it was a serious injury," Dr. Muñoz said later. "It is probable that if Stan hadn't had surgery he would have died."

Peter was worried about the hospital's relatively primitive conditions but was impressed with the young neurosurgeon and agreed that surgery was necessary. As I was being wheeled to the operating room on the second floor, he walked with me and assured me I was in good hands. But I was groggy and didn't seem to understand what was happening.

Orderlies wheeled me into a bright operating room with white tile walls and a white stone floor. As I was prepped and anesthetized, Dr. Muñoz ran through the operation in his mind. He had never done major surgery on his own before; as a resident, he had always operated with a senior surgeon. Still, his training and quiet self-confidence had prepared him well.

Probing the wound, he assessed the damage. A depressed skull fracture. A rupture in the dura mater, the brain's tough, outer covering. A hematoma, or blood clot, on the outer lining of the brain. Fragments of bone and rock in the brain tissue. Lacerations to the brain tissue. Loss of brain fluid. Air between the brain and the skull. Oddly, the open skull fracture saved my life, for it allowed brain fluid and blood to drain from my cranium. Had my skull not caved in, I would probably have died within several hours from a buildup of pressure on the brain.

Dr. Muñoz picked out the small stones, bone fragments, and grains of volcanic ejecta from the brain. He cut away and suctioned out the destroyed brain tissue. He drained and removed the blood clot. He cauterized the end of the healthy tissues to prevent leakage of blood and a future hematoma. With saline solution, he washed the injury and forced out the air between my skull and brain. He administered large doses of antibiotics intravenously. The delicate procedure took three hours. As he worked, he discovered something that — when I learned of it later — only reinforced my sense of how remarkable my survival was. One of the large skull fragments was lodged less than an eighth of an inch from the sigmoid sinus, which functions much like a vein. Had it been cut, I would have bled to death in a matter of minutes on Galeras.

When he had finished and a bandage was put over the hole in my head, a chunk of my brain the size of a peach pit had been destroyed. Although he was confident I would survive, Dr. Muñoz was not sure of the long-term damage.

"Clearly there could be consequences," he said later. "The injury could affect his memory, speech, behavior, and could cause seizures."

Chuck Connor, Peter Baxter, and my graduate student, Toby Fischer, were waiting for Dr. Muñoz when he emerged from the operating room around midnight. The first thing he did was to hand Connor a list of several medicines, including antibiotics and anti-inflammatories, that weren't stocked in the hospital. He instructed Connor to scour the all-night pharmacies for the drugs. The surgeon told him that I would live, although he could not say how damaged my brain had been from the blow. Connor was relieved, but Baxter was still not sure I would survive.

Peter was worried, above all, about infection. Although Dr. Muñoz seemed to be excellent, the intensive care unit where I was recuperating was a rudimentary ward without sufficient precautions against infection. Peter had made calls to the United States to set up an evacuation by air ambulance, but the plane wouldn't arrive for at least a day.

Around 1 A.M., Connor hit the streets in search of medicine. It had been nearly twelve hours since the eruption, and his flu symptoms had vanished. "I got an adrenaline rush that went through me like a rocket, and I felt absolutely well," he said. Within an hour, he'd found all the medicines I needed.

Baxter was exhausted and distraught over the fate of his friend Geoff Brown. Earlier that night, Peter had learned that Brown and four other scientists had not been found before dark. The search had been called off until daybreak. "This, to me, was really a shattering thing. I assumed that Geoff had been injured and that they just hadn't found him. And I said, 'Well, you've got to carry on with this search and rescue!' and they said it was just too dangerous. So I thought he was up there and would freeze to death because the temperature went down to freezing at night. You could survive up there if you were okay. But if you were badly injured you wouldn't, and I just assumed he would be dead by morning from hypothermia. I felt bad because I was in the hospital, whereas I know that his first response would have been to go up and try to find me."

Sometime after midnight, Pete Hall and Patty Mothes went to my favorite haunt in town, the Punto Rojo, a twenty-four-hour cafeteria. Overwhelmed by the day's events, they picked at their food and talked about the eruption. The restaurant was cold inside and nearly deserted. Hall described the gist of that conversation to me later: "Here we were scientists, we should know our game very well. We should know what's going on, and in fact we thought the volcano was safe at this point. We thought we could go into the volcano and it could be studied without any major problems. We saw no precursory activity that would suggest anything was amiss."

Patty was emotionally spent, but as she sat there she had no desire to return to the hotel and rest. "To go to sleep seemed so insignificant compared to what had happened," she wrote to me later. "I felt anguish about seeing all of the mutilated bodies, the smashed skulls, and the traumatized survivors."

She talked about what she had done, and only then did it hit her how risky the rescue had been and how lucky she, Marta, and the others were that Galeras had not erupted again. Their overriding goal was to get onto the cone and evacuate their colleagues, and they pursued it so single-mindedly that they descended onto Galeras without gas masks or hard hats. She was thankful to be alive. And she couldn't fathom how, in just a few hours, things had gone so terribly wrong. As she talked, the day's images flashing through her mind, she was distraught over the disappearance of Geoff Brown. We just had dinner with Geoff last night, she told her husband. And now he had vanished.

Her distress over Brown's fate became more acute as she and Pete walked from the Punto Rojo to the hotel. The night was unusually cold, even for a city at 9,000 feet. Patty looked toward Galeras, thought about Brown, Menyailov, and the others, and shuddered. If someone is lying injured on the volcano, she thought, he'll never make it through the night.

In the first twenty-four hours, news of the eruption spread around the world. For the relatives of the dead, injured, and missing, word of the disaster arrived through sketchy phone calls and often inaccurate media reports. With five scientists unaccounted for, the reality — and the grief — came in stages for some families. For others, the truth came in one blow.

Such was the case with José Arlés's wife, Monica Gonzales Vallejo. Many people had seen the young scientist on the flank of Galeras, and there was no doubt about his fate. Monica was vacationing in Manizales with José Arlés's family when someone called that first afternoon, saying Galeras had erupted around 2 P.M. Her first thought was that José Arlés and the others would be fine, since by two they were usually off the volcano and back in Pasto. She drove with José Arlés's brother to the INGEOMINAS offices in Manizales, where her husband had worked as a student. The staff said there was no news about her husband. They seemed almost to be avoiding her, so she lit a cigarette, grabbed a cup of coffee, and began to pace. A radio was playing in the office.

"Then the news came on and the announcer said there had been an eruption at Galeras and that among the three known victims was José Arlés Zapata," Monica told me later. "I was desperate. People tried to console me. They said wait until we get the real truth. But one geologist's wife came up to me. She was crying and hugged me and extended her sympathies, and then I knew. The press started coming, and I knew."

Confirmation came late that afternoon when an official from INGEOMINAS called to say that José Arlés was, indeed, among the four confirmed dead.

"At that moment," said Monica, "there is an emptiness in your soul."

Nestor García's estranged wife, Dolores Ocampo, was in her office in Manizales. Her radio also brought the news. Interrupting the regular programming, the announcer said that Galeras had erupted and that the fate of those on the volcano was unknown. Immediately she called Nestor's mother, who was with their twelve-year-old son, Marcello, that afternoon.

Marcello asked his mother what she thought. "I answered that, knowing Nestor and how devoted he is to his work, it was possible something could have happened to him."

Nestor's parents had also learned of the eruption from the radio. The first thing his aging father said was, "Oh, my son has been killed." He began to have chest pains, and the family called a doctor. But Nestor's mother, Argelia Parra de García, held out hope for their son's survival. "He was such a good athlete that I felt he could have escaped and saved himself," she said.

That afternoon their eighteen-year-old daughter, Paula, and Nestor's two sisters flew to Pasto. By late that night, the news was bad but not hopeless. Nestor was missing, but the authorities said he might still be alive.

In Pasto, Carlos Trujillo's wife, Anna Lucía Torres, was at the departmental hospital, where she was a social worker. Not long after 2 P.M., a colleague told her that Galeras had just erupted. She made numerous phone calls, and someone told her not to worry because Carlos had spent the day in Sandona on a field trip. But when her sister came to pick her up that afternoon, she said the radio had listed the dead and Carlos was the first victim mentioned. Anna broke down in tears, but as day turned to night, his death was not confirmed. He still was missing and the search had been called off until Friday morning.

Gloria Benavides, whose husband, Efrain Guerrero, and son, Yovany, had hiked to the volcano with her son's best friend, had not heard the blast. Around midafternoon, her brother-in-law telephoned to say there had been an eruption. She knew that her husband and son would have been on Galeras about that time, and frantically she and her fourteen-year-old daughter phoned the hospital, the army, civil defense offices, and the Red Cross. No one had any news. That night, she and her daughter sat in their house and prayed. The hours ticked by. By 2 A.M., when her husband and son still hadn't returned, Mrs. Benavides was certain that they had died.

In England, six time zones ahead of Pasto, the news did not reach Geoff Brown's wife, Evelyn, until Friday morning. She had driven to the Open University, where she taught. Before going into a meeting, she went to the cafeteria for a cup of coffee and waved at some members of Geoff's department. She noticed, however, that they looked uneasy. Before long Chris Wilson, the acting head of the department, approached her.

"Well, I'm afraid I've got some bad news for you," he said. "You'd better sit down."

Thinking her husband's workaholic ways had finally done him in, she said, "He's had a heart attack, hasn't he?"

"No, I'm afraid not," he replied. "There's been an eruption."

Wilson explained that Geoff and several other scientists on the volcano had not been found.

From the start, Evelyn feared the worst. She called her daughters, telling them Galeras had erupted and their father was missing. The eldest, Miriam, was at work in London and came home to find the message on her answering machine. As shaken as she was by the news that her father might have died, she was even more disturbed to think he was lying injured on the volcano.

Ruth, the middle child, was at home in Nottingham when her mother called. It seemed unreal, and she held out hope he might have survived. "You sit back for a while and you think, 'Oh, they'll find him soon,'" Ruth recalled. "We'll hear the news in a minute. He'll be back." She spent the afternoon with her boyfriend, crying. TV and radio stations reported the eruption, saying that Geoff Brown was missing and presumed dead. Angry that they were burying her father when his fate was still unknown, she called a station to complain. (England — the entire world, for that matter — was filled with bad information. Someone called Peter Baxter's wife in Cambridge to inform her that her husband had been killed. My death was reported by one U.S. newspaper.)

Ruth called her younger sister, Iona, who was at an orchestra rehearsal. "When I found out," recalled Iona, "I felt a real sense of disbelief that this was actually happening to me, followed by immediate panic. I've never felt anything like that since. I felt sick, physically sick."

As the hours passed on Friday with no word, Geoff's family began to lose hope. Evelyn received several phone calls from Peter Baxter. "He just couldn't accept it. He kept saying to me, 'I'm sure he's going to turn up. He's a survivor.'"

On the Kamchatka peninsula, Lyudmila Menyailova received a call on January 15 from one of Igor's colleagues in Russia. The news was bad, not even couched in terms that her husband was missing. Her husband and I had died, the colleague said. Shortly thereafter, a fax arrived saying that I had survived but that Igor and others were dead. Lyudmila, married happily for more than thirty years, hardly remembers the ensuing hours and days, other than receiving injections of sedatives.

Igor's mother, Sofia Naboko, was also in Kamchatka. It was Lyudmila who called to say that Sofia's son had been caught in an eruption and was missing. A survivor of Stalin's terror and World War II, Sofia Naboko had known her share of grief. She kept this pain to herself. "Lyudmila told me and I did not cry. Lyudmila did. I am unable to cry. Maybe sometimes my voice would tremble, but I did not cry."

In Moscow, Igor's only child, Irina, was at home with her young daughter when a friend of her mother's called, asking where her father was. Irina replied that he was in Colombia.

"Well," the woman said, "there is news about him. They announced on TV a while ago that somewhere in Latin America a volcano erupted and they named Igor Menyailov as among those believed to be killed."

"And then the hell started," Irina recalled. "They did not actually say at first that he was killed; they said he was not found. The search was going on, but no one informed us about the progress. We could not get news from so far away. It was terrible. A nightmare."

Not far from Moscow, in the central Russian city of Tula, Fernando Cuenca's bride of two years was on vacation at her parents' house. The call from Colombia came at 5 A.M. on January 15 or 16. It was one of her husband's colleagues, saying Fernando was missing and presumed dead in an eruption at Galeras. "I don't know how I lived through it," Larissa said. "It was only thanks to my mother. She pulled me out of it. She was with me every second."

In Tempe, Arizona, late on the afternoon of the eruption, my wife was in the mailroom of the Geology Department at Arizona State University when someone told her that the chairman, Ed Stump, would like to see her. Lynda walked into his office, and Stump told her that Galeras had blown. Herself a geologist, my wife was initially delighted: "Great! They'll get to see an eruption."

"Not so great," replied Stump, who then told Lynda that several people had been hurt, including me. One of my ASU colleagues at the conference had told Stump that I had two broken ankles. Shaken, Lynda went home. As the evening wore on, the calls from Colombia brought progressively worse news. Several people had died in the eruption. I had a fractured skull, burns, and two broken legs. At one point, Peter Baxter called to say that I was undergoing brain surgery.

"Should I come down?" asked Lynda.

"Yes," he replied, his tone implying that I might not survive.

Lynda's mother was visiting from Arkansas and could watch the children. At 2 A.M. on Friday, Lynda was at the Phoenix airport, preparing to board a plane to Miami. Flying alone to a remote area of a dangerous country, she was terrified. It occurred to her that neither of us might come back, and we had no will. So, sitting in the empty, fluorescent expanses of Phoenix's Skyharbor Airport, she wrote out a will on several scraps of paper, stuck them in an envelope, and mailed them to our house. Then she called her mother to tell her not to be alarmed when she received the letter. Lynda said she was just being cautious.

At 2:30 A.M., she boarded the plane to Miami, where she transferred to a flight to Bogotá. Sitting beside her was a Colombian university student reading a newspaper story about the eruption, which reported that many scientists had died. As she flew south, she fully expected to be told I was dead when she landed. Almost worse was the prospect that I might be severely brain-damaged. Lynda's father and one of her brothers are neurosurgeons. Her other brother is a neurologist. They had warned her to expect the worst.

Meanwhile, Stump had arranged for an emergency air evacuation. As my wife flew over the Caribbean, a white Learjet, with a doctor and nurse aboard, took off from Miami, bound for Pasto.

Friday, January 15, is lost to me. Infused with painkillers, I remember almost nothing save a blur of hovering doctors and nurses. My legs were so badly shattered that the Colombian doctors wrapped them in crude casts, correctly reasoning that it was best to repair the damage in the United States. Peter Baxter, who continued to watch over me, arrived on Friday morning and was relieved to see that I was conscious and talking, though not always making sense. He was mainly worried about infection, but he needn't have. While my wounds were filled with ash and rock, they never became infected; volcanic ejecta are completely sterile.

Chuck Connor came to the hospital to visit all the injured. He told me that José Arlés had been killed and that Igor, Geoff, Nestor, and the other scientists were missing and apparently dead. I don't recall this moment, but Peter said my eyes filled with tears. They still do whenever I relive the eruption.

The storm of seismic activity at Galeras had abated, and early the next morning search and rescue teams descended on the volcano. They scoured the cone and the crater for hours but found no sign of the five missing scientists. They did recover the bodies of José Arlés and the three tourists. Sheathed in body bags, they were lifted by stretcher to the top of the amphitheater scarp and flown by helicopter to the departmental hospital.

For José Arlés's widow and the families of the dead tourists, this confirmation of their deaths was shattering. But for the families and friends of the missing, the uncertainty was perhaps even worse. Had the men simply disappeared without a trace? Some people held out hope that the scientists had been injured and had wandered, dazed, down the open western flank of Galeras. If so, they might be in the jungle near the Azufral Valley and could turn up at any moment in one of the villages on the lower flanks of Galeras. For many, it was hard to believe that experienced volcanologists like Igor, Geoff, and Nestor could not have found a way to survive, could actually have been vanquished by this force that had long inspired them.

Peter Baxter, who had witnessed Geoff Brown's persistence and determination on Etna and other volcanoes, kept thinking that his friend would turn up soon. "I knew that Geoff would get out if there was a way," he said. "For a day or two, I still thought he might have made it out of the crater and would be found somewhere on the slopes, badly injured but still alive. Because he had this tremendous ability to try and get around a problem."

At the Hotel Cuellar, some conference participants held a half-hearted round of final meetings. The mood was dismal, as people grieved over their dead and missing colleagues. At the INGEO-MINAS observatory, seismologists noticed the scattered *tornillo* signals on the seismograph in the days leading up to the eruption. It was the first recognition that such tiny numbers of *tornillos* might have been an indicator of trouble.

By sunset Friday, civil defense officials halted the search for the day. New rescue teams, accompanied by dogs, had arrived from Cali and other cities and were set to continue the hunt on Saturday.

Arriving in Bogotá on Friday afternoon, Lynda — who doesn't speak Spanish — was met by two officers from the U.S. embassy. Looking at their grim faces as they ushered her into a private room at the airport, she expected them to tell her I was dead. Instead, they said they had no news. They had been unable to get her a ticket to Pasto, but Lynda, determined to see me before I expired, called a Colombian colleague of mine in Bogotá. His wife rushed to the airport and helped Lynda get on a plane to Cali, which is about halfway to Pasto. Arriving at night in Colombia's drug capital, Lynda spent three hours at the airport until she finally found her contact from the air ambulance service. Pasto's airport, the man explained, was fogged in. The air ambulance was waiting in Cali for a break in the weather. The man took Lynda to a hotel, told her she might be leaving the next morning, and gave her a sleeping pill. Wary of swallowing a pill given to her by a stranger in Cali, she tentatively took half of it. In a few minutes, noticing no ill effects, she took the other half and slept through the night.

She was awakened the next morning by a call from the pilot of the air ambulance. The fog in Pasto was expected to lift, he said, and they hoped to leave soon. Shortly after noon, Lynda took off in the Learjet, staffed by two pilots, a nurse, and a young Cuban-American doctor. Threading its way through the Andes, the jet approached Pasto's airport, a bumpy, paved strip a few hundred yards long carved out of the Andes. At the end of the runway is a mile-deep ravine. Landing, a pilot must weave through the mountains, then drop quickly down on the small runway. Thick clouds can smother the airport in a matter of minutes. The pilot did a fine job that day. Later he likened the landing to setting a plane down on an aircraft carrier in a sea of mountains.

An American embassy official, whom Lynda thought was a CIA agent, was at the airport in his own Learjet. He said he was "in the neighborhood" and offered his help. Lynda thanked him, then sped off with the doctor and the nurse over Nariño's hair-raising mountain roads to Pasto, 25 miles away.

Marta, Peter Baxter, and Chuck Connor were waiting for her at the hospital. She hugged Marta and Chuck, whom she knew, then headed straight for my room. Moving swiftly down the dingy corridors, oblivious of the surroundings, Peter led her into the room. My head was wrapped in a blood-spotted turban, my face was swollen, my legs were encased in casts, my hands were black from crawling on ash, and IV lines were looped around the bed. All in all, Lynda thought I looked great. Expecting a corpse or a vegetable, she was relieved that I was sitting up and speaking Spanish coherently with the nurses. Walking to my bedside, she leaned over and hugged me, and we both began to cry. I remember looking into her green eyes and being flooded with feelings of love, relief, and hope. Her presence instantly dispelled the bleakness of the hospital, and I felt as if I were halfway home. I told her I was all right and asked about the children. She told me she was getting me out of the hospital and that we were heading home.

I talked almost nonstop, much to Lynda's relief. But then she noticed I was mixing up words, repeating myself, wandering into verbal dead ends. She had seen me like this once before when I was doing postdoctoral work at the University of Chicago. Early one morning, a driver lost control of his Cadillac on an icy road and spun into my lane, totaling my car. I suffered a mild concussion, and when I called Lynda to tell her about the accident, I was rambling and forgetting what I had told her just a few seconds before. She had flown from Dartmouth to Chicago to be with me and saw a marked improvement after her arrival.

"It was like I breathed life into him then, and I wanted to breathe life into him again if it was at all possible," she wrote later.

As I talked incessantly that afternoon, Lynda was confident I would soon return to normal, just as I had after the car accident. She didn't realize — neither of us realized — that I would never be the same. After Galeras there would be no more "normal" in our relationship.

(During my hospital stay, I had mumbled something about the $10,000 in hundred-dollar bills that I had carried with me onto the volcano. Suspecting the money was in the emergency ward, my colleagues went in search of it, pessimistic that so much cash would be found. In a storeroom not far from where I'd been treated on Thursday evening, they saw a plastic bag on the floor. Opening it, they were elated to find the wad of bills — testimony that honest people still inhabit this notoriously lawless country. Marta and John Stix used the money to cover expenses for the conference.)

Lynda and I rode in an ambulance to the airport, where Marta, Peter Baxter, Chuck Connor, and Dr. Muñoz said farewell. (My injured colleagues — Luis LeMarie, Mike Conway, and Andy Macfarlane — would return home within the next two days.) The young neurosurgeon had wanted to board the air ambulance and help care for me all the way to Phoenix, but he didn't have an American visa. I said good-bye to the doctor, and Lynda hugged him as she thanked him. I remember being slid into the cozy, spotless interior of the Learjet ambulance and thinking: This is a remarkable plane. Is it really all for me?

Lynda sat at the foot of the stretcher, the doctor and nurse at my head. Fearing that a drastic change in air pressure might exacerbate my brain injury, Dr. Muñoz and the air ambulance doctor instructed the pilot to fly below 8,000 feet, a low altitude that would force us to refuel twice. I gave in to a feeling of pure relief as I was lifted onto the clean sheets, saw the high-tech medical gadgetry, and felt the reassuring presence of the American doctor and nurse. The nurse poked an IV into my arm, strapped on a cuff, and took my blood pressure. The Learjet whined. We bounced over the runway and in a few seconds were airborne.

I will be in Phoenix tomorrow, I thought, as I fell asleep.

On the way home, I drifted in and out of slumber. Unable to sit close enough to hold my hand, Lynda occasionally talked to me and I wiggled my toes in response. We landed in Belize to refuel amid oppressive humidity and huge mosquitoes. We refueled again in Brownsville, Texas.

Lynda was wearing the suede flight jacket I had given her for Christmas. As I slept, she cried on the sleeve of the jacket and wondered — when she wasn't worrying about me — whether her tears would stain her Christmas gift.

10

·················

EXTINGUISHING THE SUN

O N SATURDAY morning, January 16, rescue teams with dogs returned to the volcano, combing its cone and flanks. Hope had faded that anyone would be found alive, but the authorities were intent on recovering bodies. Again they were thwarted. My colleagues had given the dog handlers underclothes from some of the missing men, but the great clouds of sulfur wafting out of Galeras hindered their ability to scent. Family members and INGEOMINAS scientists were growing increasingly frustrated. There had to be some trace of the men.

The conference — or what was left of it — broke up on Saturday. Some colleagues, including Tobias Fischer and the team from Los Alamos National Laboratory, stayed behind to continue their research and even went twice more onto Galeras's cone — a courageous step that would have been endlessly second-guessed had the volcano erupted again. Chuck Connor remained for a few more days to make sure his injured colleagues returned safely to the United States and Ecuador. But Pasto had become oppressive for him.

"By the time I left, I felt like, 'Get me the hell out of here,'" he said later.

On Sunday, three days after the eruption, about 75 people — including members of Carlos Trujillo's family — converged on Galeras to continue the search. This time the area was expanded to cover about a mile down the open western flank, where the blast had been channeled. Walking a grid pattern, the party methodically searched the mountain's middle flanks and soon found something. About 550 yards below the crater rim, members of the group spotted a large dark object. Drawing closer, they saw that it was the blackened upper torso and head of a man. The torso had been "completely cooked" but not "desiccated or charred as in fire victims," said Peter Baxter. The heat to which it had been exposed was sufficient to melt body fat, so the temperature was at least 930 to 1,100 degrees F. Heat and volcanic missiles had obliterated its facial features, and chunks of volcanic rock and ash were driven into the body.

Rescuers summoned Trujillo's brother-in-law, Tomás Torres. Staring at the black object on the field of scree, he declared that it could not be Carlos. But then he looked at the hands. On one of the fingers was Carlos's ring. Dental records later confirmed that the torso was, indeed, that of Carlos Trujillo.

At the time of the eruption, Trujillo had been walking along the western rim with Geoff Brown and Fernando Cuenca. Baxter later concluded that the force of the blast had flung his body 550 yards. At some point, a large rock cut the corpse in half. But what Baxter found intriguing was that Trujillo's upper torso showed signs of having been scorched by a pyroclastic flow. As the other survivors and I lay on the southeastern flank of Galeras, worrying that a *nuée ardente* might rise up out of the crater and kill us, a small pyroclastic flow may have surged down the open western flank, further cooking Trujillo's already burned and blasted corpse.

As the search continued, the rescuers and their dogs found bits of flesh and little pools of congealed blood scattered far down the slope. But they discovered almost nothing large enough to collect, save for an inch-long piece of what looked like an esophagus. They placed it in a plastic bag for the medical examiner.

Not far from Trujillo's torso, the search party came across the scorched remains of the aluminum interior of Geoff Brown's gravimeter. The fiberglass casing had been blown off. Engineers at Cambridge University estimated that a rapid temperature rise of at least 390 degrees F would have been needed to break the screws and separate this casing from the inner aluminum box. The search parties also found a plastic gas mask cartridge fused to a rock by the heat of the blast.

Otherwise, the rescuers who combed the flank that day found nothing. By evening it was clear that, aside from Trujillo's torso, the missing had been blown to pieces in the initial phases of the eruption. Igor Menyailov and Nestor García, caught inside the crater, had essentially been vaporized and scattered across the Andes. Geoff Brown and Fernando Cuenca, standing on the crater lip, had been hit with such force by so many rocks that no trace of them was found either. Horrific as they were, these deaths offered us one measure of comfort: they occurred instantly.

The other four who died — José Arlés and the three tourists — expired almost as quickly. An autopsy showed that José Arlés had been killed when a hot rock hit the right side of his face, shattering his skull and causing extensive brain trauma. The presence of carbon monoxide in his lungs indicated that he took a few breaths of hot, gaseous air before he died.

One of the tourists was killed by a barrage of rocks that inflicted massive damage to his head and torso, killing him immediately. The autopsy showed that rocks had broken his spine in several places, severing his spinal cord, creating large blood clots, and badly deforming his upper torso. Volcanic bombs also broke his ribs, ruptured and detached both lungs and his windpipe, detached his heart, and ruptured his aorta and spleen. At some point, wrote Baxter, the tourist "was flung through the air against a hard-rock surface with the internal rupture injuries being caused by rapid deceleration." The body also had many burns, caused when the tourist's clothing caught fire after he died.

Another tourist died when a large volcanic bomb pulverized his skull, inflicting massive brain injuries. The body also had a fractured left thighbone, broken ribs, and burns on the right arm, the right side of the torso, and the palm of the right hand. "These injuries," wrote Baxter, "were sustained when he was hit on the head by flying rocks and then fell on his knees on to hot rocks. Another rock hit him in the scapula [shoulder blade] area, resulting in fractured ribs and the rupture of the lung, whilst he was on his knees with his hand outstretched on to a hot rock."

The third tourist also died after being struck repeatedly in the head and chest with hot volcanic projectiles. His skull was shattered, his left leg fractured in several places, his left foot nearly severed at the ankle — an injury very similar to mine — and the upper left lobe of his lung ruptured. Third-degree burns covered 18 percent of his body.

These deaths showed that even a tiny eruption can inflict unthinkable damage to anyone caught in or near a crater. Even in a minor blast, volcanic missiles fly out of the crater at speeds of up to 1,300 feet per second. That's more than the muzzle velocity of most handgun bullets — about 1,000 feet per second — and isn't much less than the velocity of shrapnel from artillery shells, which reaches speeds of 1,500 to 2,000 feet per second. Yet volcanic bombs are usually much larger than those metal fragments, and the results are devastating. Baxter has calculated that a 1-pound volcanic fragment, traveling at more than 90 feet per second, has a 90 percent probability of killing someone if it strikes them in the torso or head. Many projectiles shot out of Galeras at ten times that speed and weighed 5, 10, 100, or even 1,000 pounds. It's easy to see how such missiles could quickly obliterate a human body.

Such incidents are all too common. Baxter cites a small eruption at Mount Etna in 1979, when nine tourists standing near the edge of the Bocca Nuova crater were killed. They died just as my colleagues did, from the impact of volcanic bombs. Other tourists, some as far as 450 yards from the crater, were injured.

Two months after the Galeras eruption, two Ecuadorian volcanologists, working in the crater of Guagua Pichincha, near Quito, Ecuador, were killed by volcanic bombs expelled in a small, steam-driven eruption.

And in July 2000 a similar tragedy befell a group of volcanologists at Semeru volcano, a 12,060-foot peak in a remote section of Java. Semeru has been active for decades and was regularly experiencing small eruptions lasting 10 to 30 seconds. A group of eight Indonesian, American, and Israeli volcanologists visited the volcano after an international meeting in Bali. As they stood near the crater rim at 6:21 A.M. on July 25, an unusually large eruption occurred, ejecting volcanic bombs in an unexpected direction. The blast was short-lived — less than a minute — but it killed two Indonesian volcanologists, who sustained massive brain injuries after being struck in the head by volcanic projectiles. Three American scientists were injured, one seriously, and an Israeli volcanologist was also hurt. Among the injured was Lee Siebert, a well-known volcanologist at the Smithsonian Institution. It took more than thirty hours to evacuate the wounded and days to retrieve the bodies.

"Looking at the distribution of the victims and the size of the bombs, it makes me realize how entirely lucky I and the other survivors were," Michael Ramsey, a volcanologist at the University of Pittsburgh, said in an e-mail to his colleagues.

That tragedy underscored the immense danger of our profession. In two decades, from 1979 through 2000, twenty-three of my colleagues were killed while working on volcanoes. Sixteen, including the six scientists at Galeras, died in eruptions. Five Colombian scientists and engineers perished in 1986 when their helicopter crashed into a glacial crevasse on Nevado del Ruiz. In 1982 two Japanese scientists drowned in an Icelandic river on their way back from studying a volcano. Considering that only about three hundred scientists work on active volcanoes worldwide, twenty-three deaths in twenty-one years is exceedingly high.

The eruption that felled me and killed my colleagues had a fatal reach of a few hundred feet and was seen and heard no farther than Pasto. But I am awed and fascinated by eruptions with global repercussions, causing climate change, famine, population migrations, and — in the case of prehistoric blasts — mass extinctions. Earthquakes have killed ten times more people in the past 400 years than volcanoes — 2.6 million deaths compared to 250,000 — but no other natural disasters have the profound global effects of volcanic eruptions.

Looking far back in time, the most devastating impacts have not come from explosive blasts but from vast outpourings of magma onto the earth's surface. Originating at "hot spots" in the mantle — with an average depth of about 400 miles but sometimes as deep as 1,800 miles — these magma plumes have shot to the surface and formed great basalt plateaus on the sea floor. They have built islands like Hawaii and Iceland. And they have gushed onto the continents, creating about a dozen large "flood basalt" plains around the globe, like the one found along the Columbia River in America's Pacific Northwest. In some instances, such enormous quantities of gas have poured from these fissures that they have absorbed many of the sun's rays, radically cooling the earth and possibly causing mass extinctions.

Such an event occurred in Siberia at the end of the Permian era, about 248 million years ago. Erupting through cracks and fissures, a flood of magma covered an area nearly as large as Montana to a depth of up to 10,000 feet. Many scientists believe these eruptions, lasting hundreds of thousands of years, drastically altered the earth's climate, playing a role in the so-called great dying. That event, the largest mass extinction in history, killed off 95 percent of all ocean species and 70 percent of all land vertebrate families, including giant amphibians and reptiles. These extinctions coincide precisely with the Siberian eruptions.

Another massive flood basalt eruption, this one in India, may have played a role in the extinction of the dinosaurs 65 million years ago. Some specialists argue that it was the impact of a comet or asteroid — not volcanic activity in India — that blotted out the sun's rays, bringing about rapid cooling and extinction. But both camps may be right. New theories postulate that in the midst of the outpouring of gas, magma, and ash from the Indian eruptions, an asteroid may also have crashed into the earth. Such a one-two combination could well have done in the dinosaurs.

No matter who's right, two things are beyond dispute. First, when magma flooded out of great fissures in Siberia and India, drastic cooling followed. Second, such an event today would have calamitous consequences.

"It is quite certain that even a modest flood basalt eruption today would dramatically affect the world climate and put the future of mankind in some jeopardy," wrote Peter R. Hooper of Washington State University.

In the past thousand years, man has had only one glimpse of something remotely resembling the great basalt floods. And though it was infinitely smaller than the eruptions in Siberia and India, it nevertheless had devastating consequences.

The eruptions occurred in 1783 in Iceland, which — geologically speaking — is little more than a lump of basalt rising out of the North Atlantic. Iceland sits astride the mid-Atlantic ridge, which is perpetually spreading apart, with the eastern flank moving at three quarters of an inch a year toward Europe and the western flank migrating toward North America at the same rate. Iceland also happens to be on top of a hot spot, and in the summer of 1783 a particularly robust plume of magma ascended from deep inside the earth and created a natural disaster that wiped out one fifth of Iceland's population.

The eruptions were centered on a 2,684-foot mountain named Laki, near the windswept, treeless coast of southern Iceland. About six hundred souls eked out an existence there, farming, fishing, and foraging for wild grasses and the eggs of migratory birds. On June 8 the earth near Laki opened up and rivers of magma began gushing from fissures and cones that eventually formed a rift 15 miles long. Fountains of fire shot up 4,500 feet, and the pall of gas and ash — sometimes reaching 8 miles high — could be seen from 180 miles away. So much magma gushed forth that at times its flow nearly equaled that of the Amazon River.

Volcanology is fortunate that a keen observer — the Reverend Jón Steingrímsson, whose parish was overrun by the lava flows — witnessed the eruptions. A contemporary of Sir William Hamilton, Steingrímsson shared his passion for studying the natural world and getting close to the action.

The eruptions announced themselves to Steingrímsson on a clear, calm Sunday. To the north, above a low line of mountains, he spotted a "black haze of sand." The cloud rapidly spread his way, darkening the sky and depositing black ash on the ground. The ash stung people's eyes and skin, made holes in pigweed leaves, and left burn marks on newly shorn sheep.

In the next few days, the lava sped down the Skafta River gorge. Before seeing the flows, residents heard great explosions as the molten rock poured into wetlands and streams. Nesting birds flew away, abandoning their eggs, which "were scarcely edible because of their ill odor and sulphurous taste," Steingrímsson wrote. Poisoned by the haze, pippets, wrens, and other small birds fell dead to the ground. Trout died in rivers and ponds. The grass, "which was green and luscious," wilted and was covered in ash. Cattle and sheep wouldn't eat forage unless it was mixed with older hay.

"The flesh and the milk of the animals dwindled one after the other . . . ," wrote Steingrímsson. "There are hardly words to describe how the sheep just withered away. No one had the foresight to see that it would have been best to slaughter them all while they still had flesh on their bones and could be rounded up, and thus have food for ourselves."

By mid-June, the advancing wall of lava "completely filled" the Skafta River gorge, 1,600 feet wide and 500 feet deep. Although no one in Iceland died in the flows, they devoured farmhouses and pastureland. "The flood of fire flowed with the speed of a great swollen river with meltwater on a spring day," Steingrímsson wrote. "Great cliffs and slabs of rock were swept along, tumbling about like large whales swimming, red-hot and glowing."

By July the sun had disappeared and livestock became increasingly ill from ingesting the fallout from Laki. First their snouts, nostrils, and feet turned yellow. Then they "simply lay down and died in their tracks." Thus began an epidemic of fluorosis, a disease in which ingesting too much volcanic fluorine causes animals' bones to grow soft and their teeth to fall out, leaving the beasts unable to stand or eat.

On Sunday, July 20, the Reverend Steingrímsson held a worship service in the Sida region. A lava flow had approached within a few hundred yards of the church and seemed certain to engulf it in a matter of hours. As the congregation gathered, they could scarcely see the chapel through the haze. The earth shook and the lightning — crackling in the highly charged, ash-filled air — was so bright, it lit up the inside of the church. Steingrímsson closed the door, and he and his flock prepared to die.

"Both myself and all the others in the church were completely unafraid there inside its walls. No one showed any signs of fleeing or leaving during the service, which I had made slightly longer than usual. Now no length of time spent talking to God could be too long . . . Every man was prepared to die there, if this would have pleased Him."

Emerging from the church, the worshipers were stunned to see that the lava had piled into a channel 420 feet wide and 120 feet deep, then stopped. They all proclaimed it a miracle, and from then on the incident was known in Iceland as the Fire Sermon.

In other parts of southern Iceland, the flood of lava continued until February. The blue haze and blizzard of ash from the eruptions poisoned the landscape for hundreds of miles. First the animals died, then the humans.

"The horses lost all their flesh, the skin began to rot off along the spines of some of them, the hair of the tail and mane rotted and came off if pulled sharply," wrote Steingrímsson. "Hard, swollen lumps appeared at joints. Their heads became swollen and disfigured, and their jaws so weak they could hardly bite off or eat grass. Their innards decayed, the bones shrank and lost all marrow."

Similar afflictions befell sheep and cattle, with their hooves and tails falling off and their bones becoming so rubbery, they collapsed under their own weight. Soon, the people of Iceland, consuming tainted flesh and poisoned water, were in just as wretched shape.

"What passed for meat was both foul-smelling and bitter and full of poison, so that many a person died as a result of eating it," wrote Steingrímsson. "Ridges, growths and bristles appeared on their rib joints, ribs, the backs of their hands, their feet and leg joints. Their bodies became bloated, the insides of their mouths and their gums swelled and cracked causing excruciating pains and toothaches . . . The inner functions and organs were affected by feebleness, shortness of breath, rapid heartbeat, excessive urination and lack of control of those parts. This caused diarrhea, dysentery, worms and sore growths on necks and thighs."

By the end of 1784 more than 10,000 head of cattle — half of Iceland's total — died. Three quarters of the nation's sheep and horses — 190,000 and 27,000 animals respectively — also perished.

Iceland then suffered the worst famine in its history. Those who didn't flee were forced to cook skins, hides, and rope. They mixed hay with old flour to make bread. They dug up roots and ate dandelion leaves. They found old fish bones buried in the sand, cleaned them, crushed them, and mixed them with milk. Some ate horse meat, which usually proved fatal. In Steingrímsson's parishes alone, 215 of 601 inhabitants died from 1783 to 1785. In Iceland as a whole, 10,521 people — one fifth of its 49,863 citizens — perished in the "haze famine." When it was over, the country's population had sunk to its lowest point in 500 years.

The effects of the Laki eruptions were felt far beyond Iceland. Drifting quickly to the southeast, the pall of gas and ash caused crop damage in the Faeroe Islands and Norway. The cloud then spread south in late June, cloaking London, St. Petersburg, Paris, Florence, and other cities in its stifling haze. By July 1, the volcanic fog had turned up in Syria and even wafted all the way to the Altai region of southern Russia, on the Mongolian border. In France, Germany, Holland, Sweden, and Poland, the blue haze hung on for six months.

The "dry fog" was the talk of Europe. Initially, by trapping the heat close to the earth's surface, the haze raised temperatures and cast an eerie gloom over the British Isles and the Continent. The Reverend Gilbert White, a vicar in the village of Selborne, England, called the summer "an amazing and portentous one, and full of horrible phenomena." One British observer spoke of the "dim and sickly eye" of the sun. Horace Walpole said, "The sun sets like a pewter plate red hot."

"The barley . . . became brown and weathered at their extremities, as did the leaves of the oats," wrote the Reverend Sir John Cullum. "Trees . . . shed their leaves plentifully, and littered the walks as in autumn . . . All [the] vegetables appeared exactly as if a fire had been lighted near them, that had shriveled and discolored their leaves."

In Paris, the fog aroused the curiosity of Benjamin Franklin, the United States ambassador to France, who correctly speculated that the bluish haze was linked to the eruption in Iceland.

"This fog was of a permanent nature; it was dry, and the rays of the sun seemed to have little effect towards dissipating it, as they easily do a moist fog," Franklin wrote a year later. "They were indeed rendered so faint in passing through it, that when collected in the focus of a burning glass, they would scarcely kindle brown papers."

Noting that the following winter was abnormally frigid, Franklin attributed it to the "universal fog" blocking the sun's rays. He had heard that Hekla and another Icelandic volcano had erupted, and he surmised that the dry fog could have been caused by "the vast quantity of smoke, long continuing to issue during the summer from *Hecla* in Iceland, and that other volcano which arose out of the sea near that island, which smoke might be spread by various winds, over the northern part of the world."

Laki's most profound effects were not felt until the following several winters. Volcanic ash, with its large particles, falls to the ground or is washed out of the lower atmosphere in a matter of weeks or months. But in major volcanic eruptions, such as Laki, large amounts of sulfur dioxide and other gases are launched high into the sky. Reacting with the sun's rays and water vapor, the SO_2 molecules condense into tiny droplets of sulfuric acid. These aerosols rise into the stratosphere — roughly 10 to 20 miles above the earth — where they can remain for several years. The aerosols then absorb and block some of the sun's rays, which heat the stratosphere but cool the lower atmosphere. In historic times, powerful eruptions have often been followed by several years of significant cooling. Such was the case with Laki.

The winter of 1783–84 was one of the coldest on record in North America and Europe. In the eastern United States, temperatures were roughly 8 degrees F below the 225-year mean. As the geologist Charles A. Wood, formerly of NASA, has pointed out, that winter was the longest in early American history, with New England recording its longest stretch of below-zero temperatures. The East's waterways, Wood wrote, experienced unprecedented freezeovers. The Delaware River at Philadelphia was frozen solid from December 26, 1783, to March 12, 1784. The Chesapeake Bay was frozen for longer than at any time in recorded history. The harbor in Charleston, South Carolina, froze in February, with ice so thick that people went skating. Perhaps most extraordinary, the Mississippi River froze at New Orleans in March, with ice floes 12 to 30 feet long and 2 to 3 feet thick piling up near the shore.

Northern Europe fared no better. Iceland's temperatures that winter were also 8 degrees F below normal, and the sea around the island was frozen longer than at any other time in memory. Temperatures in Stockholm, Copenhagen, Edinburgh, Berlin, Geneva, and Vienna were 5 to 6 degrees F lower than the mean for the late eighteenth century.

The following winter was also unusually cold in North America and Europe, with mean temperatures in the United States still 5 to 6 degrees F below the 225-year mean. Some climatologists have argued that the severe winters of 1783–84 and 1784–85 were not related to Laki but represent weather anomalies that periodically occur around the globe. But most volcanologists and climatologists are convinced that the earth cooled because of the massive amounts of gas and ash emitted from Laki.

For all its power, Laki was a minuscule event compared to the great flood basalt episodes. To get a sense of the scale, consider the following: At Laki, 4 cubic miles of lava and ash poured out of the earth. During the Siberian flood basalts, 500,000 cubic miles of lava and ash — more than 100,000 times greater than Laki — gushed out over the course of a million years. That anything on earth survived after such a cataclysm is miraculous.

Thirty-two years after the greatest nonexplosive eruption of our era, the world witnessed the most powerful explosive eruption in recorded history, one that skewed the global climate even more than Laki and had far greater social impacts worldwide. The blast occurred in April 1815 at Tambora, one of many volcanoes — including

Krakatau, which erupted 68 years later — strung out on the islands of Indonesia. (This necklace of East Indian volcanoes is part of the Pacific "Ring of Fire.") Located on the heavily populated island of Sumbawa, Tambora, at 14,100 feet, was the highest mountain in the East Indies.

In what was probably the most powerful eruption of the last 10,000 years, Tambora ejected 24 to 36 cubic miles of magma, gas, and ash — about 100 to 150 times more than Mount St. Helens. The April 10 blast was heard 1,600 miles away, and its eruption column rose 30 miles into the air. When it collapsed, it spawned at least eight massive pyroclastic flows that traveled 12 miles from the summit and devastated the population of Sumbawa. Ash fell 800 miles away and plunged the area within 300 miles of Tambora into darkness for two days. A volcano-induced tsunami — probably caused by pyroclastic flows sweeping into the sea — traveled 750 miles. Two feet of pumice clogged the Java Sea near Tambora, interfering with shipping; four years later, sailing vessels were still encountering rafts of volcanic debris. The volcano ejected so much material that it caved in on itself, forming a classic caldera more than 4 miles wide and 0.5 mile deep. In the collapse, 4,700 feet of the volcano was lopped off. It now stands at 9,383 feet.

The Tambora eruption was the deadliest in history, killing an estimated 92,000 to 117,000 people. About 10,000 died immediately in pyroclastic flows, the remainder in house collapses, famines, and epidemics as ash blanketed the islands of Sumbawa, Lombok, and Bali.

Tambora also launched roughly 200 million tons of volcanic aerosols into the stratosphere, a huge quantity that was partially responsible for several years of exceedingly cold weather in many parts of the globe. Initially, the vast infusion of gas and ash into the atmosphere and stratosphere created extraordinary sunsets, as the sun's rays were filtered through a volcanic haze. Suffused with brilliant reds and oranges, the sunsets transfixed the British in the summer and fall of 1815. The English landscape painter J.M.W. Turner rendered them on canvas in all their intensity.

But the effects of Tambora were most profoundly felt the following year, which has come to be known in the United States as the "Year Without a Summer." Temperatures in eastern North America and Europe were significantly below normal, and several hard summer frosts and a severely shortened growing season caused crop failures that led to hunger in the United States and famine in parts of Europe. In America, the cold and resulting crop failures prompted a large western migration. In Europe, the famines spurred another westward move — to the United States.

For the citizens of the young American republic, the years 1810–1815 had been colder than normal, apparently because of sunspot activity and other solar anomalies. Crop yields had been below normal in 1813, 1814, and 1815 in the northeastern United States. In 1815 and 1816, Americans had seen the vivid sunsets and noticed a persistent haze that gave the sun a red aura.

On paper, the summer of 1816 does not look radically colder than its predecessors in the eastern United States — only about 3 degrees F below the mean. June temperatures were 5 degrees below the mean. But a freak snowstorm in June and a rolling series of frosts from May through September played havoc with agriculture. In the second week of June, it snowed in fifteen of the nineteen states, accumulating to a foot and a half in parts of New England. In mid-May, severe frosts hit New England as well as Pennsylvania and New Jersey. Hard frosts swept through New England again in mid-June and on July 9, August 21, and August 30.

Chauncey Jerome, the historian of the American clock industry, reported from his home in Plymouth, Connecticut, that "on the 10th of June, my wife brought in the washing frozen stiff . . . On the Fourth of July, I saw several men pitching quoits in the middle of the day with thick overcoats on."

In New Haven, Connecticut, the average temperature in June 1816 was 7 degrees F cooler than the norm. In Montpelier, Vermont, many sheep died of the cold, and prodigious numbers of birds were found dead in the fields. The cold weather also reached the Deep South, which experienced abnormally late frosts and damage to crops, including Louisiana's sugarcane harvest. Even the Caribbean had an unusually cool year, reducing crop yields on Cuba and other islands.

But New England suffered the most. The growing season there — normally 120 to 160 days — was reduced to 70 days in Maine, 75 in New Hampshire, and 80 in Massachusetts. A drought also hit many of the areas affected by the summer frosts. As a result, the staple corn crop was all but wiped out in much of New England, and in many areas frosts also ruined apple crops and killed vegetables. Cattle in New Hampshire died for lack of fodder.

In the wake of these calamities, hunger followed, particularly in northern New England and the interior regions of New Hampshire and Vermont. People ate raccoons, groundhogs, and hedgehogs. To replace ruined row crops, they foraged for roots and grasses.

Nobody knew that the cause of their tribulations may well have been a volcano in the East Indies. They knew only that the air itself had taken on a devilish cast and that winter had come in summer. Many wondered if the end was upon them, and church attendance skyrocketed, marking what one historian called "the greatest religious revival the nation ever knew." Others thought it best not to sit still and wait for the Second Coming, so they headed west. Eastern migrants flocked to the central United States in the fall of 1816. That year, 42,000 Easterners arrived in Indiana alone.

The cold and crop damage was even worse in eastern Canada. And Europe also suffered a freakishly cool summer that had dire consequences for agriculture. Temperatures across Europe, from the British Isles to Italy, were 5 degrees F below the mean. England recorded its lowest June temperatures in history — a mean of 55 degrees F. Ireland experienced an extraordinarily cool, wet spring and summer, which caused the wheat, oat, and potato crops to fail, followed by a famine.

In France the unseasonably cold summer and fall produced the latest wine harvest on record. Cold, wet weather in Switzerland, Germany, and other countries in central Europe also had greatly reduced crop yields. Not only did the abysmal harvests follow several years of poor crop production all over Europe, but the Napoleonic wars had also just ended, leaving Germany particularly weak. Wheat prices doubled in Europe from 1815 to 1817, and in parts of Germany they quadrupled. Food riots broke out, and famine gripped many regions of Germany as well as Ireland, Hungary, and Transylvania, with tens of thousands dying of starvation.

Carl von Klauswitz, traveling through the Prussian Rhineland in the spring of 1817, saw "ruined figures, scarcely resembling men, prowling around the fields searching for food among the unharvested and already half-rotten potatoes that never grew to maturity."

From Ireland to central Europe, the famines and deprivation stimulated a wave of emigration to the United States, Canada, and Russia.

In the summer of 1816, Lord Byron had abandoned his wife in England and gone to Lake Geneva to escape the dreary British climate. He plunged into melancholia as, day after day, the weather was frigid and the skies gray with rain. There were other guests, as well, in the Villa Diodati. One was Mary Shelley, who stayed inside and wrote her novel *Frankenstein*. Trapped in the villa, Byron wrote, too.

Neither he nor anyone else imagined that the blame for the perpetual haze, the cold, the crop failures, and Europe's social upheaval could be traced, in part, to a volcano a world away. But in his poem *Darkness*, written that summer, Byron nonetheless evoked the power of a volcano to darken the earth and ruin lives.

> I had a dream, which was not all a dream.
> The bright sun was extinguish'd, and the stars
> Did wander darkling in the eternal space,
> Rayless, and pathless, and the icy earth
> Swung blind and blackening in the moonless air;
> Morn came and went — and came and brought no day,
> And men forgot their passions in the dread
> Of this their desolation; and all hearts

Were chill'd into a selfish prayer for light:
And they did live by watchfires — and the thrones,
The palaces of crowned kings — the huts,
The habitations of all things which dwell,
Were burnt for beacons; cities were consumed,
And men were gather'd round their blazing homes
To look once more into each other's face.

11
....

RECOVERY

ARLY ON SUNDAY, January 17, three and a half days after the eruption, the Learjet ambulance landed in Phoenix. A medical team was waiting for me — overkill, perhaps, but then again, they'd never worked on an eruption survivor. I was transferred to the Barrow Neurological Institute, where a brain surgeon soon pulled Lynda aside and told her, "We're lucky he's alive. It's good that he recognized you. He's going to be able to feed himself and brush his teeth, and beyond that we just don't know at this point."

An orthopedic surgeon — a groggy, disheveled man who looked decidedly unhappy to be treating an injured volcanologist at 3 A.M. — wasn't much more upbeat. After the casts on my legs were removed, revealing protruding bones and exposed patches of chewed-up flesh, he studied the mess and said, "I hate these gift packages from South America." That was enough to light Lynda's fuse; she informed him that he could either get some rest or stop caring for her husband. He returned in 30 minutes, refreshed and civil.

The doctors concurred that the best course of action was to clean me up and begin the heavy reconstruction work on Monday. At this point I didn't much care. I was happy to be alive and in the antiseptic confines of an American hospital, surrounded by doctors and nurses who spoke English and seemed eminently capable of putting me back together again.

That Monday, when the doctors began to repair my mangled right leg, I underwent the first of seventeen operations designed to return my body to some semblance of its former state. At times I felt like Frankenstein, with surgeons nearly removing my right foot before putting it back in better alignment and virtually lopping off an ear to undo the damage inside. They also cut and pasted swaths of flesh and chunks of skull. This torture went on for nearly two years. But I can tell you this much: What I endured physically pales when compared with the psychological trials I've experienced as a result of my brain injury. I'd gladly have traded a leg in exchange for never having been slammed in the head by a volcanic bomb.

Where to start? I'll begin with the easy repairs.

My jaw was broken, so the doctors wired it shut, forcing me to subsist on liquids for a month. My nose was broken and the surgeons straightened it out. When the first adjustment on the nose failed, they did it again. They slapped a few skin grafts on my burned legs. They pulled the wires out of my jaw, saw it wasn't opening fully, then did microsurgery to correct the problem. They performed plastic surgery on my ear and both legs. There wasn't much they could do about my brain injury, but I still had a quarter-size hole in my head where I'd lost a piece of my skull. So a neurosurgeon cut a circle of bone out of my skull, sliced it in two, did a little sanding, and plugged both the holes in my head.

After three weeks in the hospital, I noticed I couldn't hear a thing in my left ear. My doctors had been good, but each tended to his or her specialty. No one had looked at me as a whole, so it took nearly a month to figure out that the eruption had destroyed my hearing in one ear. It turned out that small stones had blasted through my eardrum and broken some tiny bones in the middle ear. Opening me up, the ear surgeon saw that I literally had rocks in my head. He extracted them, cleaned up the scar tissue, and reshaped one of the broken bones. The nerves in the inner ear hadn't been damaged, and he was confident I'd hear again. But after the operation I was still deaf. I had a second operation. Still deaf. A specialist at the House Ear Clinic in Los Angeles took a whack at it. Still deaf. All the doctors were mystified. Now I wear a hearing aid.

But the real challenge involved the shattered right leg. Nearly severed just above the ankle, it had lost 1½ inches of bone. On that first Monday, Dr. Charles Gauntt closed and stitched the wounds, then secured the leg inside a metal frame that consisted of two parallel, 18-inch rods. Screws ran from the rods through my flesh and into the shattered bone. I didn't walk for three weeks, then hobbled on crutches. Two months later Dr. Gauntt — hoping to return my leg to its normal length — performed a bone graft. He removed a chunk of bone from my pelvis, then inserted it into the void where I'd lost a piece of my leg. He sewed me up, screwed the frame back into my leg, and sent me on my way.

Three months later it was time to see if the bone graft had been successful. Using a carpenter's brace, Dr. Gauntt cranked out the screws. I have a high tolerance for pain, but it was more than I could bear, for the bone had grown into the screws. Nearly fainting from the agony, I asked the doctor for some Demerol. He complied, we waited awhile, and he finished unscrewing the brace. As soon as it came off, we both could see the graft had failed. Just above the ankle, my lower right leg looked like Jell-O, and the foot began flopping around once more. The leg was too severely injured for a standard bone graft. Dr. Gauntt went over my options. He could amputate the lower leg and fit me with an artificial limb. Or I could walk on crutches the rest of my life. Neither scenario held much appeal. What else could be done? I inquired. Dr. Gauntt replied that there was an orthopedic surgeon in Phoenix trained in the use of the Ilazarov device, also know as the "Russian birdcage." Developed by a Soviet surgeon, the machine was used to repair massive breaks and lengthen bones. Given my situation, the "Russian birdcage" sounded like a good bet.

I went to see Dr. Vincent J. Russo, Jr., who told me I was a prime candidate for the device. On July 9, 1993, the day before I turned forty-one, I underwent yet another operation as Dr. Russo spent several hours installing the birdcage. First, he broke the healthy bone just below my knee. Then he removed the dead and injured bone in my lower leg and aligned the broken parts. After that, he installed the superstructure of the Ilazarov device. It consisted of three steel rings encircling the lower leg, connected by steel rods. Dr. Russo then ran a series of long screws and titanium wires from the rings through my flesh, into the bone, and out the other side.

I pinned all my hopes on the birdcage, knowing that if it failed I would be crippled for life. The principle of the device was simple; it relied on the ability of bones to grow and regenerate. Every day I was supposed to turn a screw that would pull apart the bones just below my knee by 1 millimeter, or $\frac{1}{25}$ inch. As I gradually expanded the gap between the bones at the site of the clean break, new bone would fill in the void, growing like stalactites and stalagmites. In theory, at the end of nine months I would have 1½ inches of new leg. Meanwhile, the lower break, completely supported by the Ilazarov frame, would have time to fuse and mend.

The contraption sounds more painful than it actually was, but it was a nuisance. With all the rods and wires penetrating my flesh and bone, I had to clean the entry and exit holes every day with antibacterial soap. The tightly drawn wires also had a tendency to snap, which sounded like a gunshot. Once a wire popped as I was teaching a class, startling my students and opening up a small wound that dribbled blood down my leg.

Despite my battered condition, my initial recovery progressed quickly, and I was out of the hospital within a month. The neurosurgeons and neuropsychologists thought I was doing remarkably well, but they cautioned that wounds in the temple can cause seizures, depression, and problems with mental function. In those early days, however, I was optimistic, for the fog in my brain was clearing. I never doubted that I was going to recover and get back to work on volcanoes.

The nonstop tinkering with my body left me with few quiet moments, but when they came I was haunted by the thought that Igor, Geoff, Nestor, José Arlés, and the others had died in the eruption. I didn't sit in my hospital bed, replaying that day on Galeras and wondering how things might have turned out differently. We had done what we needed to do on the volcano, and I felt no guilt. I missed my friends, however, and felt terrible for their families.

As I struggled to accept these deaths I was consoled by letters and visits from friends and colleagues. One of the most touching notes came from Geoff Brown's widow, Evelyn, who wrote to Lynda two weeks after the eruption:

> Please assure [Stan] that he must not yield to any sense of guilt he may experience on Geoff's behalf or any of the others who were lost. Geoff was a gambler. He gambled in every facet of his life and would always weigh up the possible benefits of a course of action against the potential risks. If the former was only marginally greater, he would take the action. I am quite sure in my own mind that even if he had known there was a fairly strong chance the volcano would erupt any day, he would still have entered the crater on the grounds that the knowledge gained from measurements at that time was worth the risk.
>
> No one could stop him once he'd made up his mind to do something. I am a geologist at the Open University, too, and so have been very well aware for some years of the dangers that Geoff exposed himself to. The accident was nobody's fault except good old nature — a gentle reminder that we may think we are learning to control or manipulate geological hazards, but the Earth has a mind of its own . . .
>
> Geoff lived his life to the full and told his daughters only at Christmas that if it was a choice between a heart attack or road accident (both very high risks in his case), or the sort of accident that befell him, he'd far rather the latter. He died doing what he really enjoyed doing most — and few of us will ever have this rare privilege in life.

In those first weeks and months, I was distracted by more than operations, physical therapy, and condolences. The media swarmed over this story, particularly after I gave a lengthy interview to the *New York Times* that became the basis of a major article on February 9, 1993. When the article was published, I was inundated with requests from the media, particularly television, and appeared on the NBC *Nightly News* and the *Today* show. Later, I was featured in numerous documentaries, including *National Geographic, Discov-*

ery, and *Dateline NBC.* I had my 15 minutes of fame and then some, and I liked it. I had always seen part of my scientific mission as educating the public, be it my students or Tom Brokaw's audience. I was always good at translating the complexities of volcanology into straightforward terms, and after the eruption I also found that talking to reporters and film crews was a pleasant distraction that fed my not inconsiderable ego. But in time I came to realize that this ceaseless performance had insidious effects.

As the months passed, and then years, it became clear that I was not the wunderkind I had been before Galeras. I was physically weaker, my mind was not as sharp, and I was not doing the groundbreaking work I had done before 1993. Increasingly, I filled this void by playing the survivor. I was no longer a pioneering volcanologist. I was the guy who lived through the eruption that killed six other scientists. I was the guy on the front page of the *New York Times.* People recognized me in stores. Friends and acquaintances identified me as the man who made it off the volcano alive. I became Mr. Galeras.

I regret another aspect of my notoriety. Although three other eyewitnesses — Mike Conway, Andy Macfarlane, and Luis LeMarie — remembered a different scenario just before the eruption, I continued to stick to my version, which diminished their role. I remembered sending my three colleagues and the tourists down from the crater rim. I remembered being the last survivor on the lip of the volcano when it blew. I told this story to the press time and again. Though some of my colleagues reminded me that my version differed greatly from those of the other survivors, that I was unfairly downplaying their presence, I kept telling the tale because I firmly believed it to be true. I never claimed to be the sole survivor, but some news stories pinned that tag on me. Then, when Katie Couric called me the sole survivor on the *Today* show, I did not contradict her. I was the leader of the field trip, I was the most seriously injured survivor, and I was at the center of the action that day. But for some reason that wasn't enough. I continued to gloss over the involvement of the three other survivors, and for that I am sorry.

Later, Peter Baxter discussed my case with a neurologist he knew at Cambridge. The specialist believed that since I had suffered a subdural hematoma, I almost certainly would have lost consciousness for some period — perhaps only seconds — after being struck in the head. He also said that the chances were very good that I would have lost some memory of the events immediately preceding the blow. People who sustain head injuries in car crashes, for example, often can't recall the moments leading up to the crash, nor do they remember losing consciousness. The worse the injury, the more memory lost. I remember rocks tumbling down the crater walls in the seconds before the eruption, whereas my colleagues recall the rockfall minutes before the blast. I remember telling my colleagues to start heading down the cone, but had they actually done so? I realize now that the blow to my head may have caused me to forget or jumble events just before the eruption. What is odd, however, is how vivid my recollections are. Mike, Luis, and Andy would say that my version is wrong. I concede that my memory of events just before the eruption may be faulty, but given the trauma we all experienced, I don't accept their account as gospel, either.

Wherever the truth may lie, one fact is incontrovertible: My brain injury, with all its physical and psychological consequences, has dogged me every day since the fourteenth of January 1993. The smashed leg was a nuisance, but one that could be overcome. In May 1994, ten months after I was fitted with the Russian birdcage, Dr. Russo operated on me and removed the device. It had worked. The ruined section of my lower right leg had fused together, and the leg-lengthening procedure was a success. I had a new, 1½-inch chunk of leg below the knee, and with physical therapy and exercise I was eventually able to walk again without a limp.

But just one month later, my damaged brain demonstrated that it was more impervious to healing. On June 4, 1994, I was preparing to fly to Chile the next day to work on a volcano that had recently begun erupting — my first trip to a volcano since Galeras. My recovery was going well, and I was optimistic that my career was getting back on track.

As usual I woke up, took out the dog, and crawled back into bed with a cup of coffee for Lynda. She remembers being awakened from a sound sleep by a violent shaking. At first she thought it was our dog, who hops on the bed most mornings, but when she turned over she saw me thrashing about. My eyes had rolled back into my head, my body was rigid, my face was turning blue. I was having a grand mal seizure — something the neurologists had expected all along but that Lynda and I thought I would avoid. The seizure subsided, and when I regained consciousness Lynda was hovering over me.

"Stanley! Can you hear me? Do you know what happened? We have to go to the hospital immediately. You've had a seizure and they need to check you."

My son, Nick, who has watched his share of television, came into the bedroom in the midst of the seizure, learned what was happening, then ran upstairs and announced to his sister: "Daddy's having a Frasier!"

That was the only humor I could find in the situation. The trip to Chile was off, the seizure a major setback. A grand mal seizure is like an electrical storm in the brain, a potentially deadly deluge of misfiring neurons. My neurologists said seizures are a common aftereffect of a major brain injury and had to be controlled. I began taking Dilantin, the first of several antiseizure medications I would try. For me, the medicines seemed worse than the affliction itself, as I was beset with sleepiness, irritability, and other symptoms not salutary for a marriage. In the eighteen months since the eruption, Lynda had been a patient and compassionate nurse, and our relationship was returning to normal. But the seizure, and the onslaught of symptoms from the medication, marked the beginning of a downward spiral in our marriage.

People often ask me if, after such a close brush with death, I wake up every day and thank God I am alive. Do I see life through new eyes and live it with a new intensity? I would like to offer them a stirring testimonial, to say that I've been reborn. I'm afraid I can't. I am grateful, of course, that I lived, and in the beginning life did seem sweeter. But that feeling wore off, and I was left realizing that I was a different person. I mixed up words and numbers, forgot things easily, tired quickly, worked more slowly, concentrated poorly, had trouble getting organized, and — most distressing — had difficulty with the kind of higher, abstract reasoning that is essential to scientific research.

Before 1993, I always had three or four graduate students working under me and was juggling a handful of projects at any given time. I pulled down grants like ripe fruit from a tree. But as my recovery proceeded, I realized that the graduate students, the grants, and the research projects were disappearing. I was angry that I was no longer the scientist I had been, angry that I felt poorly, angry that my struggles were hurting my family. Most people experience a diminishment of their mental and physical capabilities over a period of several decades. Mine unfolded before my eyes in a year or two, and it infuriated me. But that's not all bad, for it has been my anger, my desire to be the scientist I once was, that has kept me going these past seven years.

Always, I put on a good public face. In August 1994 I made the first of a half-dozen trips back to Galeras, several of them with a television crew in tow. No sooner had I landed with the people from *Dateline NBC* than Galeras began emitting long-period *tornillo* signals. I didn't venture near the crater on that trip, but I told the reporter, Robert Bazell, what I told every reporter after that: Galeras hadn't defeated me. I was not afraid of the volcano. I would continue to study it. In the end, I would conquer Galeras.

The following year I returned to the crater for the first time. In the same cloudy weather that we experienced on January 14, 1993, I descended the amphitheater scarp, nudging aside my fears. Climbing the cone, trudging up the scree where I and the others had been felled, was unsettling. But I concentrated on the gas samples Marta and I were taking, telling myself lightning would not strike twice. The next day I ventured into the crater again, something I had often done with no difficulty. But this time the second trip exhausted me. I could barely make it up the amphitheater wall on my own. Three days later, sapped of energy, I developed pneumonia and had to be hospitalized in Pasto for two days. Once again, Galeras showed me who was boss.

*   *   *

Although I felt I was working at half speed, I continued traveling around the world, studying active volcanoes. Through an insidious depression, through endless stretches of self-doubt — a corrosive emotion I had never known before the eruption — I was sustained by the goals that had driven my career: improving the forecasting of eruptions and saving lives. I was proud of the work I had done in my first fifteen years as a volcanologist, and I was determined not to let Galeras bring it to an end. Following in Dick Stoiber's footsteps, I further refined the use of the COSPEC and continued studying volcanic gases from Central America to the Kurile Islands in the Russian Far East. In 1994 I felt a surge of the old adrenaline as I rushed off to measure sulfur dioxide pouring from the reactivated, 17,929-foot Popocatépetl near Mexico City. A few months later I flew to Papua New Guinea, where the twin volcanoes Vulcan and Tavurvur were erupting simultaneously.

The volcanoes, 5 miles apart and flanking Simpson Harbor, are perched on the outer edge of a large caldera formed by massive eruptions over the past 5,000 years. The blue waters of the bay cover the remains of an ancient, imploded volcano to form a superb natural harbor that was a Japanese stronghold in World War II. Both Tavurvur and Vulcan are about 6 miles from the city of Rabaul, population 50,000, and when they blew at the same time, we feared that the entire caldera might be on the verge of a cataclysmic eruption.

In the 1980s, the caldera had been shaken by swarms of earthquakes and had risen by 3 feet. Scientists at the Rabaul Volcano Observatory did a good job of educating people about the danger, mapping out escape routes, and staging mock evacuations. I worked there in 1983 and 1989, sampling gases and teaching scientists how to use a COSPEC, which I helped them acquire from the Canadian government.

On September 18, 1994, Rabaul was shaken by a series of earthquakes. The following morning, at 6 A.M., Tavurvur opened the eruption sequence. Shortly afterward, drawing off the same magma body, Vulcan blew, pumping a column of ash and gas 12 miles into the air. The residents of Rabaul evacuated in a quick, orderly fashion, and it was a good thing. Within several hours, the city was buried under about 20 inches of ash, its weight causing many roofs to cave in. Only five people died, thanks to the smooth evacuation.

I arrived several days after the eruptions began, flying over a city whose lush greenery had been shredded by the rain of ash. Thousands of flimsily constructed structures had collapsed in a gray jumble. My graduate student, Steve Schaefer, and I pointed the COSPEC out the plane window and measured 25,000 tons of SO_2 roaring out of the mouth of Tavurvur every day, a huge amount. Over the next ten days, that figure fell to 3,000 tons a day, a clear indication that Tavurvur — Vulcan had already shut down — was past the peak of its activity despite the plume of ash still shooting from the crater.

Schaefer and I also rode a helicopter to the base of Tavurvur, where the ash was nearly 3 feet deep, and scooped up a cross section of the volcanic fallout. We worked only a half mile below the crater, and the noise of the eruptions was deafening. Feeling the concussive wave of the blasts, we looked up to see refrigerator-size blocks of debris flying out of Tavurvur's mouth. The Galeras eruption, just twenty months earlier, was still fresh in my mind, and Steve and I worked frantically to collect the ash. Our helicopter, its engine idling, waited nearby.

The chemical composition of the ash samples showed us that the magma pool feeding the volcanoes was gradually being tapped out. That finding, coupled with the declining SO_2 emissions, enabled us to tell the local authorities, with reasonable surety, that the worst of the eruption was over. We hadn't forecast the events, but we were able to help answer two crucial questions in the wake of an eruption: Is it really over, and can people return to their homes?

Volcanology has moved so far and so fast in the past quarter century that forecasting some eruptions is now within our grasp. With increasing accuracy, we can tell when a volcano is heating up. The big question is whether the accelerated activity is just "nature's noise" or whether an eruption is imminent. On that front, we still have a ways to go. Indeed, no volcanologist would ever use the word "predict." In fact, even "forecast" makes us nervous. But when everything breaks just right — when a volcano behaves in textbook fashion and when we throw lots of money and manpower at it — we have been successful. Pinatubo, in the Philippines, was just such a case.

Located on the main island of Luzon, 5,725-foot Pinatubo hadn't erupted in 500 years. It looked benign, but the geological record showed that it had experienced three large eruptions in the past 5,500 years, disgorging voluminous pyroclastic flows, mudflows, and ashfalls.

In late 1990 and early 1991, a series of earthquakes marked the end of Pinatubo's dormancy. Filipino and American officials paid close attention, not least because Clark Air Force Base — an American installation with 14,500 servicemen and their families — was just 15 miles away. Chris Newhall, another protégé of Dick Stoiber's, arrived in late April with a contingent of USGS scientists, who had long worked closely with Filipino geologists. The Philippines is a country of intense volcanic activity, and its scientists — like the USGS crew — were experienced in dropping in on an active volcano and quickly taking its pulse. (The success at Pinatubo points up a paradox of volcanology — in order to forecast eruptions better, we need more of them. Meteorologists have become good at forecasting the tracks of hurricanes because they've been able to study scores of storms.)

Establishing a network of seven seismic stations around Pinatubo, Filipino and USGS volcanologists observed an increasing number of earthquakes under the volcano in May and early June. They also detected long-period quakes, an indication of magmatic fluids working their way to the surface. The volcano's fumaroles became roaring vents as the gas pressure increased. Using a COSPEC, the geologists tracked a sharp rise in sulfur dioxide emissions. Then, on May 31, emissions of SO_2 abruptly declined, indicating that the volcano was becoming plugged.

On June 7, 1,500 earthquakes rumbled under the volcano. With geologists forecasting an imminent eruption, the Filipinos began evacuating 58,000 people who lived in hazard zones within 20 miles, including along the river valleys that would serve as conduits for pyroclastic flows and mudflows. As American and Filipino geologists sought to demonstrate the dangers of Pinatubo, they showed Maurice Krafft's video "Understanding Volcanic Hazards" to both officials and residents. It had a major impact, persuading many that evacuation was necessary. As the film was being shown, Maurice and Katia were killed by the pyroclastic flow at Unzen.

On June 10, with Pinatubo's flanks swelling and a magma dome forming inside its crater, the U.S. government evacuated 14,500 servicemen and their families at Clark Air Force Base. Two days later, a pair of eruptions propelled a column of gas and ash 13 miles in the air and deposited ash on the surrounding countryside. Then, on June 15, Pinatubo reached the climax of its eruption, uncorking a classic Plinian blast that threw a column of ash and gas 21 miles into the sky and sent pyroclastic flows sweeping 10 miles down river valleys, engulfing recently evacuated villages. A large typhoon sideswiped Luzon at the same time, and the eruption and hurricane combined to create about ten large mudflows that roared as far as 22 miles from the crater. Two inches of ash fell over an area of 1,500 square miles, burying Clark Air Force Base. Pinatubo's was one of the most powerful eruptions of the twentieth century, ejecting seven times as much debris as Mount St. Helens. Yet relatively few people — about three hundred — died, most from being crushed by roofs collapsing under the weight of the ash.

Scientists on the scene were able to forecast the eruption because the volcano ratcheted up its activity in incremental stages, sending out clear signals that it was preparing for a major blast. USGS and Filipino geologists did a superb job monitoring the volcano, and by the time it was ready to blow, officials had evacuated more than 70,000 people. Had nothing been done, thousands of people — possibly tens of thousands — could have been killed or injured.

Our ability to pull off another forecast like Pinatubo is improving rapidly. Reading a volcano's seismic signals and studying its gas emissions remain the two most reliable ways of deciphering its activity. Earthquake monitoring, with the help of sophisticated computer programs, is becoming so advanced that scientists were later able to come up with something like a CT scan image of the inside of Pinatubo, showing the size of its magma chamber. As seismology advances, my colleagues may one day be able to produce such images in real time and track the movement of magma toward the surface. They will, in other words, be able to do something geologists have dreamed of doing for ages — look inside the earth.

All this requires more money, and volcanology gets little of it. NASA's annual budget is about $14 billion a year. The amount of federal money spent on volcano research is minuscule by comparison — several million dollars annually in National Science Foundation grants and roughly $20 million a year in USGS spending. Even another $10 million funneled our way each year would considerably advance our science.

When and where will the next volcanic disaster strike? We don't really know, but there are some things we can say with certainty. First, 1,500 active volcanoes worldwide potentially threaten about 500 million people. Second, rapid population growth in the developing world has put far more people near volcanoes than ever before. Third, in any given year, about 50 volcanoes erupt worldwide. Fourth, every decade the world experiences an eruption the size of that at Mount St. Helens, every century we see an eruption the size of Pinatubo's, and every 500 to 1,000 years we can expect a blast as massive as Tambora's. Fifth, the earth has been shaped by eruptions far larger than these, and at some time in the coming millennia — perhaps in 2,000 years, perhaps in 50,000 — we are likely to see an apocalyptic blast that could kill millions of people and seriously alter the earth's climate. But 50,000 years is a long way off and, in any case, some other cataclysm may well do us in long before.

My comprehension of the threat posed by the world's volcanoes came in stages. In 1978 Dick Stoiber helped me understand that about 90 percent of Guatemala's population is living on pyroclastic flow deposits. Two years later, at Mount St. Helens, I saw the phenomenal destruction wrought by a blast that, geologically speaking, was fairly small. In 1983, in Indonesia, Dick Stoiber once again encouraged me to open my eyes and see that the country's 175 million people were living amid a forest of highly explosive volcanoes, such as Tambora and Krakatau. In 1985, at Nevado del Ruiz, I learned at first hand how a distant volcano can wipe out a city in a matter of hours.

The United States has 67 volcanoes that have been active in the past several thousand years — 15 in the western states, 52 in Alaska, and 10 on Hawaii. Alaska's are the most active, but are generally remote. Hawaii's are in populated areas, but not explosive. Of the 15 active volcanoes in the western United States, some are periodically explosive, some are close to population centers, and most bear watching. One of the biggest wild cards is Mammoth Mountain, a picturesque, 11,121-foot peak in California's Sierra Nevada, east of Yosemite National Park. On winter weekends, 30,000 skiers and tourists pour into the Mammoth Mountain area, most of them unaware that they are whizzing down slopes perched on top of an active volcanic system. Mammoth sits on the edge of the Long Valley caldera, a 20- by 10-mile bowl created 700,000 years ago by a blast five hundred times more powerful than the eruption at Mount St. Helens. But Long Valley has experienced eruptions as recently as 500 years ago, and over the past two decades numerous signs — including carbon dioxide emissions, the swelling of the caldera floor, and countless earthquakes, one of which badly damaged a local high school — have served as reminders that this volcanic system is anything but dormant. USGS scientists do not expect an eruption soon, but they are monitoring Mammoth Mountain and Long Valley carefully — a reminder that what we see as terra firma is often inherently unstable ground.

Mount St. Helens is the most striking example of a dangerous volcano, but its neighbors in the Cascades are far from benign. One volcano that concerns us is Mount Rainier, which the United Nations selected — along with Galeras — as a "decade" volcano that needs more intensive study. Rainier, 14,409 feet high, is just 75 miles southeast of Seattle, where the suburbs continue to creep toward the volcano. Rainier, which last erupted in 1825, does not have a history of highly explosive blasts. But its summit is covered in snow and glaciers, and even a small eruption — like that of Nevado del Ruiz in 1985 — could create sizable mudflows. The landscape around Rainier shows signs of older mudflows, including one, the Osceola deposit, that is thirty-five times the size of the Nevado del Ruiz *lahar*. About 5,000 years ago, the Osceola *lahars* poured off Rainier and rolled all the way to Puget Sound, 50 miles northwest. Roughly 100,000 people live near Rainier on these deposits, and the number grows every year. The USGS has installed seismic monitoring stations on the mountain and should have some warning of an eruption. But officials need to heed the ancient signs of the Osceola deposits and restrict development in *lahar* zones along river valleys. If volcanology has taught us anything, it's that the past is prelude to the future.

No starker example of that axiom exists than Mount Vesuvius. Today, as volcanologists look around the globe at potential disasters, Vesuvius is at the top of everyone's list. The world's most famous volcano has what it takes to create real havoc. It has erupted regularly over the past 2,000 years, unleashing a smorgasbord of deadly and destructive volcanic hazards, including pyroclastic flows, ashfalls, tsunamis, and lava flows. Today, the population around Vesuvius, which includes Naples, is many times larger than it was in A.D. 79 or 1631, when powerful Plinian eruptions killed thousands. Three million people live within reach of Vesuvius today, and the region — with as many as 50,000 people per square mile — is one of the most densely populated in the world. About a million people live within 4 miles of the volcano, and experts like Peter Baxter estimate that nearly all of them would be at risk in a major eruption.

Vesuvius's last sizable eruption was in 1944, about two generations ago, which is enough time for people to forget the threat the volcano poses. Today, houses and vineyards creep up the mountain's flanks, just as they did in the time of Pliny the Elder. Torre del Greco, the town just south of Vesuvius on the Bay of Naples, has been destroyed several times in the past few thousand years. Yet today its population is larger than ever. Naples itself sits between the great volcano and the Campi Phlegraei, or "Flaming Fields," whose vents can spew out ash, pyroclastic flows, and lava.

To grasp what Vesuvius could do to the Naples area today, you need look no farther than the words of Pliny the Younger and the geological record. Pliny the Younger and his mother were caught in the outer edge of a pyroclastic surge that swept from Vesuvius all the way across the Bay of Naples to Misenum, 20 miles west. This surge passed over what are now heavily populated parts of Naples and its outskirts. Such a pyroclastic surge today could destroy everything in its path and set Naples on fire. Pliny's uncle expired in the weakened, leading edge of a pyroclastic flow that had traveled from the volcano to Stabiae, 10 miles south. A similar *nuée ardente* today would devastate many towns, villages, and suburbs in the shadow of Vesuvius.

The A.D. 79 eruption is only one of four large, Plinian eruptions that have rocked Vesuvius in the past 2,000 years, the others being in A.D. 472, 512, and 1631. In the 1631 blast, at least 4,000 people died in pyroclastic flows and ashfalls. The volcano has also experienced dozens of smaller blasts, undergoing eighteen eruptive cycles from 1631 to 1944. Many of those eruptions were lethal, including the 1794 blast witnessed by Sir William Hamilton, which killed more than four hundred people.

Volcanologists can almost always tell if Vesuvius (or any volcano) is heating up. The problem is that often we can't say if, and when, it's going to blow, which weakens our credibility with the public. Such was the case in the early 1980s, when swarms of earthquakes shook the southern edge of the Campi Phlegraei just as the earth began to swell from the pressure of rising magma. In the port town of Pozzuoli, the ground near the harbor inflated roughly 8 feet, leaving the docks too high for boats to moor. In October 1984 officials wisely evacuated 40,000 people from Pozzuoli and its environs. But when no eruption followed, both residents and politicians were furious, accusing the scientists of crying wolf. As usual, the decision to order an evacuation was tricky. Sometimes, as at Pinatubo, scientists and politicians make the right call. And sometimes, as at Pozzuoli, we play it safe and incur the public's wrath.

Such problems have been compounded at Vesuvius as Italian vol-canologists have fought bitterly over the best way to deal with the danger. The Vesuvius Observatory, the first of its kind in the world, has worked with civil defense officials on a hazard plan that defines the areas of greatest risk and establishes evacuation procedures. When Vesuvius wakes up again, the observatory will issue scientific alerts in seven stages based on the perceived risk. The plan calls for at least 600,000 people to be evacuated by train within seven days. But critics, including the controversial volcanologist Flavio Dobran, have attacked this strategy, arguing that the volcano might not give the region a week's grace period before it blows and that evacuating more than a half million people by train would be absurdly chaotic. Dobran, a theoretician who has done computer models of future eruptions and pyroclastic flows, insists that much more than a mas-sive evacuation plan is needed. He proposes permanently relocating people from the most hazardous areas well before a future eruption and constructing strong, airtight shelters in which people can seek refuge from pyroclastic flows.

Meanwhile, Vesuvius may be preparing for its next show. Recent studies indicate that since the last eruption, in 1944, a large quantity of magma — as much as 2.5 million cubic yards — has moved up be-neath the volcano. Should gas pressure build and the magma body erupt, it could trigger a blast equivalent to the 1631 eruption.

A painting of that eruption shows the smoking cone of Vesu-vius — its height reduced 1,640 feet by the blast — rising above the curved Bay of Naples. Hundreds of people can be seen fleeing the eruption in panic, but otherwise the panoramic picture, executed from the west, shows a pastoral landscape dotted with a few farms and houses.

Today, 370 years later, the view of Vesuvius hasn't changed much. But where once there were a few dozen buildings and fields, now there are 3 million people, most of whom ignore the peril that forms a striking backdrop to their daily lives.

12

·················

SURVIVING GALERAS

MINERAL-ENCRUSTED fumaroles and steaming craters, with all their intimations of the earth's power, still exert a strong pull over me. Although I move more slowly now, there are few places I'd rather be than on a volcano, crouching next to a fissure and sampling gases as clouds sweep over the mountains. It's a feeling of contentment I don't experience much in the lowlands anymore.

Not long ago I was back again on Galeras with Marta, poking titanium sampling tubes into the Deformes fumarole and taking a look at the crater. A portion of the southwestern lip had sloughed into the volcano's mouth, leaving a parapet of jagged, andesitic boulders connecting the southern and western rims. The volcano has been tranquil for a few years, save an occasional, tiny explosion, and gases were streaming out of the crater bottom at moderate temperatures and pressure. As we walked on the edge of the crater toward the western rim, the clouds dispersed, revealing blue sky. The equatorial sun flooded the Azufral and Guaitara valleys with light. We were on top of it all, gazing down at coffee plantations and jungle nearly 2 miles below. My happiness was dampened only by the torturous climb up the amphitheater escarpment, where I was forced to pause every few steps. I had never felt so winded, my expletives coming in short, indecipherable bursts as my lungs heaved.

Galeras belongs to Marta now. She and I have remained good friends — indeed, since the eruption we have been closer than ever.

As the faculty adviser for her Ph.D., I was in the awkward position of heading a committee that would pass judgment on the woman who had saved my life. I asked Ed Stump, the chairman of our department, if I should recuse myself as her adviser. He said that he knew of no precedent and told me to continue shepherding Marta through the dissertation process. She received her degree in 1995.

Eighteen months after the eruption, as she wrapped up her research on Galeras's eruptive history, I joined Marta on a grueling, day-long, 10-mile hike over the steep, forested ridges that are the flanks of a half-million-year-old incarnation of Galeras. She described the ancient lava flows and U-shaped valleys that glaciers had carved into the volcanic landscape 9,000 years ago. A cold rain fell and at times we slogged through knee-deep mud. But despite the muck and my growing fatigue, I took pleasure in seeing how thoroughly she had unearthed Galeras's history.

Although I travel to the volcano less than I used to, I still manage to see Marta about once a year, either in the United States or Colombia. While she always inquires about my ongoing recuperation, Marta is a private person, and we rarely talk about the eruption and how it changed her life. Once, when I pressed her, she told me that the hardest thing was the loss of her close friend José Arlés Zapata and the effect it had on his widow, Monica. Although Nevado del Ruiz had been a far larger tragedy, it never affected Marta the way Galeras did. She had not known the victims at Armero, but she had been close to José Arlés and Nestor and had met the other scientists who died. After the eruption, it was Marta who accompanied Igor's daughter, Geoff's daughter, and Fernando Cuenca's widow to Galeras. She never talked much about those visits except to say how moved she was by the suffering of these women.

Since the eruption, Marta and her twelve-member observatory staff have continued to watch the volcano closely. They have learned a great deal about Galeras's seismic rumblings and emission of gases. Much of that progress came after the series of eruptions from February through June of that year, which taught us the potential importance of the *tornillo,* long-period earthquakes at Galeras. The results of our conference and subsequent studies on Galeras filled an entire volume of the *Journal of Volcanology and Geothermal Research* in May 1997. Thanks to the work of Marta and other Colombian and American scientists, we are closer to being able to forecast when the volcano will blow than we were a decade ago.

Was this progress worth the lives of Igor Menyailov, Geoff Brown, José Arlés Zapata, Nestor García, and the others? Of course not. Did they die in vain? I don't think so. If someone were to argue that they did, I would counter that such reasoning dictates that we should clear volcanologists off volcanoes altogether. That would have disastrous consequences for those who live near volcanoes. You never know what results you're going to get until you actually climb the volcano and work on it. The balance of risk versus reward was summed up by Don Swanson of the USGS not long after the Galeras tragedy:

> Curiosity leads to understanding, and understanding is the paramount goal of science as well as the soundest basis for reducing risk. Volcanologists who are curious will get themselves into trouble and sometimes die because of it. It is often stated that we must weigh the potential benefits and risks before doing something that may be perceived as risky. Of course we must, but it is mathematically impossible to solve one equation with two unknowns, and generally the potential benefits and risks are both unknowns. In the end it comes down to common sense, which varies among individuals and in any case is far from foolproof. Let it be no other way, and let us praise the curious as we mourn the dead.

In the villages and towns near Galeras, most people still keep an eye on the volcano, but they are confident that even if it blows, the destruction won't come their way. In the summer of 1999, I spent a day circumnavigating the lower flanks of Galeras and talking to the people there. Even in the areas that INGEOMINAS has identified as high-hazard zones — the valley of the Rio Azufral on the west and the towns of La Florida, Nariño, and Jenoy to the north — people thought Galeras wasn't likely to harm them.

"I'm not afraid, because the volcano doesn't hurt anybody," said Carmilla Bastidas, eighty-six, who lives in the Azufral Valley on Galeras's western slope. "The volcano is our brother. Anyway, if God wants to kill everybody he will."

On the opposite side of Galeras, in Jenoy, I stopped at a small, pink stucco house to sample the grilled guinea pig being sold by the owner. On a cool, sunny afternoon, we stood on the lower flanks of the volcano and talked about the threat. She worried about Galeras and its intermittent eruptions. But she also knew that the only people killed by the volcano in recent centuries were my colleagues.

"Many people told me," said Doris Rojas, thirty-three, "that the scientists died because they disturbed the volcano."

Eight years later, the eruption continues to reverberate through dozens of lives. For most of us who were on the volcano that day and survived, the blast is an increasingly distant sound. But for the families of the nine who died, it is an inescapable fact of daily life.

Luis LeMarie returned to Ecuador, where he spent more than a year recovering from his burns and two broken legs. For the first two months, haunted by the eruption, he slept only a few hours a night. But gradually, as he talked about his ordeal with friends, he was able to sleep peacefully. A chemical engineer, Luis returned to work on one volcano, but he is now an inspector with the Organization for the Prohibition of Chemical Weapons and lives in The Hague with his family.

After returning to Florida International University, Andy Macfarlane was treated for his burns and underwent plastic surgery for the gash in his head. He had no nightmares about the eruption until a later trip to the Cerro Negro volcano in Nicaragua with Mike Conway. The night before they were to go into the crater, both of them had "violent, vivid nightmares" about the eruption, according to Macfarlane. Now an associate professor of geology, Andy has stopped working on active volcanoes.

Andy Adams went back to his job at Los Alamos. He, too, stopped working on volcanoes, although it had nothing to do with the eruption. Funding for his geology and geochemistry group was tight, so in late 1993 he was transferred to the environmental department at the laboratory, where he is working on the disposal and storage of nuclear waste. Adams said he is grateful that I asked him to leave the volcano an hour before the blast, but he thinks I should have discussed an emergency plan with the group in case of an eruption. He also believes that everyone should have been wearing hard hats and fire-resistant clothing. Certain that his hard hat saved his life, he returned home and contributed his suggestions to a panel drafting safety rules for volcanologists. Those guidelines, which include wearing hard hats and fire-retardant suits, were approved by the International Association of Volcanology and Chemistry of the Earth's Interior. I do wear such gear when I'm on volcanoes today, including a rugged hard hat and a special fire-retardant, acid-resistant jumpsuit. Marta and many of her Colombian colleagues still do not use such gear.

Mike Conway, recovering from a broken hand and burns, completed his Ph.D. at Michigan Tech while teaching at Florida International. When he went to Galeras, his wife was pregnant with their third child, whom they named James Galeras Conway. For the first few months after his return, Mike had nightmares in which his children were caught in a burning building. They were screaming for help but he couldn't rescue him. He would awake from the dreams in tears. Mike is now a professor of geology at Arizona Western College in Yuma and occasionally works on volcanoes. Like Macfarlane, he was angry and mystified when he saw me on television, being touted as the sole survivor from the crater rim.

Patty Mothes and her husband, Pete Hall, are still running the geophysical institute in Quito, Ecuador, and work constantly on volcanoes. Less than two months after the Galeras eruption, Patty descended partway into the crater of Guagua Pichincha, a highly active, 15,695-foot volcano that looms over Quito. Taking deformation measurements, she observed fresh ash on the ground, a noticeable increase in sulfuric smells, more active fumaroles, and rumbles coming from the volcano. Returning to the observatory, she gave firm instructions for none of the scientists to venture into the crater

until further notice. The next day, however, two younger geologists
— eager to observe the intensifying activity — defied her warning. A
small Vulcanian eruption occurred, similar to the one at Galeras,
and the men were killed instantly by flying bombs. Both were wearing hard hats, a safety precaution Pete and Patty insisted on after
Galeras. But the helmets were shattered by the same projectiles that
crushed the men's skulls.

Despite the obvious dangers and the constant struggle to fund
their institute, Pete and Patty continue to devote their lives to studying the volcanoes of Ecuador and working with officials on hazard
maps and evacuation plans. They and their Ecuadorian colleagues
have drawn up eleven hazard maps for the country's volcanoes, including Guagua Pichincha, which threatens Quito's 1.5 million inhabitants. Their work focuses on translating their knowledge into
practical benefits. They've gotten local newspapers to print color-
coded warnings for Guagua Pichincha and other highly active volcanoes. They've helped devise simple evacuation procedures, such
as hiking up a valley wall to avoid *lahars*. Few volcanologists have
had as tangible an impact as this couple; their work could well save
thousands of lives.

The loss of her colleagues at Galeras and Guagua Pichincha has
made Patty more cautious. Before setting foot on a volcano, she
now asks herself whether the samples are really necessary. Once on a
volcano, she has an acute understanding of the power of even small
eruptions — an understanding forged that afternoon on Galeras as
she dashed across the cone past the bodies of José Arlés and the
tourists. Not long ago, I asked Patty how Galeras had changed her.

"Life is fragile, and the power of volcanoes is incomprehensible
when a human body confronts the physical force of a volcano," she
wrote. "For months now I have been experiencing the Vulcanian explosions on Tungurahua volcano. They rock one's equilibrium and
one is amazed and impressed by how these car-sized blocks are
thrown out like popcorn from the crater. The volcano emits a tremendous amount of energy, and the whole region and people who
even live at a distance are altered by this energy. They don't feel in

command of the situation. As we say, '*El volcán mande aquí.* The volcano rules here.'"

In 1999 I went to Colombia, England, Italy, and Russia to speak with the family and friends of the men who died on Galeras. It was an emotional trip for everyone, but in doing research for this book I felt I needed to understand these men better, to see what had driven them to climb the volcano that day. I had heard Igor, José Arlés, Nestor, and Geoff talk about their families but had met only Nestor's wife. As for Fernando Cuenca, Carlos Trujillo, and the three tourists, I didn't know them at all but wanted to learn more. These were all relatively young men, deeply enmeshed in the lives of their wives, children, and parents. Most of them were at or approaching the peak of their careers, and their violent deaths left great voids in the lives of those close to them.

Gloria Benavides lost a husband and a son. They, along with their son's friend, were the tourists who had joined us on the cone minutes before the eruption. Gloria, a housewife, has never remarried, and she and her daughter, Paula, have lived off the pension her husband accrued as dean of academics at a university in Pasto. Gloria and her daughter wonder about eighteen-year-old Yovany and think it likely he would have followed in his father's footsteps and gone into teaching. Paula, who was twenty-one in 2000, is studying natural sciences at the University of Nariño and is thinking of becoming a geologist. She does not plan to work on volcanoes.

After the blast, I thought about the three tourists. They told us they had walked from Pasto, a trip of about five hours. Had they slowed just a bit, lingered over their lunches ten more minutes, or listened to Carlos Estrada's advice to turn around, they would be alive today. But they made it to the crater — breathing hard in the thin air — at the worst possible moment.

Gloria and her daughter live at the foot of Galeras. Every time they step outside and look to the west they are reminded of the eruption. "It was very difficult the first three years, but now it has settled down and become easier," Gloria told me. "I am still very angry at that volcano. I want to ask it, 'Why did you take away my husband and son?' I wonder if it was their destiny to die there."

For Carlos Trujillo's widow, Anna Lucía Torres, the volcano is also a constant reminder that her husband is gone, for she, too, lives in its shadow. After the blast, she and her son, Mauricio — six at the time of the eruption — moved in with her sister. Anna has never remarried.

"I can't accept 100 percent that he's not here," she told me as we sat with her extended family in a large living room. "I still have this hope that he will come back. It's very difficult, especially for Mauricio."

Mauricio, in eighth grade when I met him, is a good-looking, talkative boy. He described how his father used to get on his hands and knees and make motorcycle noises while Mauricio rode on his back. As the boy talked, I found myself holding back tears, both for him and his family — and for mine. My boy, Nick, is the same age, and had the bomb that hit me changed its trajectory by a fraction of an inch, he would also now be recalling memories of his dead father.

Larissa Gorbatova, Fernando Cuenca's Russian widow, stayed in Russia for a year and a half after the eruption. Her husband's body was never found, they had no children, and at first it seemed pointless to return to Colombia. Even her parents urged her to remain in Russia. But eventually she felt the pull of Fernando's homeland, and in 1995 she returned, thinking she would see her husband's family, then return to Russia. Five years later, she is still in Colombia: "I got off the plane here and it was somehow easier, as if I was closer to Fernando."

One of the first things she did was visit Pasto and Galeras. Marta drove her to the top of the amphitheater. Clouds were drifting by, offering an occasional glimpse of the dark cone and the steaming crater.

"It was very quiet, like the quiet of outer space," Larissa told me at her apartment in Bogotá. "It was this beautiful, wild nature. There was something grand about it."

INGEOMINAS paid Larissa a paltry death benefit, less than $1,000. She lived for a while with Fernando's family. Then, feeling some responsibility for the young widow, INGEOMINAS gave her a job in Bogotá as a geochemist, a field she had studied in college. But after eight months she decided to start a new life on her own and soon found a job as a translator at a large Colombian helicopter company, eventually working her way up to engineer. A few years later, she married a young Colombian in the cell phone business. They have a son, a blond boy who looks thoroughly Russian. He was two when I visited Larissa.

Larissa is a tall, striking woman with high cheekbones and blue eyes. Her modern apartment in Bogotá has a large color photograph of a Russian birch forest on the wall, as well as oil paintings of onion-domed, Russian Orthodox churches. She told me how madly in love she and Fernando had been, and I asked her if she thought she would ever find that kind of love again.

"What I had with Fernando I don't think it will be possible to find again. Pacho [her husband] is ordinary. Absolutely ordinary. He is nothing like Fernando. But he's kind. He's a good husband and father. This is my life."

Losing Fernando, she said, had in a strange way been good for her. "Other than Fernando I didn't see anything. I wasn't interested in the world, in other people. I focused on him alone. Of course there were my parents. I was the only daughter. Everyone always did everything for me. I didn't think deeply about other things. I had experienced nothing. I was such an egotist. You can't be like that. And when Fernando died I had to go out into the world, to get to know other people, to struggle for the first time. If Fernando had lived, I'm not sure how much I would have accomplished. I'm not sure I would have learned Spanish like I know it now. After the shock wore off, I saw my own capabilities and potential. I completely lost my fear. I got to know other people and began to understand how the world works."

For now, Larissa will remain in Colombia. The unstable economy and continuing violence worry her, but when she considers returning to Russia with her husband and son she sees a country beset by no fewer problems. Recently, she has set her sights on Canada, a place where she can start over once again.

José Arlés Zapata's young wife, Monica Gonzales Vallejo, has followed a path similar to Larissa's. Sheltered and passionately in love with her husband, she was forced to grow up quickly after the eruption. Dazed and aimless after her husband's death, she traveled around Colombia for more than a year, staying in Cali, Manizales, and Pasto with family and friends. "I thought that going from one place to another I might feel better, but I did not find peace anywhere," she told me. Eventually she met Pedro Nel Herrera, a butcher ten years her senior whose family also owned a pig farm. She married him and soon became pregnant with their daughter, Valeria.

I found Monica in a middle-class neighborhood in Bogotá, not far from the airport. She was living in an apartment behind the butcher shop with her family and Pedro's three children from a previous marriage. A large photograph of Galeras hung in the hallway. I found it odd, for I thought that the last thing Monica and her husband would want was a glaring reminder of José Arlés and his death. But over a lunch of steak and rice, Monica talked easily about José Arlés. She cried from time to time, and when she did Valeria, who was three, reached out and stroked her face.

"I have learned a lot of things," Monica said as Pedro, a stocky man with a droopy black mustache, listened. "I learned you can have a person beside you and you can close your eyes and open them and all of a sudden that person is gone. They can be taken away, in a second. I have learned how complicated life is and that you have to make the best of it. I have learned to take life easier and to appreciate every minute. Having a child provides a lot of hope, and when you're having a difficult time in life, a child gives you a reason to go on. I have learned a lot of things, and I think that Pedro has better luck than José Arlés."

I asked Monica if she wanted to ask me any questions. One thing had been on her mind.

"José Arlés said, 'I'm happy working on volcanoes and I don't

care about dying in an eruption as long as something is left for science.' And that is something I have always asked myself. Was his
death worthwhile? Is there anything left behind from all that José
Arlés did? He did all that work and he gave his life and it seems that
after the eruption people stopped studying Galeras. Why have you
stopped studying it?"

I assured her that we had not stopped working on Galeras and explained that José Arlés's contributions — as well as the eruptions
in 1993 — had taught us much about the volcano. She cried even
harder, then said, "I'm glad you're studying it. I thought all this time
that his death was for nothing."

Nestor García's death literally killed his father. Hospitalized after
hearing his son was missing in the eruption, Señor García was soon
transferred to a clinic in Bogotá. He died there of heart failure on
February 11, 1993, four weeks after his son's death.

"I don't know how I took it, but I had my family, my daughters,
and my grandchildren, and I had to take it," said Nestor's mother,
Argelia Parra de García, told me when I visited her. "God gave me
the strength to make it through."

Shortly after the eruption, Nestor's twelve-year-old son, Marcello,
began having a recurrent nightmare. His mother, Dolores, would
hear him talking and go into his room. "He would wake up and put
his hands on the wall next to his bed and he would say, 'Help me
hold up this wall because it's going to fall and kill my father!'"

Their daughter, Paula, then eighteen, was old enough to understand what had happened. But it took Marcello at least a year to
come to grips with the his father's loss, which was only compounded by the lack of Nestor's remains. "He wanted to see his father," said Dolores. "He wanted his father to appear."

"For me and the children, we felt good that at least if he died, he
died doing what he loved. But the ritual of having your loved one's
body taken to a church is a basic custom. For a while we just pre-
tended that he was on a trip and that one day he would come back.
Marcello is unique but strange, like Nestor. Later, he saw me crying
and he said, 'Mom, why are you crying? If Dad will come back, he

will, so don't cry. And if he's not going to come back, then no amount of crying will bring him back.'

"And then I said, 'Son, don't you miss your father?' And he replied, 'Mom, this is the way life is.'"

Marcello is now studying geology at the University of Caldas and may become a volcanologist. His mother, recognizing her husband's determination in her son, will not stand in his way. "As for Marcello's career, my desires are not important. What is important is Marcello's realization of himself. I can't let my interests stand in the way of Marcello's development."

Dolores herself is studying law. She has never remarried and maintains that — despite his infidelities — Nestor will remain the love of her life.

Occasionally, in the middle of the night, she hears noises coming from her son's bedroom. Walking in, she finds Marcello asleep with his hands pressed against the wall, struggling to hold it up.

For Geoff Brown's wife and daughters, the first few weeks of grieving were eased only by the knowledge that his death had come instantly. Several weeks after the eruption, the family held a memorial service at the Open University. Colleagues, friends, and family recounted tales of Geoff's mad driving, his perpetual tardiness, and his passion for volcanology and life. Later, the family planted a blue cedar in his honor near the old stone church on the university grounds. At the base of the tree they placed a brown memorial stone: "Geoff Brown. Remembered with Love. 1945–1993."

In December 1999, in London and at the Open University, I met with Evelyn Brown and her daughters. They said that before his departure for Colombia he was pensive, putting his affairs in order and wondering how he could reorganize his life and spend more time with his family. That Christmas, Ruth — who had an infant daughter, Laurie — visited her parents. Geoff fawned over his granddaughter.

"When Laurie was born, I think it made him sit back and put a perspective on life," Ruth said. "He realized there was too much going on and something had to give. He didn't want that to be his research or his love for volcanology. He didn't want it to be his family. And so he was thinking strongly of delegating his responsibilities in the department at the Open University."

During the holidays, Evelyn recalled, Geoff did something unusual — he discussed the risks of his work. It was then that he remarked that he would rather die on a volcano than in a car crash. He also put the finishing touches on his chapters for a book, wrapped up work for a course he would be teaching, and showed his wife where he kept his will and insurance policies.

On New Year's Day, 1993, Iona — who'd had a stormy relationship with her father as a child — phoned him and apologized for having been such a difficult child for so many years.

"Our relationship had been good for the last eight years — we had been really close — but I just wanted to say I was sorry for being so unbearable," Iona recalled. "He said, 'If you feel that you want to come down and talk through all this more, you can.' . . . But we just talked and sorted things out, and the last thing I told him was that I loved him." Shortly before Geoff flew to Colombia, Iona had a dream about her father. In it, he fell backwards into a volcano.

After Geoff's death, Evelyn and her girls lived by one of his credos. "He always said, 'Life is what you make of it,' by which he really meant, 'Life is what you make of what it throws at you,'" said Evelyn. "You can either wallow in what life throws at you or you can pick yourself up, dust yourself down, and say, 'All right, let's learn from this and move on.' That's what he wanted from us — and what he always did."

The girls were forced to mature rapidly after their father's death. Evelyn had to come into her own as well, but her reaction to Geoff's death was far more complicated than her daughters'. Though she misses Geoff, she said his passing ended a troubled marriage.

"We had reached an impasse," said Evelyn. "I couldn't live with him and I couldn't live without him . . . I think we would have had to [divorce]. I think we would have destroyed each other . . . It was an intense loss, but I grew up a lot. I had to reconstruct myself. So I gained a lot more confidence. And I had to develop new friends, new interests. Death doesn't have to be destructive. It can be very constructive. And that was the way we viewed it right from square one."

Their oldest girl, Miriam, gained a new independence after her father died and found the nerve to switch careers and become a nurse. Ruth — Evelyn's "wild child" — ceased being what she called a "a layabout slob" and began studying hard at the Open University. She eventually graduated with honors in math and took a job at a government safety research center for automobiles.

"One of my greatest regrets was that my dad didn't get to see me come into all of this," said Ruth. "I was always the one who had the potential, but didn't really fulfill myself in school, but I think he knew I had it in me."

Iona said that with her father's death she went from being a girl to a woman — a crash course in growing up. One result, according to Evelyn, was that her daughter's violin playing underwent a "quantum shift" and she performed with a newfound maturity and confidence.

"I spent two years, from age twenty-one to twenty-three, without laughing and without having a good time," Iona said. "I lost what should have been really carefree years. I became so serious and somber . . . But I think in the long run it gave me much more compassion and understanding for people. So I definitely grew, but I missed some youth that you only get once."

Miriam finally came to terms with her father's death when she visited Galeras several years after the eruption. Driving in from the airport on an uncharacteristically clear day, she was struck by the beauty of the volcano that had taken her father's life. "I had this image of a monster because it killed my dad," said Miriam. "I thought it would have this violent appearance. But with wispy clouds above it and this beautiful blue sky, it seemed so serene. It was such a contradiction, that nature could be so serene and so violent."

Later, accompanied by Marta, she drove to the top of the amphitheater scarp. Clouds had descended on the volcano. "It was like you were in an alien world, all this mist. And when I was standing on top there was a part of me that was quite apprehensive. I thought it would also try to do to me what it had done to my father."

For two days she didn't cry, but as she boarded the plane to head home she started sobbing. She continued to weep as the plane took off and banked, giving her a final view of Galeras. She cried as she took pictures of the volcano and wept all the way to Bogotá.

"It was like I was leaving him behind," Miriam told me. "I think I didn't really accept his death until I went to Galeras. Before, as far as I was concerned, it was almost as if he were living on. He was still in my memories. It was like he was on an extended trip abroad. I even had this Reginald Perrin fantasy that he had survived and had changed his identity and was living another life somewhere in South America. It wasn't until I visited Galeras that I no longer felt that way."

A few days after talking with Geoff's family, I flew to Moscow to meet Igor's widow. Just before Christmas, on a frigid afternoon, I traveled by subway to the neighborhood of shoddily built, modern high-rises far from the city center. Emerging from the metro, I walked past gauntlets of kiosks where food, vodka, cosmetics, and toiletries were sold, then tramped on snowy sidewalks to a white and green tile apartment building of about a dozen stories. Lyudmila occupied a cramped two-bedroom apartment, living off a pension equivalent to about $30 a month.

A comely blond woman in her sixties, Lyudmila greeted me with a smile and a certain reserve. Through a translator, we talked all afternoon, her reticence fading as she told me about Igor and their life together. Although I knew Igor had been devoted to his wife, I never understood how close they were until that day. Nor had I a clue how devastated she had been after Igor's death. She quit working as a volcanologist, lost twenty-six pounds, and for two years lived in almost complete isolation in Kamchatka and Moscow, barely speaking with friends and colleagues, answering few letters or phone calls. She apologized for not responding to an e-mail and letter that I had sent after the eruption, explaining it was too painful to communicate with someone who evoked so many memories of Igor and

Galeras. After I had phoned in the fall of 1999, saying I wanted to talk with her, she found herself crying at the prospect of our meeting.

"I nearly died when he died," she told me as we sat in a living room with two pictures of Elvis Presley on the wall. "It was like taking away a piece of myself. People should not be so close. It's dangerous to be attached to each other so much."

When her grief eventually eased, a flood of anger and bitterness took its place. She was angry that she had lost a husband, angry that she had lost her professional partner, angry that the career of one of the world's most prominent volcanologists had been cut short. As time passed, she was disappointed that none of Igor's younger colleagues was following his path. Some lacked the drive, she said. Some lacked the courage and patience to sit for hours in a crater, sampling gases.

"Such a young man did not deserve to die. He was too young. It is impossible to die so early. We did not finish all our work. Galeras stopped us, and we were practically at the finish . . . There are no people involved in this work now. They are all gone. You have to train such a person. This work involves a lot of physical labor and you need someone who loves it as much as Igor, who will be as diligent as Igor. It's difficult to find the right person with the proper proportion of ambition and devotion."

I wanted to tell her that I knew the right person — my former graduate student Tobias Fischer, who was as talented and tough a volcanologist as I'd ever met. Tobias was also a specialist in volcanic gases, and I'd seen him as Menyailov's heir, but I knew that Lyudmila had in mind a Russian successor.

Not long after Igor's death, Lyudmila left Kamchatka for good and moved to Moscow. She dreamed frequently of Igor, dreams so vivid that when she woke she felt he was still in the room. Then, five years after the eruption, their daughter, Irina, gave birth to a boy. Irina was married to an Italian geochemist named Franco Prati, and they named their boy Igor. When Lyudmila visited them in Florence, she felt almost as if her husband had been reincarnated. The boy does bear a remarkable resemblance to his grandfather, and holding pictures of them at age two side by side — smiling, curly-haired, blue-eyed blonds — it's difficult to tell who's who. After seeing her grandson, Lyudmila stopped having the constant dreams about her husband. Now she spends several months a year in Florence, and Irina and Igor visit her in Moscow. For the first time since 1993, she has a reason to live.

As the afternoon wore on, Lyudmila showed me black-and-white pictures of herself and Igor on horseback in Kamchatka, embarking on expeditions to Klyuchevskoi and other volcanoes. We had tea and sandwiches, and toward evening she told me she had enjoyed sharing her memories with me. "The worst thing now," she told me, "is to be alone."

Before leaving, I felt compelled to explain what had happened on Galeras and why we had been unable to foresee the eruption. But Lyudmila dismissed my explanation, and her anger at me quickly surfaced.

"Do you think Igor and I would have dared invite people to the volcano without knowing what condition it was in? You should have been prepared and not let people go up there. And they let such a big crowd climb the volcano. I think it's a crime. If you had sampled the gases regularly and measured the temperatures, you would have known there was going to be an eruption. It's unbelievable that you couldn't measure the increase in gases. I just don't believe you couldn't see it coming. When a volcano activates, it's immediately evident. There had to have been signs. You just missed them, that's all.

"Igor must have just lost his caution, his sense of danger. He shouldn't have climbed a volcano that was not being regularly studied. You should only go up on those volcanoes that are getting regular attention. If you had been examining the volcano regularly, you wouldn't have gone there. You would have known it was close to an eruption. Igor had been studying volcanoes since 1962. It was just stupid that he died."

I kept quiet while Lyudmila cooled off. I felt terrible, but it seemed best to let her vent her wrath. She blamed me, but, like many Russians, she had a deeply mystical streak and thought that perhaps the gods had punished her and Igor for their overconfidence on volcanoes.

"You know, we got too deeply into the mysteries. We were aiming at the secrets of volcanoes so boldly that the volcano punished us. Every time on a volcano we would go deeper and deeper. A lot of other people went on volcanoes with us. But they were more like tourists, observers. They looked at the volcano from a distance, with respect. We did not show any respect."

The next day I visited Igor's mother, Sofia Naboko, in another apartment building in Moscow. She was a remarkably spry ninety-year-old, surrounded by shelves of volcanology books and walls decorated with old pictures of Kamchatka's volcanoes. Less than five feet tall, Mrs. Naboko had clear blue eyes and short hair dyed a bright gold. She served me sandwiches, tea, and cookies but kept apologizing for not fixing me "real Kamchatka food" — salted fish, caviar, and boiled potatoes.

After she told me about her life and talked about Igor, I asked what the years since Igor's death had been like. "There is so much grief in the world," she replied. "I comfort myself with the thought that he could have died in other ways, but he died for science."

Mrs. Naboko, like Lyudmila, rued the absence of any remains. She said that Lyudmila had sent a plaque to Colombia commemorating Igor and asked officials there to place it on Galeras. I had never seen such a plaque but didn't have the heart to tell her. Then she pointed to several large cardboard boxes tied with string, sitting under a table in her living room. "I am trying to make Lyudmila open these cases," Mrs. Naboko said, "but she cannot bring herself to do it. These cases are full of Igor's manuscripts. If I were her I would have by all means worked on them, published them. It's a pity that Igor did not finish his last work, which was on all the volcanoes of the world. It's a loss for all of us."

Before I left she pulled out a picture of Igor as a little boy, referring to him in the diminutive that Russian mothers reserve for their children. "You really couldn't find his body?" she asked, searching my face. "I still think he's alive sometimes. Oh, it's so sad. It's so sad. It's so bad for Igorochek."

A few days earlier, I had visited their daughter, Irina, and grandson in Florence. Irina, in her mid-thirties, told me that the blow of her father's death was cushioned by her daughter, Dasha, and her husband. Two months after the eruption, distraught that her father's body had vanished without a trace, she went to Colombia to visit the spot where he had last been alive. Marta drove Irina to the top of the escarpment, where she tossed a vial of Moscow dirt into the amphitheater and collected some ash and pumice from Galeras. The weather was typically foggy and gloomy, the base of the cone occasionally visible.

"We did not go down in," she told me. "The volcano was still very active, everything was steaming. It was terrible. I remember the roar. I thought that it must have been awful for my father. I imagined him coming there, climbing up, and never coming back. I thought about other people killed in the eruption. It was very difficult.

"On the one hand it is terrible that we cannot visit his grave. But he used to say that he could not imagine himself as an old man. He said he wanted to die somewhere on a volcano. He used to say that he might just jump into a crater someday."

The arrival of the new baby was a balm for her and her mother. There was no question what his name would be. As he grew older, his uncanny resemblance to his grandfather further ratified the wisdom of their decision. Still, when Irina looks at her son she can't help but see her father. She misses him intensely and likes to picture him at his happiest — at their dacha. She sees him carrying water, puttering in their garden, holding Dasha on his lap.

Trained as a geologist, she has no plans to work on active volcanoes. Nor does she intend to return to Galeras. "That volcano," she told me, "has done nothing good for anybody."

On bad days I'm inclined to agree with her. On really bad days, I wish I had died on the volcano with Igor and the others. Many times, my wife has said that the old me did die that day on Galeras. She's right. I am not the same. I was always an impatient and aggressive person, but courtesy and normal inhibitions kept me in check. After the head injury, however, the brakes on my bad behavior seemed to fail, and I found myself barking at my wife and losing my temper over the smallest things. Slowly I pushed her away. As the doctors reconstructed me, I joked that I was like Frankenstein. Now, I occasionally look in the mirror and wonder: Who is this monster? My frustrations have been compounded by my difficulties concentrating and working and by a volatile mix of powerful seizure medications and antidepressants. After the initial relief, Lynda and I began to see that I was a different person and that our marriage had changed as well, perhaps fatally.

"Part of you died at Galeras," Lynda wrote to me recently. "You were put back together like Humpty Dumpty, patted on the back and told that your recovery was impressive. People told me, 'There you go, Mrs. Williams, you are so lucky that your husband has recovered this well.' The phrase haunts me as countless people tell me how lucky I am that you survived. I'm so tired of people pretending that everything is fine when it's not. Only those who have lived with ambivalent loss can understand this . . . I love the man I married, but was not allowed to grieve what was lost."

Over time, and with new medications, I have regained my equilibrium. Whether this will be enough to salvage our marriage I don't know. I hope so.

Now I face the challenge of reinventing myself. The hardest thing has been to accept that I am not the person I was before the eruption. Once I was at the top of my profession. Conceiving research projects, securing funding for them, pulling them off, and writing them up used to be a cinch. Now it's a struggle. Once I saw an open field. Now it seems full of obstacles. Once I brimmed with ambition. Now I entertain fantasies of quitting my job, leaving my family, and moving to Ecuador to work on volcanoes.

I have been derailed, but I haven't quit. I still relish working on volcanoes, still love poking around craters and fumaroles. I am not doing as much topflight research as I once did, but I am doing some, and it will have to be enough. I still love to teach, and I want to spend more time sharing my knowledge about volcanoes with others. Though I wouldn't ever forsake my family, I'd like to go to South America to train young volcanologists. I even dream of starting an international center for such a purpose.

One thing is certain. I need to get clear of Galeras. It has shadowed me every day for the last eight years. It has exerted a gravitational pull, and no matter how hard I try to scramble away I seem to wind up right back under the volcano. As other parts of my life have fallen by the wayside, Galeras has filled the void. Being the survivor has become an integral part of my identity. In the early years, I used to talk about conquering Galeras, about not letting it cow me. Now I'm just tired of it. I want to move on.

A NOTE ON SOURCES

BIBLIOGRAPHY

ACKNOWLEDGMENTS

INDEX

A NOTE ON SOURCES

This book is the result of two years' work by me and my co-author, Fen Montaigne. In researching *Surviving Galeras*, we traveled to Ecuador, Colombia, England, the Netherlands, France, Germany, Italy, and Russia and interviewed more than seventy-five people about the eruption and the men who were part of it. We also did extensive research on the history of volcanology and some of the great eruptions of the past.

In Chapter 2, we relied on numerous contemporary accounts of the 1902 eruption at Mont Pélee in Martinique. Most important was Tempest Anderson and John S. Flett's groundbreaking "Report on the Eruptions of the Soufrière in St. Vincent in 1902 and on a Visit to Mont Pélee, Martinique," published by the Royal Society of London in 1903. In the section on Mount St. Helens, the USGS volcanologist Wes Hildreth was especially helpful in describing the life and career of his colleague David Johnston, who perished in that eruption. My friend Dr. Peter Baxter of Cambridge University was extremely helpful in describing how the Mount St. Helens eruption killed and injured its victims. We also relied on papers in the *New England Journal of Medicine*, *Journal of the American Medical Association*, *American Journal of Surgery*, and *Bulletin of Volcanology*.

In Chapter 4, much of the information on Galeras's geological history comes from the master's thesis and doctoral dissertation of Marta Calvache. In writing about Galeras's recent eruptive history, I relied at times on the unpublished work of Professor Emiliano Diaz del Castillo Zarama, a native of Nariño who kindly made his research available to us.

Although I did not quote them by name, several of the brothers and sisters of José Arlés Zapata offered insights, which helped us round out our portrait of José Arlés in Chapter 5. Likewise, although we did not directly quote the INGEOMINAS geologist Rosalbina Pérez, her reminiscences about her colleague Fernando Cuenca helped us shape our brief profile of him.

In Chapter 6, in the section on Pliny the Elder and Pliny the Younger, we relied on more than a dozen published accounts of the A.D. 79 eruption of Vesuvius. Particularly helpful was Alwyn Scarth's *Vulcan's Fury: Man Against the Volcano* (1999), as well as articles in the *Classical Weekly* and *Isis*. In assembling the portrait of Sir William Hamilton, we read his classic work, *Campi Phlegraei,* and all his letters from Naples to the Royal Society of London. We also consulted two biographies: *Sir William Hamilton: Envoy Extraordinary,* by Brian Fothergill, and *Nelson and the Hamiltons,* by Jack Russell. Among the articles about Hamilton, two were especially helpful: Mark C. W. Sleep's portrait in the *Annals of Science* (December 1969) and Harold Acton's monograph *Three Extraordinary Ambassadors,* published in 1984 by Thames and Hudson as part of the Walter Neurath Memorial Lecture series. Our biographical sketch of Maurice and Katia Krafft owes much to four people who talked at length with us: André Demaison, the Kraffts' good friend and biographer; Bertrand Krafft, Maurice's brother; Jean-Louis Cheminée of the Volcanological Observatory at the Institute of Global Physics in Paris; and Jörg Keller at the University of Freiburg.

In Chapter 7 and elsewhere, we used written accounts of the eruption from three other eyewitnesses — Mike Conway, Andy Macfarlane, and Andy Adams. In interviews, they also talked in detail about the events of that day on Galeras.

In Chapter 10, much of our description of the 1783 eruption at Laki in Iceland was based on the journals of the Reverend Jón Steingrímsson, a translation of which was kindly provided by my colleagues at the Nordic Volcanological Institute in Reykjavik. We also relied on an exhaustively researched account of the Laki eruptions that my Icelandic colleague Thorvaldur Thordarson graciously made available to us. Other sources used in the Laki section include articles by my colleague Haraldur Sigurdsson in *EOS* and other publications; a January 1982 paper in *Geography* by E. L. Jackson; a July 1995 article in the *Geographical Journal* by John Grattan and Mark Brayshay; a paper by Charles A. Wood of NASA in *The Year Without a Summer,* published in 1992 by the Canadian Museum of Nature; and a 1970 paper in the *Bulletin Volcanologique* by S. Thorarinsson. For the section on the Tambora eruption and its climatic effects, we found the following books particularly helpful: *Volcano Weather*, by Henry and Elizabeth Stommel; *The Year Without a Summer*; and J. D. Post's *The Last Great Subsistence Crisis in the Western World*. Among the articles we relied on were Haraldur Sigurdsson's and Steve Carey's June 1988 paper in *Natural History*; Charles M. Wilson's account of the summer of 1816 in the June 1970 issue of *American History Illustrated*; Steve Self et al.'s report in a November 1984 issue of *Geology*; Richard B. Stothers's account in a June 1984 issue of *Science*; and Joseph B. Hoyt's June 1958 article in the *Annals of the Association of American Geographers*.

In Chapter 11, in describing the successful forecasting of the eruption at Mount Pinatubo, I consulted many of the papers written by my colleagues at the USGS. Conversations with friends and colleagues there also helped me better understand how the USGS and Filipino scientists made such a good call at Pinatubo.

BIBLIOGRAPHY

Acton, Harold. *Three Extraordinary Ambassadors*. Thames and Hudson. London. 1984.

Anderson, Tempest, and John S. Flett. "Report on the Eruptions of the Soufrière in St. Vincent in 1902 and on a Visit to Mont Pelée, Martinique. *Philosophical Transactions of the Royal Society of London.* Part 1. Ser. A, 200: 353–553. 1903.

Barberi, F., and L. Civetta. "The Eruptive Scenario of the Mid-term Maximum Expected Eruption of the National Emergency Planning of the Vesuvius Area." *General Assembly: Volcanic Activity and the Environment.* 31. IAVCEI. 1997.

Baxter, Peter J. "Medical Effects of Volcanic Eruptions." *Bulletin of Volcanology.* Vol. 52: 532–44. 1990.

———. "Volcanoes." In *The Public Health Consequences of Disasters.* E. K. Noji, ed. Oxford University Press. New York. 1997.

Baxter, Peter J., A. Neri, and M. Todesco. "Physical Modelling and Human Survival in Pyroclastic Flows. *Natural Hazards.* No. 17: 163–76. 1998.

Baxter, Peter J., et al. "Mount St. Helens Eruptions, May 18 to June 12, 1980." *Journal of the American Medical Association.* Vol. 246, No. 22: 2585–89. 1981.

Bernstein, Robert S., Peter J. Baxter, et al. "Immediate Public Health Concerns and Actions in Volcanic Eruptions: Lessons from the Mount St. Helens Eruptions." *American Journal of Public Health.* Vol. 76, Supplement: 25–37. 1986.

Blong, R. J. *Volcanic Hazards: A Sourcebook on the Effects of Eruptions.* Academic Press. Sydney. 1984.

Bogoyavlenskaya, G. E., et al. "Catastrophic Eruptions of the Directed-Blast Type at Mount St. Helens, Bezymianny and Sheveluch Volcanoes." *Journal of Geodynamics.* Vol. 3: 189–218. 1985.

Bullard, Fred M. *Volcanoes of the Earth.* University of Texas Press. Austin. 1976.

Calderazzo, John. "Fire in the Earth, Fire in the Soul: The Final Moments of Maurice and Katia Krafft." *Isle.* Vol. 4.2: 71–77. 1997.

Calvache, M. L. V., and Stanley N. Williams. "Lithic-Dominated Pyroclastic Flows at Galeras Volcano, Colombia. An Unrecognized Volcanic Hazard." *Geology.* Vol. 20, No. 6.: 539–42. 1992.

Calvache, Marta Lucía V. "The Geological Evolution of Galeras Volcanic Complex." Ph.D. diss. Arizona State University. 1995.

———. "Geology and Volcanology of the Recent Evolution of Galeras Volcano." Master's thesis. Louisiana State University. 1990.

Chouet, B. "Long-Period Volcano Seismicity: Its Source and Use in Forecasting Eruptions." *Nature.* Vol. 380: 309–16. 1996.

Christiansen, R. L. "Eruption of Mt. St. Helens." *Nature.* Vol. 285: 531–33. 1980.

Decker, Robert W., and Barbara Decker. *Volcanoes.* W. H. Freeman. New York. 1997.

Diaz del Castillo Zarama, Emiliano. "*El Galeras y Bombona.*" Unpublished ms. 1999.

Dobran, F., et al. "Vesuvius 2000: An Interdisciplinary Initiative for Vesuvius Aimed at Volcanic Risk Mitigation in a Densely Populated Area." *General Assembly: Volcanic Activity and the Environment.* 111. IAVCEI. 1997.

Eisele, John W., et al. "Deaths During the May 18, 1980, Eruption of Mount St. Helens." *New England Journal of Medicine.* Vol. 305, No. 16: 931–36. 1981.

Fenton, Carroll Lane, and Mildred Fenton. *The Story of the Great Geologists.* Ayer Co. Salem, N.H. 1945.

Fischer, T. P. "The Geochemistry of Fumarole Gases at Galeras Volcano, Colombia." Master's thesis. Arizona State University. 1994.

———. "Geochemistry of Volatile Discharges from Subduction Zone Volcanoes: Kudryavy, Kurile Islands and Galeras, Colombia." Ph.D. diss. Arizona State University. 1998.

Fischer, T. P., et al. "The Relationship Between Fumarole Gas Composition and Eruptive Activity at Galeras Volcano, Colombia." *Geology.* Vol. 24, No. 6: 531–34. 1996.

Fisher, Richard V. "Obituary — Harry Glicken." *Bulletin of Volcanology.* Vol. 53: 514–16. 1991.

Fisher, Richard V., and Grant Heiken. "Mt. Pelée, Martinique, May 8 and May 20, 1902. Pyroclastic Flows and Surges." *Journal of Volcanology and Geothermal Research.* Vol. 13: 339–71. 1982.

Fisher, Richard V., Grant Heiken, and Jeffrey B. Hulen. *Volcanoes: Crucibles of Change.* Princeton University Press. Princeton. 1997.

Fothergill, Brian. *Sir William Hamilton: Envoy Extraordinary.* Harcourt, Brace & World. New York. 1969.

Foxworthy, Bruce L., and Mary Hill. *Volcanic Eruptions of 1980 at Mt. St. Helens. The First 100 Days.* USGS Professional Paper No. 1249. Washington, D.C. 1982.

Franklin, Ben. "Meteorological Imaginations and Conjectures." *Memoirs of the Literary and Philosophical Society.* Manchester. Vol. 2: 373–77. 1784.

Goff, G., et al. "Gold Degassing and Deposition at Galeras Volcano, Colombia." *Geology Today.* Vol. 4, No. 4: 244–47. 1994.

Grattan, J., and D. J. Charman. "Non-Climatic Factors and the Environmental Impact of Volcanic Volatiles: Implication of the Laki Fissure Eruption of A.D. 1783." *Holocene.* Vol. 4: 101–6. 1994.

Grattan, John, and Mark Brayshay. "An Amazing and Portentous Summer: Environmental and Social Responses in Britain to the 1783 Eruption of an Iceland Volcano." *Geographical Journal.* Vol. 161, Part 2: 125–34. 1995.

Hall, Minard L. "Chronology of the Principal Scientific and Governmental Actions Leading Up to the November 13, 1985, Eruption of Nevado del Ruiz." *Journal of Volcanology and Geothermal Research.* Vol. 42: 101–15. 1990.

Hamilton, Sir William. "An Account of the Eruption of Mt. Vesuvius in 1767." *Philosophical Transactions of the Royal Society of London.* Vol. 58, 1–2. 1768.

———. "An Account of the Late Eruption of Mount Vesuvius." *Philosophical Transactions of the Royal Society of London.* Vol. 85: 73–116. 1795.

———. *Campi Phlegraei. Observations on the Volcanoes of the Two Sicilies.* Fabris, Naples. 2 vols. 1776 and 1779.

Harrington, C. R., ed. *The Year Without a Summer. World Climate in 1816.* Canadian Museum of Nature. Ottawa. 1992.

Haywood, Richard M. "The Strange Death of the Elder Pliny." *Classical Weekly.* Vol. 46: 1–3. 1952.

Heiken, Grant. "Will Vesuvius Erupt? Three Million People Need to Know." *Science.* Vol. 286: 1685–86. 1999.

Hill, D. P. "Unrest, Response Levels, and Public Perceptions in Long Valley Caldera, California." *General Assembly: Volcanic Activity and the Environment.* 117. IAVCEI. 1997.

Hoffmann, Hillel J. "The Rise of Life on Earth." *National Geographic.* Vol. 198, No. 3: 100–113. 2000.

Hoyt, J. B. "The Cold Summer of 1816." *Annals of the Association of American Geographers.* Vol. 48, No. 2: 118–31. 1958.

Ida, Yoshiaki, and Barry Voight. "Introduction to the Harry Glicken Memorial Special Issue." *Journal of Volcanology and Geothermal Research.* Vol. 66: ix–xvi. 1995.

Jackson, E. L. "The Laki Eruption of 1783: Impacts on Population and Settlement in Iceland." *Geography.* Vol. 67: 42–50. 1982.

Jaggar, Thomas A. *My Experiments with Volcanoes.* Hawaiian Volcano Research Association. Honolulu. 1956.

Keller, J., and M. Krafft. "Effusive Natrocarbonatite Activity of Oldoinyo Lengai, June 1988." *Bulletin of Volcanology.* Vol. 52, No. 8: 629–45. 1990.

Keller, Jörg. "Memorial for Katja and Maurice Krafft." *Bulletin of Volcanology.* Vol. 54: 613–14. 1992.

Krafft, M., and J. Keller. "Temperature Measurements in Carbonatite Lava Lakes and Flows from Oldoinyo Lengai, Tanzania." *Science.* Vol. 245: 168–70. 1989.

Krafft, Maurice. *Volcanoes: Fire from the Earth.* Harry N. Abrams, Inc. New York. 1993.

Krafft, Maurice and Katia. *Le Feu de la Terre.* Éditions de la Martinière. Paris. 1992.

Lipman, Peter W., and Donald R. Mullineaux, eds. *The 1980 Eruption of Mt. St. Helens, Washington.* USGS Professional Paper 1250. 1981.

Lipscomb, H. C. "The Strange Death of the Elder Pliny." *Classical Weekly.* Vol. 47: 74. 1954.

Lowe, D. R., et al. "Lahars Initiated by the November 13, 1985, Eruption of Nevado del Ruiz, Colombia." *Nature.* Vol. 324: 51–53. 1986.

Menyailov, I. A. "Prediction of Eruptions Using Changes in Composition of Volcanic Gases." *Bulletin Volcanologique.* Vol. 39, No. 1: 112–25. 1975.

Menyailov, I. A., et al. "Geochemistry of Volcanic Gas Emissions at Momotombo Volcano, Nicaragua." *Vulkanologiya i Seismologiya.* No. 2: 60–70. 1986.

Muñoz, F. A., et al. "Galeras Volcano: International Workshop and Eruption." *EOS.* Vol. 74: 281–87. 1993.

Murck, Barbara W., and Bryan J. Skinner. *Geology Today: Understanding Our Planet.* John Wiley. New York. 1999.

Murray, J. "Vertical Ground Deformation on Mountain Etna, 1975–1980." *Geological Society of America Bulletin.* Vol. 93: 1160–75. 1982.

Mussey, B., and S. L. Vigilante. "1800 and Froze to Death: The Cold Summer of 1816 and the Westward Migration from New York." *Bulletin of the New York Public Library.* No. 52: 454–57. 1948.

Newhall, C. G. "Geology of Lake Atítlan, Guatemala." Ph.D. diss. Dartmouth College. 1980.

Newhall, C. G., and R. S. Punongbayan, eds. *Fire and Mud: Eruptions and Lahars of Mount Pinatubo, Philippines.* Philippine Institute of Volcanology and Seismology. Manila. 1996.

Nikada, S., et al., eds. "Unzen Eruption: Magma Ascent and Dome Growth." *Journal of Volcanology and Geothermal Research.* Special Volume. Vol. 89, Nos. 1–4. 1999.

Noji, Eric K., ed. *The Public Health Consequences of Disasters.* Oxford University Press. New York. 1997.

Olsen, Paul E. "Giant Lava Flows, Mass Extinctions, and Mantle Plumes." *Science.* Vol. 284: 604–5. 1999.

Parshley, Philip F., et al. "Pyroclastic Flow Injury, Mount St. Helens, May 18, 1980." *American Journal of Surgery.* Vol. 143: 565–68. 1982.

Perret, Frank. *Volcanological Observations.* Carnegie Institution, Publication 549. Washington, D.C. 1950.

Post, J. D. *The Last Great Subsistence Crisis in the Western World.* Johns Hopkins University Press. Baltimore. 1977.

Punongbayan, R. S., et al. "Lessons from a Major Eruption." *EOS.* Vol. 72: 545, 552–53, 555. 1991.

Rampino, Michael R., Stephen Self, and Richard B. Stothers. "Volcanic Winters." *Annual Review of Earth and Planetary Sciences.* Vol. 16: 73–99. 1988.

Roggensack, K. "Volatiles from the 1994 Eruptions of Rabaul: View into a Large Caldera System." *Science.* Vol. 273: 490–93. 1966.

Russell, Jack. *Nelson and the Hamiltons.* Simon & Schuster. New York. 1969.

Rymer, H., and G. C. Brown. "Causes of Microgravity Change at Poás Volcano, Costa Rica." *Bulletin of Volcanology.* Vol. 49: 389–98. 1987.

———. "Gravity Changes as a Precursor to Volcanic Eruption at Poás Volcano, Costa Rica." *Nature.* Vol. 342, No. 6252: 902–5. 1989.

Scarth, Alwyn. *Volcanoes.* Texas A&M University Press. College Station. 1994.

———. *Vulcan's Fury: Man Against the Volcano.* Yale University Press. New Haven. 1999.

Seibert, Lee, Harry Glicken, and Ui Tadahide. "Volcanic Hazards from Bezymianny and Bandai-Type Eruptions." *Bulletin of Volcanology.* No. 49: 435–59. 1987.

Self, Stephen, et al. "Volcanological Study of the Great Tambora Eruption." *Geology.* Vol. 12: 659–63. 1984.

Sheets, Payson D., and Donald K. Grayson, eds. *Volcanic Activity and Human Ecology.* Academic Press. London. 1979.

Sieh, Kerry, and Simon LeVay. *The Earth in Turmoil.* W. H. Freeman. New York. 1998.

Sigurdsson, Haraldur. "Assessment of the Atmospheric Impact of Volcanic Eruptions." In *Global Catastrophes in Earth History. An Interdisciplinary Conference.* V. L. Sharpton and P. D. Ward, eds. 99–100. Geological Society of America Special Paper No. 247. Boulder, Colo. 1990.

———. *Melting the Earth.* Oxford University Press. New York. 1999.

———. "Volcanic Pollution and Climate: The 1783 Laki Eruption." *EOS.* Vol. 63: 601–3. 1982.

———, ed. *Encyclopedia of Volcanoes.* Academic Press. San Diego. 2000.

Sigurdsson, Haraldur, and Stephen Carey. "The Far Reach of Tambora." *Natural History.* 67–73. June 1988.

Sigurdsson, Haraldur, and S. Cashdollar. "The Eruption of Vesuvius in A.D. 79: Reconstruction from Historical and Volcanological Evidence." *American Journal of Archaeology.* Vol. 86: 39–51. 1982.

Sigurdsson, Haraldur, and Paolo Laj. "Atmospheric Effects of Volcanic Eruptions." In *The Encyclopedia of Earth System Science.* Academic Press. Sydney. 1992.

Simkin, Tom, and Lee Siebert, eds. *Volcanoes of the World.* Smithsonian Institution, Washington, D.C., and Geoscience Press. Tucson. 1994.

Sleep, M.C.W. "Sir William Hamilton: His Work and Influence in Geology." *Annals of Science.* Vol. 25, No. 4: 319–38.

Sontag, Susan. *The Volcano Lover.* Anchor Books/Doubleday. New York. 1992.

Steingrímsson, Jón. *Fires of the Earth.* University of Iceland Press and the Nordic Volcanological Institute. Reykjavik. 1998.

Stix, J., et al. "Galeras Volcano, Colombia; Interdisciplinary Study of a Decade Volcano." *Journal of Volcanology and Geothermal Research.* Special Volume. Vol. 77, Nos. 1–4. 1997.

———. "A Model of Degassing at Galeras Volcano, Colombia, 1988–1993." *Geology.* Vol. 21: 963–67. 1993.

Stoiber, R. E., and A. Jepsen. "Sulfur Dioxide Contributions to the Atmosphere by Volcanoes." *Science.* Vol. 182: 577–78. 1973.

Stoiber, R. E., et al. "Mount St. Helens, Washington 1980 Eruption: The Magmatic Gas Component During the First 16 Days. *Science.* Vol. 208, No. 4449: 1258–59. 1980.

Stommel, Henry, and Elizabeth Stommel. *Volcano Weather. The Story of 1816, the Year Without a Winter.* Seven Seas Press. Newport, R.I. 1983.

Stothers, R. B. "The Great Tambora Eruption in 1815 and Its Aftermath." *Science.* Vol. 224, No. 4654: 1191–98. 1984.

Stothers, Richard B. "The Great Dry Fog of 1783." *Climatic Change.* Vol. 32: 79–89. 1996.

Swanson, Donald A. "Harry Glicken. 1958–1991." *Journal of Volcanology and Geothermal Research.* Vol. 66: ix–xvi. 1995.

Tanguy, J. C., C. Ribiere, et al. "Victims from Volcanic Eruptions: A Revised Database." *Bulletin of Volcanology.* Vol. 60: 137–44. 1998.

Tazieff, Haroun, and Jean-Christophe Sabroux. *Forecasting Volcanic Events.* Elsevier Science Publishers. Amsterdam. 1983.

Thorarinsson, S. "The Lakagigar Eruption of 1783." *Bulletin Volanologique.* Vol. 33, No. 3: 910–29, 1970.

Thordarson, T., and S. Self. "The Laki and Grímsvötn Eruptions in 1783 and 1785." *Bulletin of Volcanology.* Vol. 55: 233–63. 1993.

Tilling, R. I., ed. *Volcanic Hazards.* Short Course in Geology: Vol. 1. American Geophysical Union. Washington, D.C. 1989.

Tilling, Robert I., and Peter Lipman. "Lessons in Reducing Volcanic Risk." *Nature.* Vol. 364: 277–80.

Tilling, Robert I., Lyn Topinka, and Donald A. Swanson. "Eruptions of Mount St. Helens: Past, Present, and Future." USGS Special Interest Publication. 1990.

Trevelyan, Raleigh. *Shadow of Vesuvius Pompeii* A.D. *79.* Michael Joseph. London. 1976.

Voight, Barry. "Countdown to Catastrophe." *Earth and Mineral Sciences.* Vol. 57, No. 2: 17–30. 1988.

——. "The Management of Volcano Emergencies: Nevado del Ruiz." In R. Scarpa and R. I. Tilling, eds., *Monitoring and Mitigation of Volcano Hazards.* Springer. Berlin. 1996.

——. "The 1985 Nevado del Ruiz Catastrophe: Anatomy and Retrospection." *Journal of Volcanology and Geothermal Research.* Vol. 42: 151–88. 1990.

Walker, G.P.L. "Plinian Eruptions and Their Products." *Bulletin Volcanologique.* Vol. 44: 223–40. 1981.

Williams, Howel, and Alexander R. McBirney. *Volcanology.* Freeman, Cooper, & Co. San Francisco. 1979.

Williams, S. N. "Erupting Neighbors — At Last:" *Science.* Vol. 267: 340–41. 1995

——. "The October, 1902 Eruption of Santa María Volcano, Guatemala." Master's thesis. Dartmouth College. 1980.

——, ed. "Nevado del Ruiz Volcano, Colombia." *Journal of Volcanolology and Geothermal Research.* Vols. 41–42. 1990.

Williams, S. N., et al. "Eruption of Nevado del Ruiz, Colombia, November 13, 1985: Gas Flux and Fluid Geochemistry:" *Science.* Vol. 23: 964–67. 1986.

——, et al. "Global Carbon Dioxide Emissions to the Atmosphere by Volcanoes." *Geokhimica, Cosmokhimica Acta.* Vol. 56: 1765–70. 1992.

——, et al. "Premonitory Geochemical Evidence of Magmatic Reactivation of Galeras Volcano, Colombia." *EOS.* Vol. 71, No. 17: 647. 1990.

Wilson, Charles M. "The Year Without a Summer." *American History Illustrated.* Vol. 5, No. 3: 24–29. 1970.

Wolfe, E. W. "The 1991 Eruption of Mt. Pinatubo." *Earthquakes and Volcanoes.* No. 23: 5–37. 1992.

Wood, C. A. "Climatic Effects of the 1783 Laki Eruption." In C. R. Harrington, ed., *The Year Without a Summer?* Canadian Museum of Nature. Ottawa. 1992.

Yanagi, T., et al., eds. *Unzen Volcano, the 1990–1992 Eruption.* Nishinippon & Kyushu University Press. Fukuoka. 1992.

Zirkle, Conway. "The Death of Gaius Plinius Secundas (23–79 A.D.)." *Isis.* Vol 58, Part 4: 553–59. 1967.

ACKNOWLEDGMENTS

At the outset, I would like to thank the people who saved my life and worked to put me back together following the eruption. At the top of that list are Marta Lucía Calvache and Patty Mothes, who led the rescue effort on Galeras. I will always be indebted to them, as I am to Dr. Porfirio Muñoz, who performed his first solo brain surgery splendidly and pulled me back from the brink of death.

In the United States, I would like to thank the team of doctors who worked on me in Phoenix, especially Dr. Vincent J. Russo, Jr., whose surgical skill saved my leg. More recently, I want to thank Dr. Drake Duane and Dr. Marlies Korsten, who have been working on a more troublesome part of my body, the brain, and treating the lingering effects of that injury.

I could not have written this book without the cooperation of the families of the men who died on Galeras. Meeting with me was both cathartic and painful, and I apologize for any distress I caused them as we talked about their lost husbands, fathers, and sons.

I am grateful to Igor Menyailov's widow, Lyudmila, for her kindness and openness in Moscow. I would also like to thank Igor's daughter, Irina, and her husband, Franco Prati, for their help and hospitality in Florence. I am indebted to Igor's mother, Sofia Naboko, for her cooperation and remarkable memory.

In England, I would like to thank Geoff Brown's widow, Evelyn, and his daughters — Miriam, Iona, and Ruth — for their kindness and for taking the time to share their reminiscences about Geoff.

In Colombia, Nestor García's widow, Dolores, and his mother, Argelia Parra de García, also generously agreed to talk to me about Nestor. José Arlés Zapata's widow, Monica, and her new husband, Pedro Nel Herrera, welcomed me warmly and spoke at length about the life and death of José Arlés. Several of José Arlés's brothers and sisters also shared their memories, and for that I am grateful. Larissa Gorbatova, Fernando Cuenca's widow, graciously submitted to a lengthy talk about her late husband.

In Pasto, I would like to thank Carlos Trujillo's widow, Anna Lucía Torres, and her son, Mauricio, for talking with me. I am also indebted to Gloria Benavides for discussing the deaths of her husband and son. I am also grateful to Gloria's daughter, Paula.

I am indebted to the colleagues of the volcanologists who perished on Galeras for their insights into the lives of these men. In Russia, I'd like to thank Igor Menyailov's fellow scientists — Anatoly Khrenov, Viktor Sugrobov, and Genrikh Shteinberg. I would especially like to thank Mikhail Korshinsky, not only for his reminiscences of Igor but also for his help arranging visas for my co-author and me to Russia. Many thanks also to Lyudmila Mekhertyecheva for all her help in Moscow.

In England, I want to thank Geoff's collaborator, Hazel Rymer, and his friend and colleague John Murray. John Simmons was a great help, and I'm only sorry that more of our conversation did not make it into the book. As always, my friend Peter Baxter gave generously of his time and knowledge.

In Colombia, I would like to thank INGEOMINAS scientists Rosalbina Pérez, Milton Ordóñez, Gloria Jiménéz, and Ricardo Mendez for sharing their memories of José Arlés Zapata and Nestor García. INGEOMINAS staff members Carlos Estrada and Ricardo Villota also were of great help as my co-author, Fen Montaigne, and I researched the book in Pasto. I would also like to thank Adela Londoño for sharing her memories of Nestor García.

I am indebted to my colleagues who survived the eruption and who shared their recollections of the events with my co-author and me. They are Luis LeMarie, Mike Conway, Andy Macfarlane, and Andy Adams. Thanks also to Pete Hall for talking with us about the eruption and his work in Ecuador.

I am particularly grateful to four people in France and Germany for talking to us about Maurice and Katia Krafft. They are Bertrand Krafft, Maurice's brother; Jörg Keller, their friend and African traveling companion; André Demaison, their friend and biographer; and Jean-Louis Cheminée, a friend and colleague of the Kraffts.

At Arizona State University, I want to thank Ed Stump, chairman of the Geology Department, and Nicole Goyart, the administrative associate, for their crucial help in evacuating me from Pasto and for their continued support of my recovery. Aggie Ahumada made it possible for Lynda to fly down to Pasto and retrieve me. I would also like to thank Linda St. Pierre, Vicki Stewart, Tori Brunson, Becky Polly, Courtneay Dowrick, Mariana Cosarinsky, and Kaatje van der Hoeven for their help with the book.

I am grateful to Dick Stenstrom for introducing me to geology and to Hank Woodard for propelling me into volcanology. Dick Stoiber became my best friend and mentor as he pushed me to delve deeper into my work on volcanoes. To this day he continues to teach me new things about the science to which we have dedicated our lives.

I am indebted to Bill Lende and the other friends who for years encouraged me to write this book. Many thanks, as well, to Dava Sobel for taking time out of her busy life as an author to persuade me to work with her literary agent, Michael Carlisle. She assured me that Michael was not only an agent but also a friend, and he has become that to me. I am grateful to Michael for getting this project off the ground and for introducing me to my co-author, Fen Montaigne. Fen had never set foot on a volcano before and therefore was all the more able to ask the right questions and craft this story for the general public. Both Fen and I are extremely grateful to Eamon Dolan, who helped shape the book and did a masterful job of editing it. Eamon is living proof that superb editors still ply their craft in American publishing.

Finally, I would like to express my gratitude and love for my wife, Lynda, and our children, Christine and Nick. The eruption and its aftermath have drastically changed our lives, and these past eight years have been a trial for our family. I will always be grateful for their patience, love, and understanding as I have struggled to recreate myself after Galeras.

INDEX

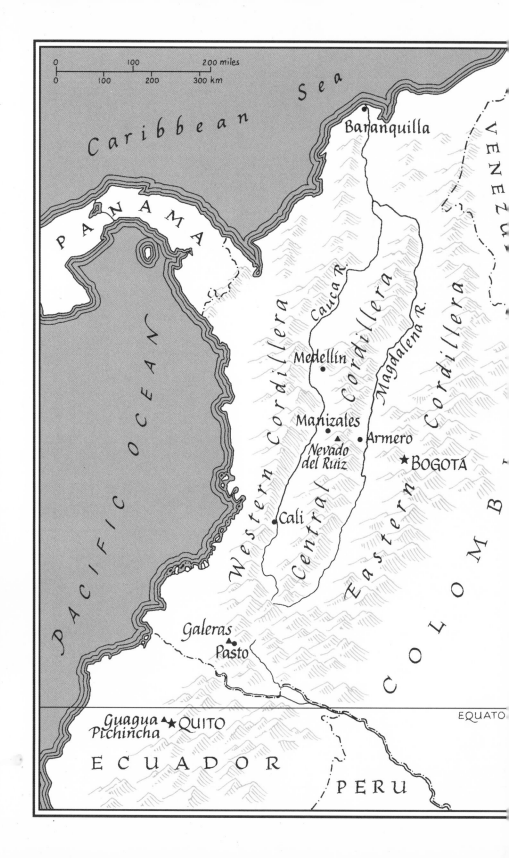